AF477745

Kindly mention THE ANNALS *when writing to advertisers*

VOLUME 422   NOVEMBER 1975

THE ANNALS

of The American Academy *of* Political *and* Social Science

RICHARD D. LAMBERT, *Editor*

ALAN W. HESTON, *Assistant Editor*

THE SUBURBAN SEVENTIES

Special Editor of This Volume

LOUIS H. MASOTTI

Director
Center for Urban Affairs
Professor of Political Science
and Urban Affairs
Northwestern University
Evanston, Illinois

PHILADELPHIA

Library of Congress Catalog Card Number 75-18434

DOROTHY ANN HOFFMAN, *Copy Editor*

JOANNE S. SMITH, *Book Review Copy Editor*

The articles appearing in THE ANNALS are indexed in the *Reader's Guide to Periodical Literature*, the *Book Review Index*, the *Public Affairs Information Service Bulletin*, and *Current Contents: Behavioral, Social, and Management Sciences*.   They are also abstracted and indexed in *ABC Pol Sci, Historical Abstracts, International Political Science Abstracts* and/or *America: History and Life.*

International Standard Book Numbers (ISBN)

ISBN 0-87761-195-5, vol. 422, 1975; paper—$4.00

ISBN 0-87761-194-7, vol. 422, 1975;   cloth—$5.00

Issued bimonthly by The American Academy of Political and Social Science at 3937 Chestnut St., Philadelphia, Pennsylvania 19104. Cost per year: $15.00 paperbound; $20.00 clothbound. Add $1.00 to above rates for membership outside U.S.A. Second-class postage paid at Philadelphia and at additional mailing offices.

Editorial and Business Offices, 3937 Chestnut Street, Philadelphia, Pennsylvania 19104.

CONTENTS

BOOK DEPARTMENT PAGE

INTERNATIONAL RELATIONS AND POLITICAL THOUGHT

ASIA, AFRICA, EUROPE AND LATIN AMERICA

UNITED STATES

SOCIOLOGY

PAGE

ECONOMICS

PREFACE

America has become a suburban nation during the last 15 years while almost no one was looking. A larger proportion of the population now lives in suburbia (more than 38 percent) than in either the central cities (30 percent) or in rural areas (32 percent). While the scale of this population shift is dramatic, a more significant reason for revived interest in the suburban phenomenon is the urbanization of the suburbs, that is, the growing economic, cultural and political independence of suburbia as it becomes more like the cities sociologically and demographically.

This transition from urban to suburban emphasis has been reflected in the "new" suburban literature.[1] This literature, supplemented by extensive mass media coverage[2] and the growing number and improved quality of suburban newspapers, has provided considerable documentation and some analysis of the suburban phenomenon. The intent of this volume of THE ANNALS is to enhance our understanding of "urban deconcentration" by exploring the implications of suburbanization—for the suburbs themselves, for the central cities on which they have traditionally depended for the metropolitan region of which they comprise a major part, and for a nation whose issues and politics are determined largely by the dynamics of urban-suburban change.

I am grateful to Deborah Ellis Dennis and the staff of the Center for Urban Affairs for generous assistance in assembling the articles in this volume. While it was impossible to cover every major implication of as massive and diverse a phenomenon as suburbanization, I believe a successful effort has been made to address the most significant conceptual and substantive issues of suburbia in the seventies.

As we begin the second half of the decade, there are already signs that the past is not necessarily prologue where suburbanization is concerned. The recent dramatic slowdown in suburban growth reflects not only the depressed national economy and the energy shortage, but also increased suburban resistance to growth. The full impact of this suburban deceleration has not yet been felt, but one can predict with confidence that it will have a significant effect on the future of suburbia, the cities and the nation.

LOUIS H. MASOTTI

1. *See*, for example, Dennis P. Sobin, *The Future of American Suburbs: Survival or Extinction?* (Port Washington, N.Y.: Kennikat, 1971); Charles Monroe Haar, *The End of Innocence: A Suburban Reader* (Glenview, Ill.: Scott, Foresman, 1972); John Kramer, ed., *North American Suburbs* (Berkeley, Calif.: Glendessary, 1972); Frederick M. Wirt et al., *On the City's Rim: Suburban Politics and Policies* (Lexington, Mass.: D. C. Heath, 1972); Louis H., Masotti and Jeffrey K. Hadden, *The Urbanization of the Suburbs* (Beverly Hills, Calif.: Sage, 1973), and *Suburbia in Transition* (New York, N.Y.: Franklin Watts, 1974); Anthony Downs, *Opening up the Suburbs: An Urban Strategy for America* (New Haven, Conn.: Yale University Press, 1973); James W. Hughes, ed., *Suburbanization Dynamics and the Future of the City* (New Brunswick, N.J.: Rutgers University, Center for Urban Policy Research, 1974); and two special journal issues: "The Suburban Shaping of American Politics," *Publius*, Winter 1975; and "The Changing Face of American Suburbs," *American Journal of Sociology* (forthcoming, 1975). *See also*, the extensive bibliography prepared by L. H. Masotti and D. E. Dennis, *Suburbs, Suburbia and Suburbanization*, rev. ed. (Evanston, Ill.: Northwestern University, Center for Urban Affairs, 1973).

2. In addition to occasional cover stories in news magazines like *Time* and *Newsweek*, several women's periodicals now have regular features on such topics as "suburban survival." *McCall's* recently changed its subtitle to "The Magazine for Suburban Women" to reflect its new readership and focus.

Suburbia and the Metropolitan Turf

By Robert L. Lineberry

ABSTRACT: As the nation suburbanizes, the definition of suburbia becomes ever more confused. There is a useful distinction, however, between a cultural or life-style approach and a demographic-legal approach to suburbs and suburbia. From a political perspective, the most critical element of metropolitan conflict is its sociospatial character, and suburban politics epitomizes this tendency. There are useful parallels between metropolitan conflict and international relations, because both involve competition for dominance of space. In both, a common concern is that the rich grow richer at the expense of the poor; this article examines that process within the metropolis. The question of how to deal with this "immiseration" of the central cities is answered differently by metropolitan reformers and by public choice theorists.

Robert L. Lineberry is Associate Professor of Political Science and Urban Affairs at Northwestern University. He is co-author of Urban Politics and Public Policy *and a contributor to political science and law journals on the subjects of metropolitanism, urban policy, and the law and politics of municipal services.*

DESPITE the voluminous literature on suburbia,[1] we are no closer than ever to a definition. It is a mere assumption of convenience that we all know what we are talking about, however variegated the pictures in our heads. We thus begin with a two-pronged conceptualization of suburbia. The two meanings wind about each other like the strands of the double helix; but they can be unraveled. In doing so, we suggest that suburban politics is a subset of urban politics generally, and that urban politics epitomizes conflict over sociospatial value allocations. A territorial imperative exists in the metropolis, and suburbanism is its most visible manifestation. The games suburbs play determine, within the metropolis, who controls the turf.

THE TWO SUBURBIAS

Whatever suburbia is, suburbanites live there, and suburbanists study them. Remarkably little effort has been made to justify suburbia as an object of serious inquiry. Suburbs are studied as mountains are climbed —because they are there. The standard opening gambit in any suburban treatise is "lots of people live there"—38 percent of the American population, more than in central cities or rural areas—but as a rationale, the argument is not wholly satisfying. Even more people live in India, and its growth rate is greater than the American suburb, so attention to suburbanism cannot be rationalized by body counts alone.

Generally, suburbanists have studied suburbs either because of their life-style implications or because of their consequences for metropolitanism. The former rationale has been the preserve of the sociologist, the latter of the economist, with political scientists, as is often the case, borrowing shamelessly from both. Each conceptualization entails a distinctive definition of suburbia, together with a rationale for the subject itself. I suggest that the principal reason that suburban literature has been so richly descriptive yet so rarely definitive is the persistent muddling of these two meanings. The initial assumption of the 1950s literature that the two meanings were correlated has led to an all-consuming effort in the 1970s to disentangle them, leaving the field swaddled in uncertainty.

Before proceeding, let us define more sharply the meanings of the two suburbias. By a cultural or life-style meaning, I want to convey either the "ideal type" or the stereotypical conception of certain class-related traits—familism, child-centeredness, single family dwelling units, sharp segregation of work place from residence, organizational consciousness—all the things which a content analysis of the Whyte-Wood studies would reveal, overlaid by a distinct touch of affluence.[2] This is the dominant, if stereotypical, picture of suburbia. Such places exist, and not merely in the pages of the Luce empire. It is possible that a fair proportion of my readers live in such places. (I myself live in Evanston, Illinois.)

By a legal and demographic con-

---

1. *See*, the bibliography compiled by Louis Masotti and Deborah Ellis Dennis, "Suburbs, Suburbia and Suburbanization: A Bibliography," 2nd ed. (Evanston, Ill.: Center for Urban Affairs, Northwestern University, 3 November 1973).

2. Robert C. Wood, *Suburbia* (Boston: Houghton Mifflin, 1958); and William H. Whyte, Jr., *The Organization Man* (New York: Doubleday, 1957).

ception, I mean that we take our definitions from the Census Bureau. Thus, a suburb is by definition an incorporated municipality within a Standard Metropolitan Statistical Area (SMSA) other than a central city.

These definitions are entirely utilitarian, provided that they are not routinely confused. Unfortunately, they frequently are. The nearly universal assumption throughout the 1950s and well into the 1960s was that a strong and positive correlation existed between these two forms of suburbia. This view was fortified by the fact that most early suburbanists wrote in and about large Northeastern metropolitan areas—Wood at MIT and Harvard, Whyte of Chicago— where such assumptions were not entirely inaccurate. Bennett Berger's notable *Working Class Suburb* was the first work to challenge these assumptions.[3] From that point on, the principal thrust of suburban literature was to produce chaos from order, to chip away at the old myth that life style and demographic suburbs were identical. If the watchword of the early years was homogeneity, the watchword today is variety. Coming full circle, we can now speak paradoxically about the "urbanization of the suburbs."[4] Yet if the suburbs are being "urbanized" at a rapid clip, there is less rationale than ever for a distinctive inquiry into something called suburbia.

I suggest that we explicitly combine the two definitions and see what follows. Figure 1 does just that, suggesting that any sociospatial area within the metropolis ("sociospatial"

3. Bennett Berger, *Working Class Suburb* (Berkeley: University of California Press, 1960).
4. Louis H. Masotti and Jeffrey K. Hadden, eds., *The Urbanization of the Suburbs,* vol. 7 of *Urban Affairs Annual Reviews* (Beverly Hills, Calif.: Sage, 1973).

FIGURE 1

A SUBURBAN TYPOLOGY

		CULTURAL-LIFE STYLE	
		High	Low
DEMOGRAPHIC-LEGAL	Yes	A	B
	No	C	D

remains vague momentarily) will fall somewhere along a continuum from high to low "suburbanness." Each area can also be classified as a demographic suburb or not. Every urban sociospatial area can be located somewhere in this typology, but only some are suburban. Cell A subsumes places which are doubly suburban, both in life-style traits and demographically. Included here are the Dariens, the Gross Points, the Alamo Heights, the Winnetkas, and a host of others with less affluence. Such locales represent "suburbia in the suburbs." Cell D is the opposite, being neither culturally nor demographically suburban.

The confusion of suburban literature comes from comingling cells B and C. C specifically recognizes that "suburbia" can also exist within the central city. Throughout most of the Southwest and West, in the most rapidly growing metropolitan areas, central cities are where suburban life styles predominate. Were we to specify empirically some threshold suburban traits—a given proportion of single family dwelling units, certain familistic values, a specific income level, and so forth—we would find that most suburbanites in Houston, Dallas, Phoenix, Sacramento, and Tulsa actually live within the central city. People who in Detroit would opt for Gross Point, or in Chicago for Glencoe, could be comfortable in River Oaks (inside the perimeters of Houston), for River Oaks is a very suburban area, but not a suburb. Partly because of the time and space conceptions of the early suburbanists, who virtually wrote off that part of the nation west of the Mississippi and south of the Mason-Dixon line, we have assumed that the pattern in older metropolitan areas repeats itself elsewhere.

Cell B of our typology also constitutes an anomaly to conventional wisdom. Nonsuburban life styles in the suburbs seem almost self-contradictory, yet it is remarkable how readily they were discovered once old myths ceased to camouflage old realities. Industrial enclaves, non-familistic suburbs, nearly all-black suburbs, commercial centers, heavily ethnic and other aberrant spots cluttered demographic suburbia decades ago, as they do today. Such areas did not spring up overnight, with a sudden urbanization of the suburbs. Rather, our preoccupation with life-style suburbs made these areas harder to see.

THE METROPOLITAN TURF

Deepening schism

The first fact of urban life is that persons of varying racial, ethnic and economic attributes are not scattered randomly about the metropolitan landscape. Both private and public sector forces contribute to this differentiation. Distribution of wealth, access to jobs, racial discrimination, and other factors combine to sort out people and production on a limited spatial plane. On the public side, zoning practices, suburban incorporation, the location of transporta-tion networks and other service facilities, and other governmental decisions combine to reinforce or reverse these patterns. Oliver Williams describes metropolitan politics as the conflict among sociospatial units, competing for access to their dominant life-style values.[5] Sociospatial units (lacking a more elegant term, Williams suggests that we call them "mumfords") include families, business firms, organizations, churches, and so forth. Each has a hierarchy of values which must be maximized in a confined space. Thus metropolitan politics is rather like politics of the turf, and the teenage gang is the "primitive urban formation":

The membership is well defined, the norms of the group quite real, albeit far from explicit, and the boundaries of the turf specific in the minds of the gang members. Gangs follow a variety of strategies, which approximate the practices of adult urban coalitions. They defend their turf against incursions by nonmembers; they build the reputations of the gang by its activities . . . ; and they purify by trying to drive out incompatible persons.[6]

Of course, in the mature adult political system, violence as a tool of spatial control is normally replaced by rules, by legitimate and authoritative use of political power, and by the formation of coalitions. Force gives way to public policy as a device for securing and maintaining locational advantages.

If metropolitan politics is a politics of space, it becomes immediately apparent that its closest analogue is not national politics, but inter-

5. Oliver Williams, *Metropolitan Political Analysis* (New York: Free Press, 1971).
6. Williams, *Metropolitan Political Analysis*, p. 43.

national relations.[7] While at some point the parallel becomes strained, both metropolitan and international politics share certain attributes. The principal governmental actor is a more or less autonomous unit, with real but permeable boundaries, and these units compete for the control of scarce space.

There are other parallels as well. The developed nations-underdeveloped nations distinction bears some resemblance to the suburban-central city dichotomy, and a common argument about both is that the economic gap between members is widening. The immigration restraints of international politics have their parallel in the exclusionary zoning attributed to suburbs, and supranational organizations like the European Economic Community (EEC) have long been advocated to remedy the problems of excessive nationalism, just as metropolitan consolidation has been a remedy for metropolitan fragmentation. Of course, there are certain analogues which would stretch this simile to the breaking point. There is no obvious international analogue to crosstown bussing, nor an obvious urban analogue to nuclear weapons.

Games suburbs play

If we think about metropolitan conflict as the politics of spatial dominance, our attention is directed to questions of strategy. Strategic considerations are at the core, incidentally, of international relations, and game theory is a principal mode of conflict analysis. Far and away, the greatest amount of attention in the metropolitan sphere has gone to the zoning game and its corollary, the housing game. The standard hypothesis in zoning literature is that zoning does to suburban areas what national boundaries and immigration quotas (the quota system of the 1924 United States immigration laws, for example) do for nations—that is, restrain influx of potential immigrants or restrict them to a very special class of persons.[8] To challengers of "snob zoning," such zoning functions like the "wall of iron" in Jehovah's advice to Ezekiel:

Lay siege against it, and build a fort against it, and cost a mount against it; set the camp also against it, and set battering rams against it round about. Moreover, take thou unto thee an iron pan, and set it for a wall of iron between thee and the city. (Ezek. 4:2–3)

It is well known, for example, that in the New York metropolitan region, 40 percent of the vacant residential land is zoned at one-half acre minimums and 20 percent at an acre or more, with a recent trend toward "upzoning."

While notorious individual cases are commonly singled out, hard evidence on the allegedly deleterious effect of zoning is hard to come by. Strange as it may seem, "there have been very few empirical studies of zoning."[9] Branfman, Cohen and Tru-

7. For earlier efforts to draw out the international relations simile, *see*, Matthew Holden, "The Governance of the Metropolis as a Problem in Diplomacy," *Journal of Politics* 26 (August 1964), pp. 627–647; and Philip E. Jacob, et al., *The Integration of Political Communities* (Philadelphia: Lippincott, 1963).

8. On zoning, *see*, Daniel Mandelker, *The Zoning Dilemma* (Indianapolis: Bobbs-Merrill, 1971); David Listokin, ed., *Land Use Controls: Present Problems and Future Reform* (New Brunswick, N.J.: Center for Urban Policy Research, Rutgers University, 1974).

9. Robert L. Bish and Hugh O. Nouse, "Collective Choice in Urban Zoning Regulation" (Paper presented at the 1974 Annual

bek undertook an elaborate quantitative analysis of the effects of zoning and found some qualified support for the standard hypothesis in the 30 metropolitan areas they studied.[10] Bruce-Briggs, however, suggests that the artificial inflation of land values associated with zoning cannot have too much impact, because only two percent of the monthly cost of a home is land-related.[11] Siegan, who studied "non-zoning" in Houston, the only major city without a zoning code, found relatively little difference in housing patterns between Houston and other metropolitan areas. Houston, however, is not a perfect test case, both because state enabling legislation permits city police powers to be used to enforce restrictive covenants and because it is a vast, low-density city with little demographic suburbanization as compared to older metropolitan areas.[12]

On the fiscal side, and whatever the reasons, there is little doubt that an increased "immiseration" of the central city has occurred. In the international system, the gap between rich and poor has widened and the dependancy of the latter on the former has increased.[13] This is also true in the American metropolis, where the decapitalization of central cities parallels the enrichment of the periphery. New York alone lost 300,000 manufacturing jobs between the 1960 and 1970 censuses. The disinvestment in central city neighborhoods is painfully dramatized in the mortgage practices of both massive and minor financial institutions. *In extremis*, of course, there is Newark, where taxes are staggering —almost $2,000 on a $20,000 house —services deteriorating, racial antagonisms upsurgent, and vacancy rates increasing.

These metropolitan fiscal disparities have been heightened by suburban incorporation, by differences in tax bases, and possibly by the zoning and land use restrictions which accompany suburbanization. The issue of metropolitan inequality was finally joined by the courts and legislatures in the school finance cases. In *Serrano* v. *Priest*, the Supreme Court of California held against a financing system which tied tax yields directly to tax bases, although the United States Supreme Court finessed an opportunity to nationalize the dictum in *San Antonio Independent School District* v. *Rodriguez*.[14]

The differences in economic development and fiscal vitality, long highlighted between central cities and areas outside of central cities, are increasingly replicating themselves among the latter. It is noteworthy that the seminal school finance case, *Serrano*, actually joined two suburbs in conflict, Baldwin Park and Beverly Hills. Today, if one graphed the mean incomes of central

Meeting of the American Political Science Association, Chicago, Ill., 29 August–2 September 1974), p. 8.

10. Eric Branfman, Benjamin I. Cohen, and David M. Trubek, "Measuring the Invisible Wall: Land Use Controls and the Residential Patterns of the Poor," *Yale Law Journal* 82 (January 1973), pp. 483–508.

11. B. Bruce-Briggs, "The Cost of Housing," *Public Interest*, no. 32, (Summer 1973), pp. 37–38.

12. Bernard H. Siegan, *Land Use Without Zoning* (Lexington, Mass.: D.C. Heath, 1972).

13. There is a very large body of literature in international relations on dependency theory, such as the papers in James D. Cockcroft, Andre Gunder Frank, and Dale L. Johnson, eds., *Dependence and Underdevelopment: Latin American Political Economy* (New York: Anchor Books, 1972).

14. *Serrano* v. *Priest*, 5 Cal. 3d 584 (1971); *San Antonio Independent School District* v. *Rodriguez*, 411 U.S. 1 (1973).

city census tracts and those of the suburbs of the same metropolitan areas, they would take roughly the same bell-shaped curve, save that the grand mean of the latter would be much higher than the grand mean of the former. This is what is entailed in the recent discoveries about suburban variety rather than homogeneity and about the "urbanization of the suburbs."

Obviously, then, some demographic suburbs are in more advantageous positions to maximize their culturally suburban values than others. In the older, Northeastern metropolitan areas, culturally suburban values have found little sustenance in the central city, leading to accentuated demographic suburbanization. There, the link between the two suburbias is forged tighter annually. Yet this is very different from the patterns in the newer and most rapidly growing SMSAs in the South, Southwest and West. The reasons people suburbanize in Phoenix may be different from the reasons they abandon Philadelphia. Studying attitudes of suburbanites in the gargantuan Oklahoma City metropolitan area (spread over seven counties), Morgan asked whether there were "any reasons in particular why you might not want to live in Oklahoma City." More than half (54.3 percent) could not think of any.[15] It is hard to imagine a similarly nonchalant attitude toward that question in Boston, Buffalo or Chicago suburbs. For the moment, at least, there is plenty of room for culturally suburban values to find expression in the newer central cities. Whether this pattern can long endure is another issue.

AGGREGATE THE TURF OR PARCELIZE IT?

Regionalization

E pluribus unum has been the rallying cry of two generations of metropolitan reformers. Consolidation of metropolitan governments would accomplish, presumably, the same blessings as regionalizing brought the European Economic Community (EEC), shaking off the curse of fragmentation. It would facilitate intraregional migration by reducing land use barriers to mobility, rationalize economic growth by bringing regionwide economic resources to bear on pockets of underdevelopment (as the EEC was supposed to do for southern Italy), and reduce political tensions by creating superordinate governing bodies.

Yet the zeal of the reformers has been matched only by the record of nonresponse to their exhortations. A handful of reform efforts have occurred in major metropolitan areas— Nashville, Jacksonville, Miami and Indianapolis—but the overwhelming proportion have been in the South.[16] Some have speculated that this Southern concentration is not accidentally related to the racial implications of metropolitanization. Metropolitan reform can be a nasty weapon in the hands of a white, suburban power structure. Whatever its benefits in rationalizing metropolitan economies and diseconomies, con-

15. David R. Morgan, "Community Social Rank and Attitudes toward Suburban Living," *Sociology and Social Research* 55 (July 1971), p. 405.

16. Vincent Marando, "The Politics of Metropolitan Reform" (Paper presented at the Conference on Government Reform in the 1970s, Syracuse University, 7–8 March 1974). For a review of the metropolitan reform tradition and efforts, *see*, Robert L. Lineberry, "Reforming Metropolitan Governance: Requiem or Reality," *Georgetown Law Journal* 58 (March–May 1970), pp. 675–718.

solidation has unquestionably had the effect of eliminating much of the turf now held by central city blacks. Jacksonville, for example, was 41 percent black before consolidation. After consolidation with Duval County, the black share of the new turf was down to 21 percent.

Adhering firmly to the position that half a loaf is better than none, reformers have retreated to a fallback position: if you cannot consolidate, then at least coordinate better. Councils of Government were invented to do this, and the advocacy of a "two-tiered" system of metropolitan governance is a fuller expression of a half-a-loaf settlement. Given the scope of fiscal disparities and other externalities of fragmented governments, however, it is not certain that these represent much more than a slice or two.

METROPOLITAN INEQUALITY: THE PUBLIC CHOICE APPROACH

Historically, the metropolitan reform tradition has been the province of political scientists, deriving its heritage from the discipline's old ties to the Progressive municipal reform movement. But while political scientists have favored fewer governments, political economists have favored the opposite response to the metropolitan problem. Tiebout, in a classic paper, defended the multiplicity of governments in the metropolis because it optimized consumer choice, as if it were a marketplace of metropolitan services.[17] Consumer satisfaction, he argued, is a product of competition—whether among commodity producers or governments—and not of monopoly. Families and firms could select the preferred mix of services by "voting with their feet." The most recent entry in the public choice approach is by Robert Bish and Vincent Ostrom, two political economists who forcefully argue that:

Instead of assuming that fragmentation of authority and overlapping jurisdictions are the source of the contemporary urban crisis, we urge the opposite proposition be entertained—that the absence of fragmented authority and multiple jurisdictions in large central cities is the principal source of institutional failure in urban government. The absence of neighborhood governments makes it difficult for residents of urban neighborhoods to organize so that common problems can be handled in routine ways.[18]

To public choice theorists, the last thing we should desire is the creation of gargantuan metropolitan governments, so large that bureaucracies become less responsive than ever. Even present-day central cities may be too large to be politically responsive and economically efficient—New York City is only the most glaring example.

The problem with such a conscious policy of piecemeal fragmentation is that it occurs without resource redistribution. It further solidifies the hard lines of economic inequality among governments. Bish and Ostrom are aware of the problem and frankly assert that "the costs of voting with their feet, for example, may be

17. Charles M. Tiebout, "A Pure Theory of Local Expenditures," *Journal of Political Economy* 64 (October 1956), pp. 416–424. *See also,* Vincent Ostrom, Charles M. Tiebout, and Robert Warren, "The Organization of Government in Metropolitan Areas: A Theoretical Inquiry," *American Political Science Review* 60 (December 1961), pp. 831–842.

18. Robert Bish and Vincent Ostrom, *Understanding Urban Government: Metropolitan Reform Reconsidered* (Washington: American Enterprise Institute for Public Policy Research, 1973), p. 95.

too great for many poor people. The cost of making their demands known to city hall may also be too high for them to pay."[19] This is a candid but rather hard-boiled admission of the inegalitarian overtones of the metropolitan marketplace model. It means, quite frankly, that those now in the weakest position to maintain their life-style values would continue to be so. How political responsiveness can be secured without intolerable tradeoffs in economic inequality thus becomes the central political dilemma of the metropolitan problem.

The two responses to the problem of metropolitan fragmentation have both involved tinkering with metropolitan boundaries—one advocating erasing some, and the other proliferating them—as if manipulating boundaries and redrawing them will resolve old conflicts without kindling new ones. Such resolutions, however, typically leave economic inequalities in suspended animation. In this sense, the Supreme Court decision in *Rodriguez,* which turned back a challenge to inter-urban fiscal inequality in education, represented the principal direct confrontation with these hard realities. And the hard realities continue. For these reasons, the boundary-tinkering approach will probably be increasingly subordinated to the more fundamental question of economic resources and their distribution within the metropolis. In the long run, the size of one's local government probably matters less than one's resources to secure a piece of the metropolitan turf.

19. Bish and Ostrom, *Understanding Urban Government,* p. 31.

Beyond Suburbia

By SYLVIA F. FAVA

ABSTRACT: The next stage of suburbanization is taking place at the edges of metropolitan areas as these areas merge into the megalopolis. The United States is already a nation in which suburbanites constitute the largest portion, but not yet the majority, of Americans. Many of these suburbanites will be suburban-born and bred, rather than having decentralized from the center city. Their moves will be from suburb to suburb or suburb to exurb, and they will thus have little direct life experience with high density living and central city problems. The questions this poses for social science theory are examined in detail in this article. Early studies of life style and attitudes beyond suburbia suggest that they differ considerably from those of the earlier generation of suburbanites. The implications of megalopolitan structure for racial minorities and for women are also examined, with little evidence that racist or sexist patterns have been changed. Brief consideration of these and other public policy questions indicates that the political structures to meet the various needs of a megalopolitan constituency have not been developed and remain a major question.

Sylvia F. Fava is Professor of Sociology and Chairperson, Interdepartmental Program in Urban Studies, Brooklyn College, City University of New York. Educated at Queens College and Northwestern University, she has published research articles on suburbs and new communities. She is co-author of Urban Society *and editor of* Urbanism in World Perspective. *She has also served as consultant to the Metropolitan Applied Research Center's new communities project and is a past vice-president of the Eastern Sociological Society.*

BEYOND suburbia lie paradoxes: suburbs dominating an increasingly urban society; the emergence of major changes among blacks and women whose potential impact on suburban housing demand and activity patterns is largely ignored; and megalopolis as the new urban-suburban "reality" which exists neither as a political unit nor as a focus of governmental policy and which does not even serve as a viable analytic unit of social science theory. This article explores these and other paradoxes in the future of suburbia in terms of the changing shape of the metropolitan region; the problems of incorporating suburban dominance into social science theory; and the restructuring of governmental programs and agencies to take account of the new distribution of people and problems.

THE SHAPE OF SUBURBAN AMERICA

Numerically the United States is already suburban. Since the 1960s suburbanites have comprised the largest share, although not the majority, of the American population. Defining suburban as the territory within the census Standard Metropolitan Statistical Areas (SMSAs) but outside the central cities, the 1970 census counted more than 75 million Americans as suburbanites, comprising 37.6 percent of the total American population; only 31.4 percent of Americans lived in the central cities of metropolitan areas, and the smallest percentage, 31.0, did not live within metropolitan areas at all. This distribution represents a complete reversal of the situation in 1900, when the nonmetropolitan population was by far the most numerous, accounting for 57 percent of the population, while the central city population was a distant second with 27 percent, and the suburban population accounted for only 15 percent of all Americans.[1] The shift to suburbia occurred throughout the twentieth century, but with a dramatic spurt after 1940. After World War II the so-called age of suburbia reached popular awareness although the systemic changes affecting American life—locational flexibility based on new forms of transportation, communication and information handling; affluence arising from advanced post-industrial productivity; and a highly differentiated, albeit large scale, mass society—had been accumulating for decades.[2]

Suburban growth of the kind we have been accustomed to has passed its peak. It represented one stage of urban decentralization, occurring when there were still large tracts of undeveloped land relatively close to large cities and when there was also a substantial reservoir of nonmetropolitan population migrating to metropolitan areas, especially to their central cities. Suburbanites—that is, people residing in metropolitan areas but outside the central cities—will undoubtedly become a majority of the American population in the near future, but these suburbanites will represent a new stage of metropolitan expansion. American cities, established in a virgin land and experiencing most of their growth under the conditions of industrial technology, expanded outward, with the highest growth rates at the outer edges. This suburban-

1. Based on data from U.S., Bureau of the Census, *Selected Area Reports, Standard Metropolitan Statistical Areas*, 1960, Final Report PC(3)-1D, Table 1, and *Statistical Abstract of the United States*, 1972, Table 15.

2. *See*, for example, Noel P. Gist and Sylvia F. Fava, "The Urban Transformation of the United States," *Urban Society*, 6th ed. (New York: T. Y. Crowell, 1974), pp. 55–81.

izing pattern has been linked with an upward thrust in the high-rise "downtown" of the central city, concentrating the bureaucracies which coordinate the complex metropolitan economic network.

As the ripples of growth expand outward, however, especially around the larger metropolitan areas, they not only encounter the expanding suburban edges of other, typically smaller and newer metropolitan areas, but they also eddy around both the man-made environment of the nonurban past—such as retirement communities, resorts and truck farms—and the natural environment of parks and wildlife preserves. In addition, a wider range of activities is decentralizing from the old central cities, either into "strip" development along major highways or into lesser "downtowns" serving the increasing population of "suburbia."

SUBURBIA IN MEGALOPOLIS

These coalescing metropolises are megalopolis, the name being as unwieldy as the form. This is the new suburban America,

Grow[ing] amidst an irregularly colloidal mixture of rural and suburban landscape; it melts on broad fronts with other mixtures, of somewhat similar though different texture, belonging to the suburban neighborhoods of other cities . . . This region serves thus as a laboratory in which we may study the new evolution reshaping both the meaning of our traditional vocabulary and the whole material structure of our way of life.[3]

Megalopolitan development was first described by Jean Gottmann, the French geographer, for the area of the Northeastern seaboard extending from north of Boston to south of Washington, D.C. Early megalopolitan development has also been analyzed for the California coastal strip extending from north of San Francisco through Los Angeles and south to San Diego.[4]

Using the term *urban region*, Jerome Pickard has indicated how general megalopolitan development has become.[5] In 1920 there were 10 urban regions, making up a third of the United States population; all but one of the regions were in the Northeast. By 1960 there were 16 urban regions comprising more than half (56 percent) of the nation's population; important new regions had emerged in the South, the West and the Middle West, although the Northeast still contained the largest regions. By the year 2000, based on an average of two children per family, continued horizontal growth, and the linking together of regions, Pickard estimates that more than 80 percent of the American people will be living in at least 25 urban regions.[6]

3. Jean Gottmann, *Megalopolis: The Urbanized Northeastern Seaboard of the United States* (New York: Twentieth Century Fund, 1961), pp. 5, 9.

4. Staff, University of California, Los Angeles, Population Research Laboratory, "California's Urban Population: Patterns and Trends," in *California's Twenty Million*, ed. Kingsley Davis and Frederick Styles (University of California, Berkeley, Institute of International Studies, 1972), pp. 259–96.

5. "An Urban Region is a coterminous area within which urban population predominates. By definition, it must contain a total population of at least one million. It is composed of one or more contiguous Metropolitan Areas and adjacent or intervening counties with relatively high population density or single counties of lower density which contain a major transportation corridor linking two or more Metropolitan Areas." Jerome Pickard, "U.S. Metropolitan Growth and Expansion, 1970–2000," in U.S., Commission on Population Growth and the American Future, *Population, Distribution, and Policy*, ed. Sara Mills Mazie, vol. 5 of the Commission Research Reports (Washington, D.C.: Government Printing Office, 1972), p. 142.

6. Pickard, "U.S. Metropolitan Growth," pp. 142–47.

These urban regions are veritable metropolitan galaxies. Pickard's projections indicate that, by the year 2000, the six largest regions will contain 116 metropolitan areas, and most of the remaining urban regions will have an average of more than three metropolitan areas each.

Data on actual settlement patterns since the 1970 census cover too brief a period to be definitive, but they suggest that the major focus of growth has shifted from the census-defined metropolitan areas to the adjacent exurban counties. This shift is not only compatible with megalopolitan development, but even expected, despite reports in the popular press about the reversal of historic trends. Specifically, the census estimated that between March 1970 and March 1974 more than 5.9 million people moved out of metropolitan areas, while only 4.1 million moved in, resulting in a net migration from metropolitan to nonmetropolitan counties of 1.8 million.[7] As the report points out, this does not indicate a total population loss to metropolitan areas, but rather a decline in the metropolitan growth rate.

Since 1970, nonmetropolitan counties—that is, those not in metropolitan areas—have apparently been growing at a faster rate than metropolitan counties.[8] Most nonmetropolitan growth represents spillover from metropolitan areas, however; Calvin Beale, a demographer with the Economic Research Service of the Department of Agriculture, has calculated that five-eighths of the new nonmetropolitan population growth has been in counties adjacent to metropolitan counties.[9] The specific factors facilitating growth in these counties are currently being debated, but they probably include the decentralization of manufacturing, construction of major highways in outlying areas, more flexible working hours, early retirement and longer life expectancy. The energy crisis and the recession would presumably operate against metropolitan expansion, but their effects are either unimportant or not yet apparent. In any event the dispersed pattern of megalopolis already exists.

SUBURBAN BORN AND SUBURBAN BRED

The most important implication of current and projected settlement patterns is that soon the majority of Americans will have only suburban experience. The central cities of metropolitan areas have been losing population in absolute numbers since the 1960s or, at best, barely holding their own. Virtually all recent metropolitan growth has been in their suburban areas, and by the early 1970s almost all of the 33 metropolitan areas of more than one million had

7. U.S., Bureau of the Census, *Current Population Reports*, Series P-20, no. 273, "Mobility of the Population of the U.S., March 1970–March 1974" (Washington, D.C.: Government Printing Office, December 1974), p. 1.

8. There is now evidence that nonmetropolitan counties adjacent to large metropolitan areas had begun significant growth before 1970. The differences in growth rates and socio-economic characteristics among the six types of nonmetropolitan counties (ranging from "Urbanized Adjacent" to "Totally Rural Not Adjacent") described by the census are also another indication of the extensive influence of the metropolis. Regional Plan Association, *Growth and Settlement in the U.S.: Past Trends and Future Issues* (New York City: Regional Plan Association, June 1975), p. 44; and "Social and Economic Characteristics of the Population in Metro and Nonmetro Counties, 1970" (Washington, D.C.: Economic Research Service, U.S., Department of Agriculture, Agricultural Economic Report #272, March 1975), pp. 7–8.

9. Cited in Roy Reed, "Rural Areas' Population Gains Now Outpacing Urban Regions," *New York Times* (18 May 1975), pp. 1, 32 BL.

the majority of their populations in the suburbs. Since 1970, as already indicated, major growth may already have shifted to the adjacent, currently nonmetropolitan, counties.

The redistribution of population into megalopolitan patterns means that proportionately fewer people will experience urban densities and related life styles: high-rise housing, public transportation, pedestrian access, and the concentration of activities and diverse people. In 1950 about 15 percent of the United States population lived at genuinely urban densities of more than 10,000 persons per square mile, but by 1970 this had dropped to only 10 percent of the nation's population.[10] Below the 10,000 level, major clustering into centers cannot occur, although densities of 1,000 or more people per square mile are considered urban since they signify that the land is built up and no longer available for agriculture or open space. Yet the lower densities are precisely the point at which recent metropolitan expansion has taken place; between 1950 and 1970 the population living in counties with average densities more than 1,000 persons per square mile rose from 29 to 37 percent of the total national population. These "urban" densities are suburban sprawl.

Translated into personal terms, these population trends mean the reality of megalopolis in suburban America will be distant. Although the suburban majority will live within the complex economic web of these enormous urban regions, their daily social, civic, and often their work lives will be spent in relatively small communities. Elazar has pointed out that within the context of metropolitan development, most Americans actually live in small towns.[11] The 1970 census shows, for example, that 21 percent of all Americans live in places of 2,500 to 25,000 people; 17 percent in places of 25,000 to 100,000; and only 28 percent in places above 100,000, with the remaining one-third of the population living in other urban areas or in rural places.

Megalopolis, then, does not portend big city living. On the contrary, it portends a generation of Americans, most of whom are suburban born and suburban bred. Their experience of high density, central city living will be limited to visits and perhaps educational training, work and residence in early adulthood. The emergence of a suburban-reared suburban majority is of particular significance because of the suburban population composition. Despite the "suburbanization of everyone" and the increasingly broad mix of life styles and classes in the suburbs,[12] suburbanites still represent a disproportionate share of those who are "better off," highly participatory and influential.

SUBURBAN DOMINANCE AND SOCIAL THEORY

The suburban theory which emerged during the 1950s dealt essentially with a population that had *become* suburban, that is, which had decentralized from central city

10. Regional Plan Association, *Growth and Settlement*, p. 11.

11. Daniel Elazar, "Smaller Cities in Metropolitan Society: The New American 'Towns'," Temple University, Center for the Study of Federalism, Working Paper no. 9 (c. 1969).

12. *See*, for example, Louis H. Masotti, "Prologue—Suburbia Reconsidered—Myth and Countermyth," in *The Urbanization of the Suburbs*, ed. L. H. Masotti and J. K. Hadden (Beverly Hills, California: Sage Publications, 1973).

to suburb. Thus, such now-classic studies as *The Levittowners, Working Class Suburb* and *Crestwood Heights*,[13] covering various socio-economic segments, examined the changes taking place as former urban dwellers settled into suburban homes. The theory governing suburban study has been essentially an extension of the urban theory of the 1920s and 1930s. For example, Louis Wirth's classic summary of the effects of size, density and heterogeneity, which reflects the approach developed at the University of Chicago during the period of very rapid central city growth and concentration in the United States, has been widely applied to the suburban setting.[14] There is, of course, every reason why such theories as Wirth's should be tested in suburbia. However, since the theories include the explicit or implicit assumption that suburbanites will have considerable urban life experience, the applicability of that assumption in the "postsuburban" period must also be tested. New research questions must be formulated to take account of the emerging suburban majority which will be suburban by birth and life history and whose moves will be from suburb to suburb or from suburb to exurb.

In the virtual absence of such studies, I take a quantum leap and offer the following suggestions about some aspects of the suburb-dominated society. These suggestions, based on fragmentary evidence, should be regarded as hypotheses: (1) being suburban born and reared will exert a strong influence toward preferring suburban residence in the future; (2) suburbanites are more locally-oriented in their contacts, a characteristic which is likely to intensify as there are more suburbanites whose life history is suburban; and (3) suburban attitudes toward blacks and toward big-city problems can best be described as tolerant aloofness and non-involvement, based on the few case studies of suburban communities settled by those who moved from other suburbs.

The effect of suburban community of origin was examined by Zelan in a secondary analysis of data from a National Opinion Research Center (NORC) survey of the June 1961 graduating class of American colleges, totaling more than 33,000 questionnaires received from students in 135 colleges.[15] Zelan was primarily interested in whether those raised in suburbia (suburbs of metropolitan areas of 100,000 or more) differed in anti-intellectualism from those raised in large cities (central cities of those metropolitan areas). Simple correlation showed no differences in intellectual attitudes between the groups. However, when anti-intellectualism responses were

13. Herbert Gans, *The Levittowners* (New York: Pantheon, 1967); Bennett Berger, *Working-Class Suburb* (Berkeley and Los Angeles: University of California Press, 1960); John Seeley, R. Alexander Sim, E. W. Loosley, *Crestwood Heights* (New York: Basic Books, 1969).

14. *See,* for example, Sylvia F. Fava, "Suburbanism as a Way of Life," *American Sociological Review* 21 (February 1956), pp. 34–38; Herbert J. Gans, "Urbanism and Suburbanism as Ways of Life: A Re-evaluation of Definitions," in *Human Behavior and Social Processes*, ed. Arnold Rose (Boston: Houghton Mifflin, 1962), pp. 625–48; for a summary of the many suburban applications of Wirth's thesis, *see,* the suburban portion of Claude S. Fischer, "Urbanism as a Way of Life: A Review and an Agenda," *Sociological Methods and Research* 1 (November 1972), pp. 187–242.

15. Joseph Zelan, "Does Suburbia Make a Difference?" in *Urbanism in World Perspective,* ed. Sylvia F. Fava (New York: T. Y. Crowell, 1968), pp. 401–8.

correlated with where the graduates *wished* to live, rather than by community of origin, the group preferring to live in suburbs had higher levels of anti-intellectual responses than those preferring urban living. Being married was also strongly associated with preferring suburban residence.

For our purposes, Zelan's important finding is that the factor most predictive of choosing suburban residence is one's community of origin—"those who have lived in the suburbs are most likely to be oriented toward suburbs."[16] Thus, even the suburban-reared graduates who manifested low anti-intellectualism and who were single said they would choose to live in suburbs. This study suggests that, although other factors are also influential in determining whether one will choose suburban residence, on the whole, a suburban childhood apparently prepares one to choose a suburban adulthood. The generation now growing up in suburbs will probably wish to live in them as adults. Suburbanism is not a self-destructive phenomenon.

Suburbanites are local; that is, their social circles and interests are more concentrated in their immediate residential localities than are those of urban dwellers. Fischer and Jackson's comprehensive review of existing literature, as well as their secondary analysis of two large-scale surveys, amply documents that suburbanites engage in more neighboring, that more of their individual ties and friendships are within short distances, and that their interest in and involvement with local concerns are greater than urbanites'.[17] After

examining various possible theories to account for these differences, Fischer and Jackson conclude that there are three sources of suburban localism.

The two most important explanations are non-ecological. First, the individual characteristics of suburbanites—age, ethnicity, home ownership and family cycle—are those associated with high levels of localism. For example, home owners are more locally-oriented than renters, no matter where they live. Thus, the most important reasons suburbanites behave as locally as they do are personal and not related to suburbanism per se. However, the second most important level of explanation of suburban localism is that of contextual effects, that is, consequences of the concentration in suburbs of certain population types. The suburban whole is more than the sum of the individuals residing in it. According to Fischer and Jackson:

While it may be that the average suburban individual is "localized" only to a minute degree . . . the suburban community as a whole is composed of such individuals. The cumulation of small individual effects in one place can have larger consequences at the aggregate level; e.g., the election of representatives hostile to metropolitan government.

The third and least important explanation for suburban localism is ecological and related to the outlying location of suburbs and to their low population density, both of which increase time/cost when engaging in nonlocal activities. Thus, the friction of space contributes to localism in suburbia.

Fischer and Jackson conclude that the localism effect in suburbia of each level of causation—individual, contextual, and locational—is quite small, but this should not, they say,

16. Zelan, "Does Suburbia Make a Difference?," p. 408.

17. Claude S. Fischer and Robert Max Jackson, "Suburbs, Networks, and Attitudes," in *The Changing Face of the Suburbs*, ed. Barry Schwartz (Chicago: University of Chicago Press, 1975, forthcoming).

mislead us about potentially significant community effects. As American society continues to suburbanize, a larger proportion of its population shifts from a city to suburban location and social context. Slight as the effects might be on each person, the balance moves increasingly, for better or for worse, from urban ways of life to suburban ones. . . . In neighboring and localism, as well as in other ways, small towns and suburbs are alike. In that sense, the increasing suburbanization of America may mean, in part, the de-urbanization of America.[18]

WESTLAKE: LIFE STYLE BEYOND SUBURBIA

The phrase "de-urbanization of America" seems almost prophetic when viewing the attitudes and life style of the suburbanites' suburbs— that is, the communities attracting those who have already experienced suburbia and want something better. These suburbanites are not so much opposed to cities as they are detached and aloof. They do not seem to find cities real enough to be concerned about them. At least these are judgments which may be made on the basis of Rabinovitz and Lamare's study of Westlake Village, a "new community" in the San Fernando valley outside Los Angeles and populated largely by former suburbanites.[19] Only four percent of the residents of Westlake Village came there from central cities; almost three-quarters of the residents moved to Westlake from the suburbs of Los Angeles or other large cities. New communities like Westlake are springing up in California and in the suburban periphery of other large American areas, providing an opportunity "to predict what will come after suburbia in metropolitan America."[20]

Westlakers are white upper-middle class persons (professional and managerial occupations, average yearly family income $21,979 in 1969, college-educated) whose reasons for moving to Westlake contrast markedly with those listed by people of a similar socio-economic level who make an initial move from central city to suburb. The suburban "new community" to which they have moved is likewise different. Westlake Village is not a suburban subdivision, but a "new community" in that it is large (12,000 acres, ultimate population goal 70,000, current population 6,000) and has a master plan aiming at some controlled variety and self-sufficiency by providing a range of commercial establishments and services, a town center, employment opportunities, a variety of single-family and apartment housing (but no low income housing), and extensive recreational facilities (pools, bridle paths, golf course), as well as the preservation of the natural environment in areas designated as permanent open space.

Westlakers rarely mention moving to the new community for the sake of their children or for the quality of the schools—the prime reasons of the earlier generation of city-to-suburb movers. Westlakers appear to take these amenities for granted. Neither did they move to achieve greater participation in local neighboring or community affairs (although most actually had high local political and civic participation), nor to find social protection in a homogeneous

18. Fischer and Jackson, "Suburbs, Networks, and Attitudes."

19. Francine F. Rabinovitz and James Lamare, "After Suburbia, What?—The New Communities Movement in Los Angeles," in *Los Angeles: Viability and Prospects for Metropolitan Leadership*, ed. Werner Z. Hirsch (New York: Praeger, 1971), pp. 169–206.

20. Rabinovitz and Lamare, "After Suburbia, What?," p. 171.

group, although as Rabinovitz and Lamare indicate, this protection is "built in" because of the limited range of housing in the master plan.

The main attraction of Westlake in drawing and retaining its population is the natural environment—location, preservation of natural ecology, and air quality; "85.6 percent of the respondents mention environment as primary in at least one dimension of their orientation to Westlake."[21] Of the total environment produced by new communities such as Westlake, it appears that the natural environment and its protection are the main drawing cards—not the social features, the opportunities for community interaction, or even the recreation facilities (Westlakers use them relatively rarely). Old style suburbs have "delivered" on all of these features to a large extent, but not on natural environmental features. Among other things, this indicates the new suburbanites will be even greater consumers of space, a finding reflected in our earlier discussion of the trends in megalopolitan form.

Westlakers are neither overtly racist nor anti-city. They believe in integration, seemingly practice it at work, and probably would accept residential integration with minorities of their own class level. On a scale of negative feelings about Los Angeles, only 9 percent were highly negative, 39 percent were somewhat negative, and the largest percentage, 45, had low negativism scores. On the other hand, although they frequently visit downtown Los Angeles, Hollywood and West Los Angeles, they seldom or never visit South Central Los Angeles (two-thirds had been there never or only once) or East Los Angeles (one-half had been there never or only once), which are the areas of minority and poverty concentration in Los Angeles.[22] Westlakers do not consciously reject the city, its problems, and the problems of the minorities concentrated there; rather, these problems are simply not part of their experience or awareness.

The findings of the Westlake study have been presented at some length because they constitute one of the very few case studies consciously directed at examining life styles and attitudes in the suburbs of lifelong suburbanites. The results make it clear that we cannot assume that suburb to suburb or suburb to exurb migration will simply produce more of the same social consequences as central city to suburban migration. This creates a problem for social theory, but also for social justice, as Rabinovitz and Lamare indicate:

Our most striking finding is the degree to which environmental qualities are rated as important by Westlake residents, and the social community as less significant. Westlake responses suggest that environmental problems may now be the ultimate middle class issue. We guess that rurality is sought rather than community, not necessarily because community is not desired, but because it is achieved already within acceptable limits. The success of the commitment of the native white majority to homogeneity in Los Angeles seems to have so undermined the visibility of the foreign and colored minorities that homogeneity is not an objective goal. And a half-life spent in suburban neighborhoods, in the companionship of one's family, in commuting and in working among others distinguishable by personal but not by group characteristics, has been not lonely or isolating but really quite satisfying, so

21. Rabinovitz and Lamare, "After Suburbia, What?," p. 191.

22. Rabinovitz and Lamare, "After Suburbia, What?," p. 189.

seeking out "community" also loses salience. . . .

How one evaluates this depends on how one rates the issue of environment in importance as against the solution of innercity problems. We think the two are separable, and that middle class America is beginning to rank the environment first.[23]

ECOLOGICAL THEORY BEYOND SUBURBIA

Urban theory faces problems in approaching suburban America not only in terms of life style, but also in terms of formulating an adequate ecological theory to explain the form and dynamics of the megalopolis in which the suburban majority is imbedded. Social scientists have approached even the metropolis with the ecological concepts of an earlier day. The Park-Burgess concentric zonal theory of urban growth and structure, for example, has been expanded to include a suburban "zone."[24] This approach has yielded some valuable insights, as in Schnore's work indicating the variety of central city-suburban contrasts and their evolutionary aspects.[25]

While these approaches are defensible as applied to the metropolis—which, despite its complexity, has one clearly dominant center—they are unsuited to the megalopolis which is not only truly multi-centered, but whose centers are often in competition. Commuting and reverse commuting to and from the dominant center are characteristic only of the metropolis. The patterns of ecological interdependence, and consequently of individual movement and contact, have shifted to a qualitatively different level of complexity in megalopolis. As a result there can be no relatively simple typology of suburbs in megalopolis, a fact which already is becoming apparent as metropolitan expansion continues.[26]

The United States Bureau of the Census (the basic source of descriptive data on suburbs) has, under metropolitan conditions, treated suburbs as a residual category, that is, as the part of the metropolis outside the central city. Census suburban concepts suffer from the same difficulty as formal theoretical approaches in that they were predicated on a concentrated city, expanding from a single center, to which diverse population groups were oriented, as were all the major economic, social and cultural affairs of the city. The census has retooled slowly to meet the problems of urban-suburban definition raised by megalopolis.

With the 1970 census, data are available which permit a fine-grained analysis of the structure of megalopolis. The census has gathered both residential and work addresses for individuals. Geographer Brian J. L. Berry emphasizes the importance of tabulation of this data in depicting the network of daily urban systems in the United States.[27] On the basis of

23. Rabinovitz and Lamare, "After Suburbia, What?," pp. 202, 204.

24. There are some derivations from earlier ecological theory which are more suitable to megalopolitan ecological analysis. Factorial ecology, for example, makes no assumptions about a *single* ecological distributive pattern radiating from a center.

25. Leo F. Schnore, "The Socioeconomic Status of Cities and Suburbs," *American Sociological Review* 28 (February 1963), pp. 76–86; Schnore, "Urban Structure and Suburban Selectivity," *Demography* 1 (1964), pp. 164–76; Schnore and Joy K. O. Jones, "The Evolution of City-Suburban Types in the Course of a Decade," *Urban Affairs Quarterly* 4 (June 1969), pp. 421–43.

26. *See*, for example, the discussion in Gist and Fava, "Urban Transformation," pp. 306ff.

27. Brian J. L. Berry, "Urban Definitions Beyond Megalopolis," in *Research and the*

his earlier work with 1960 census data, Berry contends that "twentieth century metropolises have so burst their nineteenth century boundaries that . . . a network of DUS's [Daily Urban Systems], each with a radius of 75–80 miles, now blankets all except the most sparsely settled parts of the country, embracing daily activities and travel of 90 percent of the nation's population."[28]

Berry also contends that the DUS is an accurate predictor of future megalopolitan growth because the DUS is based on the delineation of actual job and housing markets rather than being restricted to the somewhat arbitrary inclusion or exclusion of whole counties. In this kind of assessment the hinterland plays a dynamic role in the establishment of distinguishing characteristics of the megalopolis rather than representing, as it does in the metropolitan concept, a mere petering out at the margins of central-city influence.

RACISM AND SEXISM IN MEGALOPOLIS

Two groups are "invisible" in the theory of megalopolis—blacks and women. Although there is much research and discussion on blacks, the findings are from housing and locational decisions of major constraint and limited choice. Recent studies of black population movement indicate that the dual housing market has now

extended to suburbia: since the late 1960s there appears to be a stream of "true" suburban migration of blacks, that is, the decentralization of middle class blacks rather than the engulfing by expanding urban growth of peripherally located, lower status blacks. However, the newly suburban blacks remain residentially segregated, often by racial succession in the "inner ring" of aging suburbs, by tokenism in white suburbs, and sometimes by living in new suburban developments designated, unofficially, for blacks. Black suburbanization has not decreased residential segregation.

New communities, especially those designated to receive federal financial guarantees under the 1968 (Title IV) and the 1970 (Title VII) Housing Acts, were widely heralded as ways to widen residential choice for blacks, including the poor black; in fact, one of the express goals of Titles IV and VII was to lessen the movement toward "two societies." However, both federally and privately sponsored new communities have only small percentages of blacks. Except for Soul City, North Carolina, blacks have not participated as organized groups in the planning and promoting of new communities. In January 1975 the Department of Housing and Urban Development (HUD) announced that no additional federally sponsored new communities would be designated; they and the privately sponsored new communities, too, are suffering from the combined effects of inflation in interest rates and building costs and recession in family purchasing power.[29]

New communities have not ex-

1970 Census, ed. Abbott Ferriss (Oak Ridge, Tenn.: Southern Regional Demographic Group, Oak Ridge Associated Universities, Inc., 1971), pp. 151–57.

28. Brian J. L. Berry, "Population Growth in the Daily Urban Systems of the United States, 1980–2000," in U.S., Commission on Population Growth and the American Future, *Population, Distribution, and Policy*, p. 240 (see footnote 5).

29. For a full discussion of new communities as suburbs, *see*, Helene Smookler's article in this volume.

tended black residential choice to any significant degree, in part because they lack knowledge of (and willingness to implement) the full range of black residential choice. What institutions and amenities would attract and retain specific groups of black residents? Piecing together the available evidence suggests, not surprisingly, that in terms of residential choice (degree of racial integration, central city vs. suburban location, and the like) there are several major subgroups among blacks.[30] No one type of community can satisfy all these subgroups. Megalopolis should provide for true freedom of residential choice among blacks rather than having black suburbanization represent merely the black "inheritance" of out-dated suburbs, as blacks earlier "inherited" deteriorating central city areas. The evidence so far is that the new patterns of megalopolitan development have shown no new basis for wide racial integration, and the old urban patterns are found to be repeated in the suburban environment. The problems of racial discrimination seem to be abating only for some of the well educated and prosperous blacks.

Although distinctions must be drawn in entirely different ways for women and for racial minorities, in terms of megalopolitan structure women are also a deprived group. The trends toward an ever more dispersed suburbia and the separation of work and residence are founded on deep-seated sexist assumptions about the role of women. Sociologist and planner Janet Abu-Lughod, having attended a recent major urban conference where she was the only woman, relates a discussion of the city of the future as follows:

Discussion moved to the issue of increased leisure and its implications for projected alteration in the workday and workweek and, hence, for anticipated changes in the physical arrangement of the metropolis. Great interest and indeed excitement began to generate, revolving around the prospect of the four-day week. This, one after another concurred, would be an absolutely marvellous design for living. It would permit even *more complete* separation of work from residence! "A *man* could go into the city to work, spend three nights there, and then *return to his family* out in the country for the other four nights."

. . . the vision of the future city they were so enthusiastic about was one which . . . was designed for men only. Married females with children presumably were to remain on rural "breeding farms." The status of single women was indeterminate; perhaps they were to be kept in the city for those other three nights? Sex roles were to be totally differentiated for, obviously, both women with children *and* their husbands could hardly expect to desert the children in the exurbs for four days and three nights, even given the existence of TV dinners!

. . . No woman I have told this story to has felt that it was a matter to joke about. We are frightened by this handwriting on the wall.[31] (emphasis in the original)

PLANNING FOR WOMEN

Planning for women in the expanding megalopolis occurs rarely,

30. For extended discussion on this point, *see*, Sylvia F. Fava, "Blacks in American New Towns: Problems and Prospects," *Sociological Symposium* 12 (Fall 1974), pp. 111–29.

31. Janet Abu-Lughod, "Designing a City for All," in *Planning, Women, and Change*, ed. Karen Hapgood and Judith Getzels (Chicago, Ill.: American Society of Planning Officials, proceedings of the Workshop on Planning for Women, 3–4 December 1974, sponsored by U.S., Department of Housing and Urban Development), p. 37.

but when it does, according to a recent literature review by Goldstein, it focuses very much on the "typical" young mother, and it rests on the rigid separation of home (women) from work (men) described above by Abu-Lughod.[32] Thus, in his recommendations to James Rouse, the builder of Columbia, Maryland—the large, privately developed new community between Baltimore and Washington, D.C.—Gans said, "For the man: job, job satisfaction, and job security are most important, as is freedom from financial pressure. He wants his wife and children to be happy. . . . For the wife: welfare and happiness of husband and especially children are most important. . . ."[33]

It is fitting that we are able to "return" to Columbia six years after its founding to examine the results of the planning recommended by Gans and others. A survey using a stratified random sample of households in Columbia found a much more diverse range of expressed needs, interests and problems of Columbia's women and led to the following recommendations: guidance counseling; educational opportunities, particularly at the graduate level; social and other activities to serve women who differ from the typical married woman with children (for example, women under 24, childless women, divorced women and black women), counseling in the areas of mental health, marital problems and dealing with one's children; childcare facilities; public transportation for women and also to relieve them of the need for transporting children; information services; and low-cost group meals so cooking would not always have to be done at home.[34] The women of Columbia display a much wider range of needs and interests than are met by stereotyped planning. Another illustration is the failure in Columbia of the neighborhood centers to serve as gathering places and information centers.[35]

The suburb, old and new, is geared to the married woman with children and, furthermore, allows for little change in her role or goals. The single woman, the divorcee or widow, the parent without a partner, and the woman who works or wishes to work are poorly served by suburb or exurb. Low density and its resultant lack of public transportation limit the accessibility of non-local associates, activities and jobs.

Michelson, in an interim report of new residents' experience a little more than a year after their move, compares the reaction of married couples in four different residential environments—apartments downtown, single-family homes downtown, suburban apartments, and suburban single-family homes. On a scale rating from one to 10 the degree of satisfaction with how they spend their time, women in suburban houses had by far the lowest scores among all four residential groups,

32. Joan Goldstein, "Planning for Women in the New Towns: New Concepts and Dated Roles" (Paper delivered at the Annual Meeting of the American Sociological Association, San Francisco, August 1975).

33. Herbert J. Gans, "Planning for Everyday Life and Problems of Suburban and New Towns Residents," in *People and Plans,* ed. H. J. Gans (New York: Basic Books, 1968), p. 188.

34. Mary Stuart, "A Study of Women's Needs in Columbia" (Columbia, Md.: Columbia Association, April 1974).

35. Charlotte Temple, "Planning and the Married Woman with Children—a New Town Perspective," in *Planning, Women, and Change,* pp. 45–6 (see footnote 31).

while the husbands in suburban homes had the highest scores![36] Few of these wives in single-family homes had a job, while most of the wives in the other three residential settings were employed.

The data show . . . that suburban housewives are *increasingly satisfied* with the social characteristics of their neighbourhood and *increasingly dissatisfied* with the locational aspects of the very same neighbourhood over time. In contrast, their husbands, who expect to be out of the neighbourhood every day, and who have the added social benefits of their family's extensive contact pattern within the neighbourhood when they return, remain very pleased with their location.[37] (emphasis in the original)

Michelson's study is longitudinal and will cover a five-year period. His final results, when available, should be most revealing for the long range assessment of suburban (and urban) locational effects on men and women.

The physical structure of suburbia limits the horizons and opportunities of women, often forcing them to choose between fulfilling their family roles and developing as persons in their own right. The limited career ladder open to suburban women is a case in point. Local jobs are typically dead-end service jobs in stores or schools; other jobs require heavy commuting or further training—which also involves heavy commuting. Yet, as noted above, the low density which inhibits the growth of clustered facilities widely accessible by public transportation is becoming even lower. The expanding mega-lopolis is not facilitating the expansion of the roles of women.

Nevertheless, women's roles are changing, as indicated by several recent trends: the marriage rate in 1973 was down for the first time since World War II, and more women are staying single until their mid-twenties; the birth rate is only slightly above the 1973 record low of 15 per 1,000; the divorce rate continues to rise as it has every year since 1962; the proportion of women with paying jobs continues to increase, even among those with young children (in 1970, 43 percent of all women worked, as did 30 percent of those with children under 6 years of age).

The consequences of these trends beyond suburbia can now only be speculated. Future developments might include families' remaining in dispersed locations but with much more sharing of household and childcare tasks; declining marketability of large homes; and further decentralization of factory and office jobs as firms move closer to their labor pool. Changes such as these might be involved in the development of a megalopolitan structure flexible enough to permit women a wide choice of roles.

MEGALOPOLIS—REAL OR UNREAL?

Megalopolis is real as a highly complex entity, but not now as a social or political entity. This analysis has indicated how the new suburbanization has removed an increasing proportion of the American population from the immediate experience of inner-city problems and high density living. The social problems of racism and sexism have been major concerns of the postwar period. Expectations have been high that the

36. William Michelson, "Environmental Change," Centre for Urban and Community Studies, Research Paper no. 60 (University of Toronto, October 1973), p. 38.

37. Michelson, "Environmental Change," p. 42.

new physical developments and life styles that have emerged would provide a way out of the old dilemmas. But the changes that have occurred have not altered, for the most part, the underlying patterns of discrimination which remain to trouble future generations.

The recent focus of public policy has shifted away from the center city and problems popularly associated with it. Federal expenditures favor small metropolitan areas and those with lower densities.[38] The federal government has declared that the "urban crisis is over."[39] These are only straws in the wind, however, and may not indicate the direction of future policy.[40] Various public needs exist in the component parts of megalopolis; how and through what political structures these needs will be expressed and met remains a major question.

38. Regional Plan Association, *Growth and Settlement*, p. 12.

39. Ernest Holsendolph, "Urban Crisis of the 1960s is Over, Ford Aides Say," *New York Times* (23 March 1975), pp. 1, 46.

40. A recent analysis of some issues of leadership and power in our largest megalopolis concluded that although "megalopolis as a meaningful sociological community has not arrived . . . a power base exists." Delbert Miller, *Leadership and Power in the Bos-Wash Megalopolis* (New York: Wiley-Interscience, 1975), p. 357.

From Suburb to Urban Place

By DAVID L. BIRCH

ABSTRACT: The relationship of the suburbs to each other and to the central city is changing. Initially sub-urban in an urban hierarchy, suburbs are gradually gaining full urban status as nodes in a series of networks. In the process, they are inheriting many of the functions and problems previously reserved for the central city. One major result will be an increasing tension between the "old-timers" and the "newcomers." In a hierarchical, fractionated region, old-timers have always constituted a majority and have thereby resisted change. As the urban hierarchy breaks down, it may be more difficult for the parts to maintain differences, and it may seem more logical to balance what is good for people against what is good for places.

David L. Birch is a Senior Research Scientist in the School of Architecture and Planning, Massachusetts Institute of Technology. Educated at Harvard University, he is author of The Economic Future of City and Suburb *and co-author of* America's Housing Needs: 1970 to 1980 *and* Patterns of Urban Change: The New Haven Experience.

FOR some time, scholars and journalists have written about the suburbanization of everything—people, jobs, problems, and so forth. Less attention has been given to the processes by which dispersal has taken place. A closer look at these processes suggests that the very thing that encouraged suburbanization from 1920 to 1970—improved personal transportation—plus some new factors, such as improved communications and still better transportation, is causing and will continue to cause a gradual change in suburban character. Increasingly, suburbs will no longer be suburban. Rather they will become urban places in their own right—perhaps we should call them "urbs." Urbs will relate to and be affected by a national and sometimes international network of urban places. Their relationship to the central city that spawned them is changing, and the change will affect all urbs, central or otherwise, in terms of the acquisition and provision of services.

THE CHANGES

Few would argue the point that people and jobs and housing units are distributed differently today than they were in 1900, or even as recently as 1950. Figure 1 reveals the changes in population. Suburbs have boomed at the expense of both cities and farms. The shift in employment is less well documented, particularly prior to 1950. Nevertheless, all the evidence suggests that most central cities' share of employment has been declining steadily since 1947. Between 1958 and 1967, for example, employment growth took place much faster in suburbs than in central cities. Suburban job growth even outstripped suburban population gains (see table 1).

Underlying these changes in the aggregates have been changes in the mix as well. The original suburbs were developed mostly for the rich who could afford new construction and the trip to and from the center. While the suburban population still remains wealthier and better educated than its central city counterpart, some of the distinctions are becoming blurred. In fact, the trend at the margin is in exactly the opposite direction. As table 2 shows, between 1960 and 1970 the percentage of the central city population earning high incomes increased, and the percentage earning low incomes decreased (after adjusting for inflation). During this same period, the suburban share of the metropolitan poor increased.

The black population is spreading out as well. Blacks maintained their share of the suburban population boom during the 1960s, thereby increasing the suburban black population significantly. This is not to say that all suburbs are turning into integrated, salt-and-pepper neighborhoods. It does suggest, however, that the process of black territorial expansion is, in many cases, crossing the city boundary into the inner suburbs and, in some cases, beyond.

Employment mixes are shifting also. Formerly the place where all forms of commerce were conducted, central cities no longer offer distinct advantages to most retailers and manufacturers. Cities remain attractive, however, to those who depend on a central place and face-to-face contact—lawyers, bankers, advertising agencies, corporate headquarters and investment bankers. Thus, the central city mix is shifting in favor of services of all kinds.

The suburbs are going through a different transition. Initially dominated by retailers and branch banks

FIGURE 1

PERCENT OF U.S. POPULATION IN RURAL, CENTRAL CITY,
AND SUBURBAN AREAS: 1900–1970

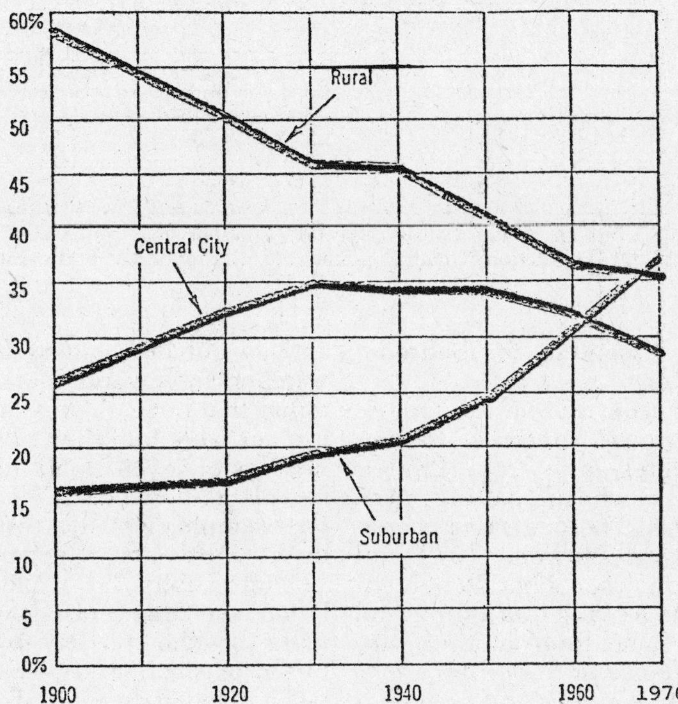

SOURCES: U.S., Department of Commerce, Bureau of the Census, *U.S. Census of Population: 1960, Selected Area Reports, Standard Metropolitan Statistical Areas*, Final Report PC (3)-1D; *Current Population Reports*, "Social and Economic Characteristics of the Population in Metropolitan and Nonmetropolitan Areas; 1970 and 1960," Report P 23, No. 37 (June 1971).

NOTE: 1960 boundaries are used throughout to permit comparability.

serving a residential population, they are gradually developing complete economic bases of their own. Interstate highways and cheap land have drawn manufacturers outward. Wholesalers and supporting services have followed, providing external economies that previously could be found only in central cities.

THE PROCESSES

Thus far we have summarized reasonably well-known redistributions of people and jobs without reference to how the shifts have taken place. The implicit model is movement from the city to the surrounding suburbs.

In many cases, particularly in the early, formative stages of the outlying urbs, out-movement probably was the dominant process. Wealthier families who could afford to commute and to purchase single-family houses used their money to buy privacy and pseudo-rurality. Most household heads returned to the central city to work each day. Suburban business catered to this pattern, springing up to provide services

TABLE 1

AVERAGE ANNUAL PERCENTAGE CHANGE IN POPULATION AND EMPLOYMENT IN
ALL SMSAs, CENTRAL CITIES, AND SUBURBAN RINGS

	POPULATION 1960–1970	EMPLOYMENT 1958–1967			
		MFG.	RETAIL TRADE	WHOLESALE TRADE	SELECTED SERVICES
SMSAs	1.4	1.8	2.5	2.8	3.5
Central cities	.6	.7	.8	1.1	2.6
Suburban rings	2.2	3.1	5.3	7.4	6.1

SOURCE: U.S., Bureau of the Census, *Special Economic Reports*, Series ES20 (72)-1, "Employment and Population Changes—Standard Metropolitan Statistical Areas and Central Cities" (1972).

and living essentials for bedroom communities.

A significant portion of today's suburban growth continues to consist of whites and, to a limited extent, blacks who are bailing out of central cities. The pattern is changing, however. Between 1970 and 1973, for example, about 70 percent of all people moving into a suburban residence came from another suburban residence or from rural areas, and only 30 percent came from central cities. As the central city bailout runs its natural course, and as the wealthy continue to reinhabit selected central city neighborhoods, dependence on the central city as a source of population growth will decrease further. In short, the outlying urbs are, for the most part, generating their own people.

The activities of the business population are much less well chronicled. Limited evidence suggests, however, that most of the relative employment shift from the city to suburbs has resulted not from the much-ballyhooed movement out of a few well-known firms, but rather from a shift in the places new firms have chosen to make their start. In New Haven, for example, where the detailed decisions of businesses to start up, expand, contract, relocate, and go out of business have been watched for several years, we have found that beneath slow net change is a veritable bubbling of activity. A net loss of seven small manufacturing plants between 1959 and 1967, for example, was the result of 190 births, 150 deaths, 58 expansions and 11 contractions—a very active population (see table 3). In days gone by, most of the births—particularly births of small firms—would have taken place in the central city where supporting services could be found. This is no longer the case. Between 1959 and 1967, more than 60 percent of all births in manufacturing took place in New Haven's suburbs.

TABLE 2

PERCENTAGE OF CENTRAL CITY FAMILIES
EARNING UNDER $5,000 AND OVER
$15,000 IN 1959 AND 1969,
IN 1969 DOLLARS

	1959	1969
Percent earning under $5,000	26.5	20.8
Percent earning over $15,000	9.8	18.9

SOURCE: U.S., Bureau of the Census, *Current Population Reports*, "Social and Economic Characteristic of the Population in Metropolitan and Nonmetropolitan Areas: 1970 and 1960," Report P 23, No. 37 (June 1971).

TABLE 3

BIRTHS, DEATHS, EXPANSION, AND CONTRACTION OF MANUFACTURING PLANTS
IN THE NEW HAVEN SMSA 1959 TO 1967

SIZE OF PLANT (EMPLOYEES)	NO. OF PLANTS IN 1959	BIRTHS	DEATHS	NET CHANGE FROM EXPANSION	NET CHANGE FROM CONTRACTION	NO. OF PLANTS IN 1967	NET CHANGE
Small (1–9)	396	+190	−150	−58	+11	389	−7
Medium (10–249)	380	+114	−113	+50	−8	423	+43
Large (250+)	34	+2	−4	+8	−3	37	+3

SOURCE: D. L. Birch et al., *Patterns of Urban Change: The New Haven Experience* (Lexington, Mass.: Lexington Books, D.C. Heath, 1974).

"Natural increase" (the net of births over deaths) accounted for two-thirds of the total growth in suburban manufacturing establishments. Apparently the more remote urbs are now sufficiently well developed to offer at least as nourishing an environment as the central urb. Suburbs are now producing their own jobs as well as their own people.

With employment shifting out faster than the population, suburban wage earners have become less and less dependent on the central city for jobs. The proportion that lives and works in the suburbs is increasing (see table 4). Perhaps more striking is the substantial increase in the number of central city residents who commute to the suburbs. We are approaching the point when a greater share of the city's population will depend on the suburbs for work than vice versa.

In brief, the suburbs are increasingly less dependent upon the central city for most of their population growth, and they do not depend upon the central city to provide work for most of their residents. Instead, they are becoming self-generating urban places in their own right.

NETWORKS VERSUS HIERARCHIES

The suburbs' decreasing depen-dence on the central city raises a broader question: On what, if anything, will they depend? Will each suburb gradually take on all urban functions in approximately the same proportions, leading to a collection of similar, largely independent cells? Or will communities continue to

TABLE 4

PERCENTAGE WHO LIVE IN CITY AND WORK IN SUBURBS, AND PERCENTAGE WHO LIVE AND WORK IN SUBURBS, FOR THE 120 LARGEST U.S. METROPOLITAN AREAS (SMSAs) IN 1960 AND 1970

	1960	1970
Percentage of central city residents commuting to suburban jobs		
smaller SMSAs	11	17
medium-sized SMSAs	10	20
large SMSAs	9	14
Percentage of suburban residents who work in the suburbs		
smaller SMSAs	60	60
medium-sized SMSAs	64	66
large SMSAs	68	72

SOURCE: Derived from U.S., Bureau of the Census, *Census of Population: 1970, Detailed Characteristics* [PC(1)–D1]; and U.S. *Census of Population: 1960, Characteristics of the Population,* pt. 1.

NOTE: SMSAs were ranked by size according to number of workers rather than number of people. The categories are: smaller (under 500,000), medium-sized (500,000 to 1,000,000), and large (over 1,000,000).

specialize, and, if they do, on whom will they depend for the things they do not provide for themselves? The answers are not totally clear during this period of transition. Certainly most outlying urbs will take on more businesses and a more homogeneous mix of people, thereby diminishing the differences between themselves and the central city. But it is difficult to imagine, under the present political system, their becoming completely uniform. Also, with present technology, it is difficult to imagine their assuming all functions. What seems far more plausible is that the suburbs will make a transition from being second-order urbs in an urban hierarchy to becoming nodes in a variety of interconnecting and overlapping networks, each of which provides the urbs with some service, and each of which connects them with other places.

The interstate highway system is the most obvious example of a network connecting each urb with the rest of the world. The interstate system makes it possible to produce nearly anything anywhere and ship it conveniently to almost any place. All urbs have practically equal status in this net from a transportation standpoint, with distance from markets being the sole distinguishing factor—and even distance is losing its hold. We think nothing of eating fresh carrots from the Imperial Valley in California, fresh apples from the state of Washington, and fresh meat from Colorado or Texas, all in the same meal in Portland, Maine. Likewise, we acquire our more durable products from all over the world and distribute them to stores throughout the United States, mostly by truck.

Communications networks are another obvious example. The Tennessee Department of Commerce and Community Development describes how a successful businessman runs his international advertising agency from the hills of Tennessee. This may be an extreme case, but it illustrates the fact that anyone anywhere in the United States can communicate directly and cheaply, and sometimes visually, with anyone else at any time. Communications satellites have extended this net internationally. One of the author's research colleagues who will be working in France next year may well do his analytical work on a computer in central Massachusetts through communications satellite. Businesses, of course, are constantly involved in similar transfers of information.

The list of emerging networks gets longer and longer each year. Electrical power is now provided through a grid. When the Big Alice turbine in Manhattan breaks down, switches are thrown in Oak Ridge, Tennessee, to direct power to New York from Oak Ridge's Bull Run steam plant. The stock exchange will soon lose its localized, regional character: all stock transactions in the United States will shortly be reported in all places through a single, simultaneous communications hook-up. National television networks have constant ties into similar nets throughout the world and occasionally on the moon. Money now flows through a complex of international channels directly to your local bank. Jet airplanes and an expanding number of jet-compatible airports make it possible for business executives to visit customers and suppliers anywhere within a 1,000 mile radius and return on the same day.

In the past, distance and access left most places in a subordinate position. The central city was the transportation and communications center for the region. Everything flowed through it, and people everywhere depended upon it for their existence. The effect of most of the networks mentioned above has been to minimize location relative to the center as a determinant of which places will thrive and which will not, and thus to open up a much greater number of places where people can live and work. If behavior is taken as an indication of preferences, people seem to want to be farther away from the central city. Between 1970 and 1973, for example, for the first time in a long time, more people left metropolitan areas (as defined in 1970) than entered them. Much of this outflow was to nearby "exurbs." The Standard Metropolitan Statistical Area (SMSA) boundaries can hardly be adjusted fast enough to keep up with the change.

IMPLICATIONS

What does all this mean for the various urbs in a region? It means that each suburban community is depending, and will continue to depend, less and less on the nearby central city and more on the other places to which it is connected through an increasingly complex set of networks—roads, cables, airplanes, satellites, computers, and so forth. Networks of this kind encourage specialization of things that benefit from specialization. They also foster a more even distribution of the people and jobs that were once restricted to a central place.

Most outlying urbs, for example, are likely to encounter an increasing number of business people who want to start up new businesses in their communities. They are likely to find builders who, faced with rising construction costs and a demand for units, will request zoning variances to permit apartment and condominium construction. They will find, over time, a gradual increase in the number of poorer people living in their communities as the poor continue to disperse in search of employment. They may even find a growing number of minority households, although evidence to date suggests that minority groups continue, not totally by choice, to be concentrated in a relatively few places. In short, these communities will take on more and more of the urban functions that were previously concentrated near the center and, in the process, will become more and more like each other. The distinction between central city, inner suburb and outer suburb will gradually fade.

During this process, outlying places may find themselves housing specialized functions to which they are unaccustomed. Airports and transportation terminals will concentrate there. Specialized clinics and medical facilities may move out, as the Lahey Clinic is presently doing in Boston. Major sports facilities will be found in only a few places, as will museums and orchestras.

As a consequence of both homogeneity and specialization, communities will face demands for services which never surfaced during their existence as bedroom communities. Welfare case loads will rise. Bilingual teachers will be needed for schools. Crime prevention will become a far more serious matter. Providing utilities and roads and traffic control for specialized facilities and business complexes will strain local planning departments, as will the pressure for higher-density residential construction to keep housing costs down.

Many of these changes will unsettle the political process. The conflict between the "old-timers" and the "newcomers" will emerge as a major issue. To the old-timers, the dispersal of urban functions and people that had previously been concentrated in the center will be viewed as decline. The newcomers will push for lower-quality schools and lower-quality services generally in order to keep their tax bills down and life in the community within their reach. This decline in the quality of services and, in some cases, the quality of the physical environment as well, will rankle the people who moved there earlier to escape from the masses. The newcomers, of course, will view the older residents' attempts to maintain service quality, zoning restrictions and taxes as attempts to exclude them, and they will attack such attempts vigorously.

The outcome of this conflict will vary from place to place. Some communities are so well entrenched that they will resist erosion of standards indefinitely. Others will fall quickly as the rationale for the present residents to stay there evaporates. Most communities will feel this conflict, however, and the result in most cases will be an erosion of service quality and a perception on the part of most existing residents that "things aren't the way they used to be—the place is gradually going downhill."

Consequences for the Central City

Many observers and residents of central cities have noted the tendencies described above and have become discouraged. Farthest along in the process of decline, the central cities, particularly the older ones, appear doomed to decay. As one planner said to the author: "We must now train planners to be undertakers to preside at the central cities' wake."

Few would argue that the immediate future for older central cities is promising. The financial strains of serving an increasingly needy population with an increasingly inefficient, entrenched bureaucracy are showing everywhere. It may be a mistake, though, to extrapolate the immediate future indefinitely.

In fact, given time to work themselves out, the processes described above may spell hope for the central cities. For one thing, the burden of providing for the most needy in society will increasingly be spread across political and taxing boundaries. As indicated earlier, the share of central city families with high incomes is rising steadily, and the share with low incomes is declining.

Also, the economic function that the central city performs well—that of providing a central place where business and professional people can get together in face-to-face negotiations—is a function that is increasing rather than decreasing in importance. It is a critical function in the service sector of the economy— the sector that is growing the fastest. New office complexes have been built in many central cities across the country, including the older ones, to meet the demand for modern, comfortable places to do business in a central place. It is not accidental that modern apartment and condominium projects have sprung up beside them for those who cannot find the semi-rurality they desire within a tolerable daily commuting range.

Properly nourished, these seeds of central city revival could well grow, turning the cities into attractive, exciting options for those to whom concentration and face-to-face negotiations are still important. This group will never equal in number the masses who once flocked to central cities and are now leaving them. Central city mayors, as well as those who create formulas to allocate federal and state dollars to central cities, must come to realize that aggregate population declines are not necessarily bad. Time and again, the author has encountered frantic efforts by city administrators and boosters to bury surveys which show that people want to get out of the city, or Census Bureau reports suggesting that they have already done so. These people's motivations are genuine enough: they fear bad publicity and a further acceleration of the trend. For the chambers of commerce, decline may well be bad, because it means decreasing membership and dues. But for cities as a whole, decline coupled with a more balanced mix may well be the basis for survival.

Unfortunately, many state and federal formulas have minimum-size cutoffs, and many cities are approaching those cutoffs. The situation is indeed a perverse one, for during this period of decline the need for funds is greatest. The return of the elite does little to help those poor who remain. The city is thus left with significant numbers of the elderly, the less well-educated, the very poor and the sick. A few decades of natural attrition and very slow dispersal will be required before these groups have redistributed themselves. In the meantime, the central city must do everything it can on their behalf, and as a nation we must not penalize central cities because they have inherited this function.

Summary and Conclusion

Most observers of urban areas in the United States have noted the striking redistribution of people and jobs during the period since World War II. A close look at the underlying processes suggests that, in the future, continued growth of outlying areas will stem not so much from their dependence on a central city as from their dependence on a large number of urban places throughout the nation—and the world—to which they are connected through a series of networks. As the number and importance of these networks increase, the actual distance to central transportation centers will matter less and less. It will be possible to perform more and more functions in more and more different places. Lacking a major change in preferences, households and businessmen will continue to seek out low density settings that offer easy access to concentrations when concentrations are important.

The emergence of networks means a weakening of the existing hierarchy. There is little reason for the less well-off to remain in the center, or for the wealthy to commute daily to the center. With dispersal of people and jobs has come the dispersal of urban functions and urban problems. Suburbs will experience to an increasing degree all the problems that were previously concentrated in the center.

The older central cities will suffer badly during this transition. They will be left with many of the residents and the businesses and governments that are least able to take care of themselves. The financial burdens will be enormous. In the midst of this gloomy picture, however, lie the ingredients for a re-use of the central city which could, over time, make such places attractive and self-sufficient once again. Many economic activities still require centralized, face-to-face contact; these sectors of the economy are growing and, by and large, demand and support a prosperous workforce. Amidst the aggregate decline, we are already witnessing a change in mix that reflects these possibilities. Many central cities are in the process of becoming smaller but important, elite service centers in their regions.

Whether these changes in the structure of regions are good or bad depends strictly on how they are viewed and by whom. For the president of a central city chamber of commerce who believes in growth, things will get worse. A long term resident of a prosperous suburb who wants to continue to raise the level of services will likely become frustrated. Those who care about the well-being of less fortunate people in the central city will become more and more concerned about these people's capacity to deal satisfactorily with their own problems. The mayor of a central city will continue to be concerned about the cost of assisting this less fortunate group. On the other hand, for an upwardly mobile person who would like to live in a lower density setting, the chances are increasingly good for finding a job and a place to live that is more to his or her liking.

These relative perspectives on community change, and the inherent conflict between the old-timers and the newcomers, raise a basic question: by what standards should we judge the performance of a region and its parts? The traditional approach is to assess the quality of a region's places and changes in that quality over time. In many ways, this is like judging a factory by how much its equipment has depreciated. No one would evaluate a factory in those terms. The depreciation of equipment is always balanced against the value of the products or services provided. Our regions produce products and services as well. They provide opportunities for people to better themselves by obtaining a better education, a better neighborhood, a better house, and so forth. Historically, this upward mobility of people has "consumed" neighborhoods in much the same way that a factory consumes machines. If we are to judge a region's performance, it must be in terms of a balance between what happens to places and what happens to groups of people.

The policy implications of such a balancing are nontrivial. "Decline" of places per se (as perceived by existing residents) may or may not be a bad thing when weighed against the potential benefits to those for whom the decline represents an opportunity to move up. So long as regions are broken into self-governing communities, the voting majority will always, by definition, be old-timers, and the mobility of newcomers and their problems will always be viewed as a bad thing. As the hierarchy that encouraged community differences within regions loses its strength, however, and as the same problems become common to all, we may reach a point politically where we will prefer to look at broader balances and to make decisions on a regional rather than a local basis. A regional viewpoint on schools is an obvious example of balancing for which precedents already exist. Regionalization of other services, and perhaps even governance of the use of land and the housing stock, will make more sense in the years ahead.

Many of the tendencies precipitating such changes could be substantially altered by rising construction and energy costs. Rising costs of producing a new housing unit or a new plant, for example, will place a premium on the existing stock of structures at their present locations. Rising energy costs will reduce the extent to which businesses and households can use the interstate highway system to achieve independence.

It is certainly too early to tell what the ultimate effects will be. These will depend on how strong the desire for living and working away from the center really is. If it continues to be as strong as it has been in the past, people may accept lower housing standards in order to achieve a more desirable environment. The rapid rise in the sale of mobile homes as permanent dwelling units suggests that this is already taking place. Likewise, businesses may continue to move out in search of markets and a more talented labor force, bringing jobs where people want them and relying on the automobile industry and Congress to devise ways to reduce the cost. Also, faced with these pressures, the elite may move more quickly to reinhabit the central core, accelerating the current trend.

New factors of this sort will always be on the horizon, and their effect will always be difficult to assess. They appear, however, to serve more as modulators of basic trends than as generators of new directions. One cannot help but be impressed by the fervor with which most people, in survey after survey, express their desire to live in lower rather than higher density urban surroundings, and by the success with which, individually and through their governments, they have arranged to get there. It seems improbable that this basic driving force will suddenly evaporate. If recent history is any guide, people will find ways to overcome the obstacles standing in their way. This being the case, it would seem wise for the suburbs and the cities to prepare for different mixes and different functions, and to move with rather than against this tide.

Implications of Suburbanization for Metropolitan Political Organization

By THOMAS M. SCOTT

ABSTRACT: The development of politically independent suburbs began in earnest at the turn of the twentieth century, but their role in the metropolitan governmental complex is still being established. Efforts to consolidate and otherwise integrate fragmented local governments through massive political reorganization in the 1950s and early 1960s were essentially unsuccessful. In the meantime, other less grandiose devices for achieving a measure of metropolitan governmental coordination have flourished: special districts, shifting particular functions from municipalities to other larger scale governments, and inter-local agreements. The evidence is increasingly clear that suburbs persist because they provide life-style opportunities that are important to a large part of the populace but are not otherwise available through urban political institutions. Suburbs are increasingly beset, however, by the same kinds of local governmental problems that have long afflicted central cities, and their political independence does make long-term metropolitan planning and coordination very difficult. Major governmental reorganization of the metropolis does not seem likely, and recent changes in federal and state policies are modifying suburban political autonomy.

Thomas M. Scott is an Associate Professor and immediate past Chairman, Political Science Department, University of Minnesota, where he recently became Associate Director of the Center for Urban and Regional Affairs. He is author of several articles on local government and is currently completing a major study of recent developments in metropolitan governance sponsored by the Brookings Institution.

THE American federal experiment simply was not designed for the urban America of the late twentieth century. The Founding Fathers, working in Philadelphia— a city of about 40,000 in the late 1700s—could not have envisioned our contemporary nation with more than 270 Standard Metropolitan Statistical Areas (SMSAs) spread across its landscape, each with a central city of at least 50,000 people and commonly surrounded by a like number of citizens in satellite suburbs.

The founders and their counterparts writing constitutions for the states certainly understood that population centers—towns and cities—required special governmental consideration, and they made provisions accordingly. But who, really, was prepared for the suburban explosion? Suburbs were not planned as part of our federal system; they emerged on their own and now are here as full partners in the governmental spectrum. How do we deal with them? How do we best include them in our political arrangements? What are the past, present and future implications of suburbia for the organization of American metropolitan government?

EARLY SUBURBS

To begin to answer these questions, one must first consider what suburbs are and why they exist. A full analysis would certainly go beyond the scope of this article, but perhaps a limited explanation will serve our immediate purpose.

Since the beginning of American urban settlement, which in each community was physically concentrated around the center of economic activity, some persons with sufficient resources of time and/or money have chosen to live in more pleasant surroundings away from the city's core.

Through the end of the nineteenth century there were two consequences of this urban population deconcentration—one social, the other governmental.

Sociologically, most of those moving away from the congested city center were the more affluent: those who could afford the cost of land and home ownership, travel and commuting, and providing for themselves the many services that are now provided publicly. Governmentally, the typical pattern was for the central municipality to annex developing fringe territory so as to re-include those who were moving to the urban fringe.

By 1900 this process produced cities that were becoming obviously socially differentiated, with economic activity and lower income persons concentrated in the central core and more affluent persons residing on the urbanizing fringes. The differentiation, however, was contained within a single governmental entity, the city.

SUBURBS FROM 1900 TO 1945

The basic shape of the contemporary metropolis was established between 1900 and 1945, when those resettling on the urban fringe were no longer willing to be annexed to the core city. They preferred limited local governance under the domination of the more rural-oriented townships and counties or, if necessary, incorporation as separate municipalities. For some suburbs this desire for local autonomy was a reaction to the charges of graft, corruption and bad management directed at many of the nineteenth century cities in the East and Midwest. For others it was a desire to maintain local control over decisions involving taxes and land use.

Whatever the reasons, twentieth century suburbs resisted attachment to central cities, and in many states the laws were rewritten to discourage annexation and consolidation and to facilitate municipal incorporation. The process of suburban fringe settlement was, of course, accelerated as automobile ownership became more common after World War I. As a consequence, by the time of the Great Depression the social distinction between city and suburb was well established but no longer contained in a single governmental unit; political fragmentation now characterized the metropolis, and suburbs had become an important, if unanticipated, part of the urban complex.

POST-WORLD WAR II SUBURBS— BEFORE THE URBAN "CRISIS"

Metropolitan and suburban development for the period from 1945 through the late 1960s has been much more complex. Specific trends seem clear enough, but the effects of their combination and interaction are much more obscure and difficult to describe. One new feature has been the role of the federal government, which became more interested in social problems during the depression and responded with several programs that had urban implications, most notably in the production of low income housing. Following World War II, federal policies through Veterans Administration and Federal Housing Administration programs stimulated the construction of hundreds of thousands of new homes, mostly single-family units, mostly located in suburbs where land was available and relatively inexpensive, and mostly for middle income families.

Housing was followed by freeways, also federally subsidized, and suburbia took another leap forward. No one has ever suggested that Congress, through these programs, designed or planned for the suburban explosion. As Francine Rabinovitz expresses it, "The United States does not now have a national urban policy towards suburbs . . . but there are a great number of federal programs which affect suburbs."[1] What is true in the present was also true in the past.

In addition to rapid growth, suburbia began to take on new dimensions and qualities in the period between 1945 and the late 1960s. In most metropolitan areas economic activity was decentralizing. Factories, warehouses and retail merchants were moving to the urban fringe for many of the same reasons that residents did so. With them went jobs, so that the traditional economic dependence of suburbs on the central city was reduced. Increasing numbers of urban citizens could live, work, shop and be entertained in suburbia and no longer required much contact with the central core. Suburbia was becoming independent and self-sufficient.

Moreover, it was becoming increasingly difficult to generalize about suburbs. Suburbs emerged that were almost exclusively industrial; others were dominated by huge retail shopping centers; still others encouraged high-rise apartment construction rather than the more traditional single-family dwelling units. Suburbs developing in the mid-twentieth century, auto-airplane metropolises of the West and Southwest have often been less antagonistic toward their central cities than were their early twentieth century counter-

1. Frederick M. Wirt et al., *On the City's Rim: Politics and Policy in Suburbia* (Lexington, Massachusetts: D. C. Heath, 1972), p. 177.

parts in the East and Midwest. In a few states, notably Texas and Oklahoma, where the nineteenth century practice of annexation is not uncommon, the twentieth century pattern of suburban governmental proliferation is considerably muted.

The sheer growth of suburbia, coupled with its differentiations, generated a whole new set of governmental problems. Rural-oriented township and county boards were not equipped to provide services for a rapidly growing population, much of which in its central city incarnation had become accustomed to paved streets, good schools, good water, sewage treatment, waste disposal, recreation programs, libraries, and the like. Competition for commercial and industrial tax-paying "sugar daddies" soon produced widely disparate fiscal capacities among suburban communities and, more often than not, the rich tended to grow richer while the poor grew progressively poorer. Municipal incorporations increased; some duplication of functions inevitably occurred; local debt and taxes rose; regional planning and coordination of area-wide issues became more difficult; the federal government continued to encourage fringe development with housing subsidies for middle income homeowners and transportation subsidies (via freeway) for intra-metropolitan commuters; and the term "urban sprawl" was popularized.

Suburbia and Metropolitan Reform

All of this looked pretty grim to urbanologists in the 1950s as they tried to anticipate the metropolis of the twenty-first century and as they began to believe that somehow the mindless growth and intra-urban competition had to be stopped, or at least managed. They believed that while the mid-twentieth century metropolis was bigger and more complex than its nineteenth century counterpart, it remained, nonetheless, a community in the broadest sense: its social and economic parts were still interdependent. For them, the heart of the urban problem seemed to lie in the apparently arbitrary and meaningless governmental fragmentation that had been created when suburbs began to insist on their own political identity. If so, the solution seemed easy enough: reduce or eliminate governmental fragmentation by consolidating the proliferating political units, thereby recreating the integrated urban community of the nineteenth century.

Subsequent experience demonstrated that a governmentally integrated metropolis was more attractive in concept than in application. With few exceptions, the attempts to restructure urban governance failed politically, even in modified forms.[2] We learned from this effort that the desire for suburban political independence remains as powerful now as it was at the turn of the century and that governance on a metropolitan scale is not in the cards for the present.

Adjustment without Reform

Upon closer examination of urban governance, however, we also learned that governmental arrangements in the metropolis, especially in suburbs, have not been unresponsive to newer problems and concerns. Increased use of special district governments has provided con-

2. *See*, Thomas M. Scott, "Metropolitan Governmental Reorganization Proposals," *Western Political Quarterly* 21 (June 1968), pp. 252–261.

solidation and large scale governance for some functions, especially those involving significant capital expenditures, such as sewers, water and transit. Other functions have been shifted from municipal to county jurisdiction, thereby broadening the base for their control and support.

Although less visible and dramatic, there have been scores, and perhaps hundreds, of formal and informal agreements made among local political units in most urban regions for cooperating on, and sharing responsibility for, a wide range of functions that the separate units are unable to perform independently. Indeed, it now seems clear that these ad hoc solutions to particular problems in each metropolis have helped reduce the interest in and impetus for more radical restructuring of metropolitan government. Clearly, suburbs as separate political entities within the metropolitan complex are here to stay; efforts to reintegrate them with the core city have failed.

SUBURBIA SINCE THE URBAN "CRISIS"

This analysis carries us through the early 1960s, but it does not illuminate the significant changes that have occurred since that time, both for central cities and suburbs—changes that will shape suburban governance into the 1980s. One important point is that suburbs are no longer simply the residential havens of the city's well-to-do. Suburbia is increasingly diverse, and except for racial integration, it covers a broad spectrum of American social and economic life.

For example, while many suburbs are getting old enough to resemble the core cities which original residents left behind, new suburban development continues on the fringe, ranging from mobile homes (the only housing a significant portion of the population can currently afford) to country estates for upper income gentlemen farmers. Under these circumstances it makes little sense to talk about a single suburban perspective or point of view. Indeed, Frederick M. Wirt and his colleagues conclude that there is nothing distinct about suburban politics, for "Trends in American politics in the aggregate are also trends in American suburbs."[3]

Secondly, suburbanites witnessed, along with everyone else, the urban upheavals of the late 1960s. Many observers have reported on the impact those long, hot urban summers had on federal policies and the subsequent creation of new social programs in the nation's cities. But what were the consequences for the suburbs? How have suburbanites reacted to scenes of racial and police violence, to the plethora of anti-poverty programs and grants, and to court-ordered desegregation? Will the city-centered events of the late 1960s and early 1970s make a difference for suburban governance in the 1980s?

Unfortunately, there is little direct evidence on this point, but one could reasonably conclude that the recent period of urban social and racial unrest is unlikely to soften the resolve of suburbanites to avoid as much as possible direct relationships with central cities.

A final point is that the role of suburbia is currently undergoing fundamental change. This change has been dramatically accelerated by the economic recession of the mid-1970s. Throughout most of its history, and

3. Quoted in Earl M. Baker, "The Suburban Transformation of American Politics," *Publius* 5 (Winter 1975), p. 9.

especially in the period following World War II, suburbia was essentially a residential outpost of the central city. The basic productive capacity of the urban region remained in the inner core, so that suburbs could concentrate on providing shelter and a wide range of associated services for its citizens—primarily good schools, recreation programs for children, low crime rates, and property value protection.

Suburbs did not often confront questions concerning their economic viability or survival. Property taxes could support suburbia as long as the economy of the central city was healthy, local demands for public service remained modest, and incomes of local residents continued to rise. However, when inflation began to outstrip income, and demands for service began to outrun ability to pay, suburban local governments with limited nonresidential property assets began to face, in many cases for the first time, the question of their long term economic and political survival.

It requires quite a wrenching of stereotypes to confront the prospect that suburbs, too, have their problems: post-1950 schools now standing empty; high public personnel expenditures; housing values and accompanying property taxes rising faster than the incomes of resident-owners, and similar problems. One might conclude, prematurely, that such difficulties will finally convince the suburbs to throw in their lot with the central cities and face their common and related problems together, within the framework of new and more appropriate urban political institutions.

A careful review of the past 75 years, however, leads to exactly the opposite conclusion, even though some of the urban events since 1967 have foreshadowed harder times ahead for suburbia. The evidence is overwhelming that the urge to escape the inner city is as pronounced today as it ever was—and now it is a realistic option for a much larger proportion of the population.

The reasons for this attitude are complex. People still seem to want a home of their own on their own property, good schools for their children, and freedom from worry about crime—especially violent crime—open space, and "breathing room." Added to this is the growing frustration toward the city; frustration, incidentally, that is being felt increasingly, even by committed city dwellers. The city is big and bureaucratized; access to political power seems remote at best; tensions are high; public services are mediocre; and images of potential urban violence linger.

While the attractions of the suburbs in the immediate post-World War II period were the housing and related residential amenities they offered, their attraction now is an opportunity to participate in relatively small political units exercising some degree of control over decisions affecting one's life style. Oliver Williams has made this point more eloquently elsewhere.[4] Most people do not become involved with proposed governmental restructuring of relatively remote public functions, such as sewers, water and transit. This is one reason single purpose special districts have been so popular in the past two decades as a device for achieving some measure of metropolitan reform. However, most urbanites are highly interested in decisions directly affecting them and

4. Oliver P. Williams, "The Politics of Urban Space," *Publius* 5 (Winter 1975), pp. 17–19.

those they contact in their daily lives—decisions on local schools, police, recreation, zoning, and other land use controls.

Williams's conclusion—and this may be the key to understanding the politics of metropolitan governance for the remainder of the century—is that suburbanites will work hard to protect access to, and control over, life-style decisions. The process of deciding such issues will therefore remain decentralized. On the other hand, there will be less concern about other kinds of public issues, so that governmental restructuring for some functions may be more likely.[5]

THE FUTURE FOR SUBURBS AND METROPOLITAN GOVERNANCE

If the above line of reasoning is correct, recent suburban experience will influence metropolitan governance in important ways during the next 25 years. Some trends are already well established and can be expected to persist; others are quite new and cannot yet be fully assessed; still others are little more than speculation at present.

The most obvious and persistent fact of metropolitan governance is that suburbs, as separate political entities, are here to stay. However, their social and economic roles are changing along with their political responsibilities. Since most suburbs cannot compete successfully for non-residential tax resources, they must keep a careful watch on public expenditures and modify any aspirations to becoming full-scale general purpose local governments. This forces them to evaluate their govern-mental roles on an ad hoc function-by-function basis. It also provides a strong incentive for relinquishing certain responsibilities (those affecting their citizens least directly) to other governmental units, most often counties or special purpose districts. Often, only parts of functions need to be surrendered, such as in law enforcement. Most suburban municipalities will sacrifice a great deal to retain a local police force, but they may be quite willing to transfer certain police-related functions—such as communications, crime laboratories and training—to more solvent jurisdictions.

The economic limits on suburban governments also encourage entry into ad hoc formal and informal agreements with other local units to solve particular mutual problems; two or more municipalities may share the cost of a health inspector, or a suburb and a county may jointly contract to maintain a street serving as a common border. Other agreements may include sharing police and fire equipment. A survey in the Minneapolis—St. Paul area in the mid-1960s revealed more than 700 such agreements covering at least 19 separate functions.[6] These undramatic, unpublicized, ad hoc inter-local arrangements have already provided a major form of metropolitan governmental coordination and integration without requiring structural reform; clearly they will continue to do so in the foreseeable future.

Increasing the role of counties, stimulating creation of special districts, and encouraging inter-local agreements does not, however, solve metropolitan governmental problems. While local control of locally impor-

5. Oliver P. Williams, "Life Style Values and Political Decentralization in Metropolitan Areas," in *Community Structure and Decision-Making,* ed. Terry N. Clark (San Francisco: Chandler, 1968), pp. 427–440.

6. Leigh Grosenick, "The Many Faces of Inter-Local Cooperation" (Minneapolis: Ph.D. diss., University of Minnesota, 1968).

tant issues is protected by these devices, overall metropolitanwide planning and coordination is minimized. In the middle and late 1960s, Congress became increasingly concerned about this problem and began to provide grants to encourage local and areawide planning. Then followed the so-called A-95 process, which required some kind of regional planning agency to review and comment on all local applications for a large number of federal grants. Most metropolitan areas responded to those two federal policies by creating Councils of Government (COGs) consisting of representatives from each municipality and county in the region (sometimes school and other special districts were included). COGs provide a mechanism for local officials to discuss common problems as well as to fulfill the federal review and comment requirements.

The council idea has evoked a varied response. Some regard it as a logical device for achieving integrated metropolitan development in a politically fragmented system; others regard it as a forerunner to some form of metropolitan government; and still others look upon it as a toothless tiger—or even worse—a protector of the status quo.[7]

Because COGs lack the power to develop and implement major regional planning policies, some observers have speculated that the federal government, by supporting the COGs concept, was not really committed to metropolitan planning. The Housing and Community Development Act of 1974 clarifies the nature and degree of this commitment by requiring ongoing areawide comprehensive planning (with citizen participation) which includes housing needs and procedures and plans for guiding major growth decisions with respect to the pattern and intensity of land use for residential, commercial and other activities.

What does this mean for suburbs? For developed communities, the impact may not be great; but for those areas on the developing fringe, the opportunities to exercise local control over locally important issues, especially those involving land use, will probably now be more restricted than they once were.

At the same time, two other developments may have the long term effect of reducing the competition and differentiation among suburbs. On the one hand, federal revenue sharing provides relatively unrestricted financial assistance to local governments. The distribution formulas tend to favor communities with extensive needs for public services and relatively limited tax bases. On the other hand, there is increasing pressure on state governments to carry a greater share of local governmental costs. The major thrust of this effort is directed at the federal courts, where it has been argued that the quality of basic services—education, for example—should not depend on the accidental ability of the property tax to support those services in any particular community. If either or both of these developments results in widespread redistribution of state and federal resources, one consequence will surely be less differentiation among suburbs in the level and quality of public services they provide.

SUMMARY AND CONCLUSION

For the first half of the twentieth century, no one paid much attention to suburbs as long as they could pay

7. John C. Bollens and Henry J. Schmandt, *The Metropolis: Its People, Politics, and Economic Life*, 3rd ed. (New York: Harper & Row, 1975), p. 303.

their own way and not adversely affect central cities. After World War II, however, it became increasingly clear that suburban development was having a profound effect on cities by redistributing population, wealth, and political power and by hindering efforts to control urban sprawl. Until very recently, the solution seemed to be to create new governmental structures which, in essence, would reincorporate suburbs into the central city, thereby gaining control over suburban development and access to suburban social, political and fiscal resources. With very few exceptions that reintegration was politically unpopular and did not occur.

In the past few years, while acceptance of suburbs as a full-fledged partner in metropolitan governance has grown, some conditions and limits are being imposed on that partnership. Areawide planning and review requirements are forcing metropolitan regions to consider the long term implications of continued sprawl at the suburban fringe. State and federal fiscal redistribution policies will ensure that poor suburbs provide at least minimal levels of public services and will require richer suburbs to carry a larger portion of the costs. Sooner or later— and there are already a few straws in the wind—suburbs will probably have to carry a fairer share of the low income housing and school desegregation financial burdens.

Most of this discussion has centered on suburbia's struggle to protect its autonomy, but the contributions of the suburban political experience to contemporary metropolitan governance should not be overlooked. Suburbs have emphasized certain practices and policies which have been and are being emulated elsewhere in the political

system. Three of these merit particular mention: the increased use of professionally trained personnel in public service; a focus on high quality, "people-oriented" public services, especially education, recreation and public safety; and the persistent determination to maintain local control over life-style public issues.

The first of these contributions is now widely accepted at all levels of government. The second has helped force central cities in particular, especially since the late 1960s, to pay more attention to people-oriented functions. The impact of the third contribution is less clear, but some serious proposals have been made to develop mechanisms within central cities by which neighborhoods can exercise the same kind of control over life-style issues now enjoyed by suburbanites; in other words, to suburbanize the central city.

Without doubt, the suburban presence is largely responsible for the increased complexity of metropolitan governance, and there are few indications of any radical reorganization in the near future. Suburbs will continue to be a crucial element in the metropolis because they provide the opportunity for life-style options that are important to a great many urban dwellers. Suburbs will remain, but they will have to adjust; they will have to give up some functions where metropolitan-wide interests will prevail; and they will see their local autonomy reduced on some issues, especially those involving land use. On the other hand, state and federal assistance will help them with many of their own internal problems. For the foreseeable future the metropolitan region will be a complex system in which the integrity of the parts will be preserved in modified form.

A Theoretical Structure
for the Study of Suburban Politics

By Joseph Zikmund II

ABSTRACT: Suburban politics, while being subjected to more and more empirical research, often is studied in a theoretical void. This article attempts to provide a general theoretical structure for the study of suburban politics which focuses on three inherent developmental factors: the developmental stage of the surrounding metropolitan area; the circumstances of origin of the suburb; and the developmental phase of the particular suburb. Also related are a number of descriptive factors pertaining to the character of the suburban community. These independent variables are used to predict three elements of suburban politics: political style, kinds of issues, and kinds of relations with neighboring communities.

Joseph Zikmund II is Associate Professor of Political Science at Illinois Institute of Technology. He has co-edited Black Politics in Philadelphia *and* The Ecology of American Political Culture *and has written several articles on American suburbia. He recently studied urban planning at Wayne State University and in Yugoslavia and Poland.*

THE evidence now is clear: suburbia is almost as diverse as the nation's total population. There are new suburbs and old suburbs; commercial suburbs, industrial suburbs, and residential suburbs; upper class suburbs, middle class suburbs, working class suburbs, and even lower class suburbs. Given this diversity, how are we to make any sense whatsoever of the politics of suburbia? How accurate was the frustrated undergraduate student who observed, "Every suburb is unique; so you can't really generalize at all"?

During the first decade following World War II, the common practice was to overgeneralize about suburbia —its people, its predominant life style, and its uniform political character. Suburbanites were middle class; their politics was "nonpartisan" Republican. Twenty years of demythologizing have wiped out the old stereotypes, but like the undergraduate quoted above, scholars have been hard pressed to generate much in the way of constructive alternatives to the conceptually limited notion of "suburban diversity." Now, it seems, the time has come to try to develop a more useful theoretical base for the study of suburban politics.

"Suburban politics," as it is used here, refers essentially to the internal politics of any individual suburban community, incorporated or not. The primary components of suburban politics focused upon in this article are:

—the form and style of politics within the community;
—the kinds of issues which dominate local politics of the suburb; and
—the kinds of relationships the suburb has with neighboring units of local government or with nearby concentrations of people living in unincorporated places.

The factors which influence these three components of suburban politics can be divided into two distinct categories: first, *developmental factors* derived from the historical evolution of the suburban community and the metropolitan area which surrounds it and, second, *descriptive factors* related to the type of community, the kinds of people who live there, and the size and location of the suburb. While these latter descriptive factors are of considerable importance, the primary emphasis here will be directed toward elaborating developmental factors and their consequences. The three significant developmental factors are:

1. the developmental stage of the metropolitan area in which the suburb is located at the time the suburb is founded and/or experiences massive suburbanization;
2. the circumstances of origin of the suburbanized community; and
3. the developmental phase which the suburb itself is experiencing at any given moment in its history.

Descriptive factors also relevant to the character of suburban politics are:

1. the economic base and/or community character of the suburb;
2. the political culture of the suburb;
3. the social class and racial composition of the suburb's residents;
4. the size—particularly the population size—of the suburb; and

5. the physical location of the suburb within the evolving geographic structure of the metropolitan area.

Each of these factors, of course, presumes a number of assumptions about the inherent workings of American metropolitan areas. Some are relatively self-explanatory; others are not. Over the past 350 years, American urban concentrations—cities, or cities plus their surrounding metropolitan areas—have grown steadily. Their populations have increased and, with rare exception, continue to do so. Similarly, the geographic areas covered by growing urban concentrations have expanded and continue to expand. The geography of these changing urban concentrations is influenced by many factors: the geology of the land; the location of activity concentrations (particularly economic activities); the types of activities (again, especially the economic activities) which dominate the region; the transportation network; the social composition or mix of the area; and the legal environment created by the state or states in which the urban area lies.

In addition, the dynamics of the area—at least the residential dynamics—can be attributed largely to factors such as the construction, maintenance, and deterioration of the housing stock (house-filtering process); the immigration of new peoples into the area and their movements throughout (neighborhood change through invasion and succession); the interactions or desire to prevent interactions among various ethnic, racial or social class groupings within the area (residential segregation); and the changing transportation technology available at any given time (pedestrian city, streetcar city, automobile city). Within the context of these structural elements and dynamic forces, metropolitan areas develop, suburbs emerge, and suburban politics evolves.[1]

However, having assumed all of this, we need not believe that all suburbanites have consciously run away from the old central city or that they are prejudiced against blacks or other minorities. Some unquestionably are, but others certainly are not. Thus, to attempt some generalizations about suburban politics, we do not have to return full-circle to the era of suburban stereotypes.

DEVELOPMENTAL STAGES OF AMERICAN METROPOLITAN AREAS

The growth patterns of large American metropolitan areas, which got their start in the eighteenth or nineteenth centuries,[2] have tended to follow a four-step sequence from the time the central city began to expand and to dominate the area up until the fully developed metropolitan complex of today. The basic characteristics of metropolitan areas in each of these stages are outlined below (see also figure 1).

1. Three important sources on basic metropolitan processes are: Brian J. L. Berry and Frank E. Horton, *Geographic Perspectives on Urban Systems* (Englewood Cliffs, N.J.: Prentice-Hall, 1970); Maurice Yeates and Barry J. Garner, *The North American City* (New York: Harper & Row, 1971); and R. J. Johnston, *Urban Residential Patterns* (New York: Praeger, 1972).

2. Evidence which suggests different metropolitan development patterns for older versus newer metropolitan areas may be found in Joseph Zikmund II, "Sources of the Suburban Population: 1955–1960 and 1965–1970," *Publius* 5, no. 1 (Winter 1975), pp. 27–43.

FIGURE 1

Development Stages of American Metropolitan Areas

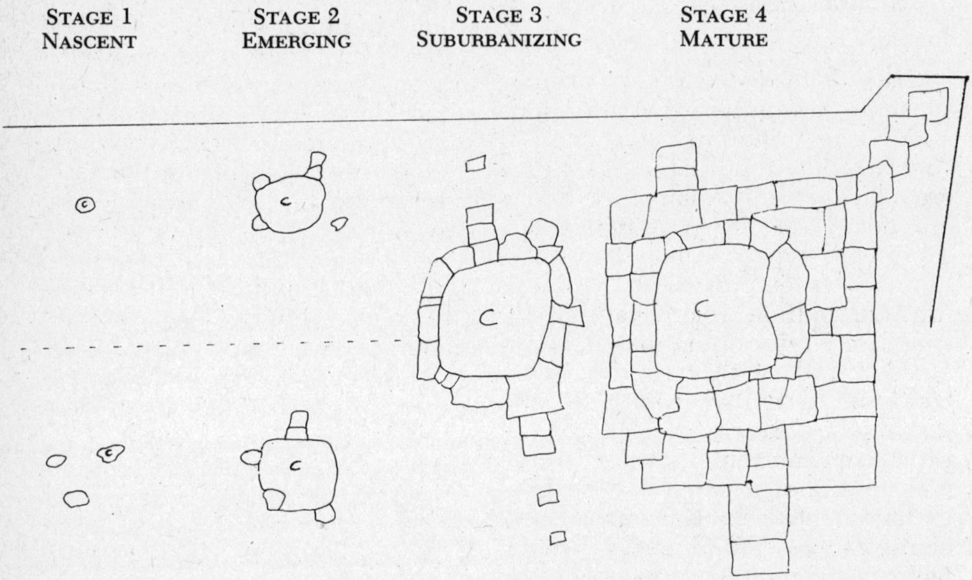

Stage 1
Nascent
Stage 2
Emerging
Stage 3
Suburbanizing
Stage 4
Mature

1. Nascent—one or more relatively small cities in a given geographic area.
2. Emerging—one or two large central cities dominating few suburbs.
3. Suburbanizing—one or two large central cities completely surrounded by incorporated suburbs.
4. Mature—one or two large central cities completely surrounded by an even larger aggregation of incorporated suburbs and satellite cities.

The progression from stage 1 to stage 2 usually begins when, for some reason, the city (or the immediate region) experiences a major influx of new residents. Population growth in the central city and in the surrounding region comes primarily from immigration from other parts of the country. Central city growth is much more rapid than growth on the periphery, and the central city expands geographically through annexation, both to accommodate its own new peoples and to take in high concentrations of suburbanites living in unincorporated places on the fringe of the central city.

From stage 2 to stage 3 the metropolitan area goes through a very important transition. The large, dominant central city becomes completely ringed by incorporated suburbs, and thus its geographic expansion ceases. Before this occurs, central city spread through annexation prevents the emergence of a large number of suburbs. Population growth in the central city still is due both to immigration and to major annexations. However, people gradually begin to move out of the central city to the suburban fringe in considerable numbers. Eventually, suburbs successfully resist central city annexation and begin to incorporate to prevent further threats from that city and to increase the level of local governmental services available to suburban residents. In the long run, these incorporated suburbs ring the central city, and the central city then grows only from an ever-declining number of immigrants who move into the city from other parts of the country.

Passage from stage 3 to stage 4 comes as a consequence of the methodical working out of the fundamental processes of metropolitan growth. The area continues to attract migrants, but in these later stages new settlers tend to move directly to the suburbs. Population movement from city to suburbs peaks and then begins to decline. However, because fewer and fewer are moving to the center, the central city shows a gradual population decline at the same time that the total areawide population increases. After several decades the city's portion of the metropolitan area population drops to as low as one-third or one-quarter. The central city no longer dominates; instead, the city becomes merely the largest and most dependent governmental unit in the metropolitan complex.

How does this pattern of metropolitan development affect suburban politics? The impact appears primarily with regard to the outlook which a suburban community takes towards its neighbors. Seven propositions embody the essence of the relationship, as delineated below.

Hypothesis 1: The earlier a suburban community appears in the developmental process of the metropolitan area, the more likely the politics of the community will be dominated by the question of its relations with the central city of the metropolitan area.

In the early stages of metropolitan development the dynamics of the area are provided primarily by growth of the central city. Annexation of unincorporated population concentrations on the city's fringe is always a threat. In many cases, the community does become part of the expanding city and, obviously, suburban politics ceases. In other cases, the community incorporates—often out of defensive fear of the central city. Thus, even where the suburb protects its own independence, the focus on the central city and its concerns is paramount. Similarly, close physical proximity to the city—perhaps sharing a common boundary—accentuates the impact of the larger body on the smaller.

Hypothesis 2: The later a suburban community appears in the developmental process of the metropolitan area, the more likely its political concerns regarding its relations with neighboring units of local government will focus upon other suburban communities rather than the central city.

Once the central city has been surrounded completely by incorporated suburbs, new communities in the second tier of suburbs, or even further out, often face three alternative governmental routes: (1) be annexed by an existing suburb; (2) incorporate and go their own way; or (3) remain unincorporated and hope they can stay that way for as long as they wish. In any case, the question of relations with neighbors will, of necessity, be directed toward other suburban communities, not toward the enclosed central city.

Hypothesis 3: The later a suburban community appears in the developmental process of the metropolitan area, the more likely its political concern for the question of relations with the central city will be symbolic rather than concrete in character.

When those suburbs not sharing a common boundary with the central city show concern about the central city at all, it is with regard to symbolic issues. These issues still may be of considerable significance, but they are quite different in character from those which dominate suburbs formed earlier in the developmental process.

Hypothesis 4: The question of relations between the central city and a suburb formed later in the metropolitan development process will be a concrete rather than symbolic issue in the politics of that suburb only when something is proposed which will force significant educational, fiscal or governmental interrelationships between the central city and itself.

Busing, city income taxes, "unigov" and metropolitan transportation authorities may expand into concrete issues in distant suburbs, but for the most part the central city either is perceived vaguely as the symbolic enemy or simply is ignored.

Hypothesis 5: As the metropolitan area moves into the later stages of metropolitan development, suburbs formed in the earlier stages of this process will share greater political interests with the central city than they will with suburbs formed later in the metropolitan development process.

Hypothesis 6: As a metropolitan area moves through its developmental sequence, suburban communities are likely to share the strongest common interests with those other suburbs formed in the same stage of the metropolitan

development process, though not necessarily with their own immediate geographic neighbors.

Hypotheses 5 and 6 serve to indicate the primary inter-suburban linkages which result from the overall development of the metropolitan area. As the area ages, the earliest suburbs, though still politically separated from the central city, come to share common problems and population groups with the central city. Meanwhile, newer suburbs both are geographically separated from the central city and from the inner suburbs and are in different social and economic phases of their own internal development. They are growing, expanding, and still able to imagine community independence from the metropolitan complex. There is, in other words, a relationship—but not an identity—between metropolitan development and the aging processes of individual suburbs. This connection can be generalized as follows:

Hypothesis 7: Suburbs formed in the same stages of a metropolitan area's development process tend to pass through the successive phases of suburban aging at roughly the same times.

AGING PROCESS OF THE SUBURB AND THE IMPACT OF CIRCUMSTANCE OF ORIGIN[3]

Suburbs age, much as city neighborhoods do, as a consequence of the development of their land and

3. While the material in these next two sections comes directly from no particular sources, the author recognizes his general indebtedness to the following: Earl M. Baker, "The Suburban Transformation of American Politics," *Publius* 5, no. 1 (Winter 1975), pp. 1–15; Marion Clawson, *Suburban Land Conversion in the United States* (Balti-

FIGURE 2

SUCCESSIVE STEPS IN THE AGING OF SUBURBAN COMMUNITIES

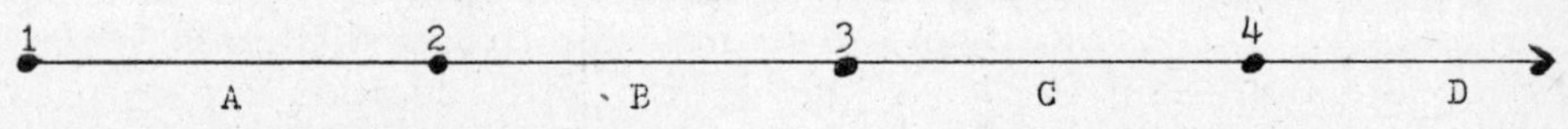

Steps in Aging Process	*Transition Periods*
1. Beginning of Suburbanization	A. Massive Suburbanization
2. Saturation of the Land	B. Community Stability
3. Beginning of Invasion-Succession	C. Conversion and Change
4. Dominance by New Residents	D. New Community Stability

the inherent aging of their housing stock and other buildings. The process, at least in its full logical form, generally involves four distinct steps with rather lengthy transition periods (see figure 2).

The aging process starts when an area begins to experience a significant influx of new suburban residents and/or suburban activities— commercial, industrial or managerial. This suburbanization can occur in any of three distinct types of circumstances. First, a piece of vacant or sparsely settled rural land can be subdivided and subjected to a major influx of families seeking new suburban homes. Second, a suburb may develop when an older, already settled satellite city on the fringe of the metropolitan area is brought into the suburban network of that expanding metropolitan area. Third, a small, already existing suburban enclave may experience a new, massive wave of residential and/or nonresidential development.

Of the three circumstances, the third is perhaps the most ambiguous and deserving of further elaboration. It is now firmly established that the areal expansion of typical metropolitan areas during the nineteenth and early twentieth centuries was not in concentric circles of geographic measure, but rather in concentric circles of transportation time or cost. As a result, the geographic picture of a typical area is not circular but star-shaped, with the pointed extensions stretching out along the primary historic and contemporary transportation routes. However, these extending fingers of suburbanization often are not uniformly developed all the way to the ends. Rather, at major access points to the primary transportation networks—train stations or expressway entrance-exit ramps—suburban concentrations occur. The further out one moves, the more likely these suburban nodes will exist for some time as relatively small, stable communities. In many ways, they will be more like rural service towns than typical suburbs closer to the metropolitan center. Thus, though technically we would have to recognize these places as suburbs, they have not yet really begun to experience massive suburbanization.

more: Johns Hopkins University, 1971); Bryan T. Downes, "Issue Conflict, Factionalism, and Concensus in Suburban City Councils," in *Cities and Suburbs*, ed. Bryan T. Downes (Belmont, Calif.: Wadsworth, 1971), pp. 285 –304; Heinz Eulau and Kenneth Prewitt, *Labyrinths of Democracy* (Indianapolis, Ind.: Bobbs-Merrill, 1973); Herbert Gans, *The Levittowners* (New York: Pantheon, 1967); Oliver P. Williams et al., *Suburban Differences and Metropolitan Policies* (Philadelphia: University of Pennsylvania Press, 1965); and Frederick M. Wirt et al., *On the City's Rim: Politics and Policy in Suburbia* (Lexington, Mass.: D. C. Heath, 1972).

The impact of these three types of suburban origins on suburban politics rests almost exclusively in the form and style of community politics and on the dominant issues in the political process in the early phases of the community's own aging process. Circumstance of community origin is best analyzed by looking at three separate origin situations:

1. origin in unincorporated, sparsely settled rural land;
2. origin in a small town, incorporated suburban town or in a small, incorporated satellite city; and
3. origin in a relatively large incorporated satellite city.

The reasons for introducing the size component are simple. When massive suburbanization reaches an already existing incorporated place —small stable suburb or satellite city —the size of that place seems directly related to the kinds of impact this wave of new residents will have on the existing political process in the community. The suggested relationships appear as Hypotheses 8 through 18.

Hypotheses applying to suburban communities which originate from sparsely settled rural areas (type 1 community origin) are as follows:

Hypothesis 8: At the time of massive suburbanization, the advantages and disadvantages of the very powers which accrue to incorporated local governments versus unincorporated places will be a major political issue.

Hypothesis 9: At the time of massive suburbanization, the politics of the community will be dominated initially by the informal, low-conflict, personal style of politics usually characteristic of relatively stable rural (township) governing bodies.

Hypothesis 10: At the time of massive suburbanization, political dominance will pass into the hands of the new suburban residents when the community decides to incorporate.

Hypothesis 11: At the time of massive suburbanization, issues related to the definition of future community character—particularly zoning and schools—will tend to dominate the political process.

The following are hypotheses applying to suburban communities which originate from the massive suburbanization of small, older suburban towns or satellite cities (type 2 community origin):

Hypothesis 12: The politics of the community will be dominated initially by the informal, low-conflict, personal style of politics typical of a relatively stable small-town governing body.

Hypothesis 13: Political conflict between established politicians and representatives of the new suburbanites may persist for some time, but generally will end with the victory of the latter over the former.

Hypothesis 14: Issues related to definition of future community character—again, particularly zoning and schools—will tend to dominate the political process.

By contrast, suburbanization of larger existing satellite cities suggests the following hypotheses (type 3 community origin):

Hypothesis 15: The political style of the suburbanizing satellite city already will be set and probably will be more formal and less personal than in the previously described communities. In addition, decision making is more likely to occur primarily in public rather than private arenas.

Hypothesis 16: Suburbanizing satellite cities are more likely to have already established persistent conflict blocs (perhaps even partisan competition) and to retain the pre-suburban political style after massive suburbanization.

Hypothesis 17: Significant political conflict is likely to occur between established groups and their political leaders, on the one hand, and the new suburbanites and their representatives on the other, with a high probability that the new ultimately will be assimilated into the old rather than have a clear victory over the old.

Hypothesis 18: The primary issues of political conflict are likely to involve less emphasis on future community character (zoning and schools) and more emphasis on the impact of the new suburbanites on community service levels and local taxation.

For communities which originate from the direct conversion of rural land to suburban development, politics is largely a matter of deciding what legal-governmental form to take and what character the community will choose or develop. The politics of the old rural environment soon is left in the distant past. For communities which emerge from existing suburban enclaves or smaller satellite cities, the question of incorporation is already in the past; the decisive problems are to establish and protect the community's character and to pass through the period of inevitable conflict between the old elites and representatives of the new suburbanites.

By contrast, the suburbanization of relatively large, established satellite cities is a different process. The city already has its character and its politics. Furthermore, the new suburbanites are less likely to overwhelm the community; their representatives will be less likely to win victories for the new groups and will be forced more often to accommodate to established patterns. Finally, service levels and taxation rather than definition of community character will be of prime concern to the already existing residents and their leaders. In fact, for a relatively large existing community, the new suburbanites attracted to the place are likely to be very similar to the people already living there.

The second step in the suburban aging process comes when the available land in the community begins to reach or reaches saturation; that is, when developable land is fully built up or when the remaining land packages are so small and isolated that massive community change, either in the form of new residents or new land uses, is virtually impossible. Of course, this does not take place as long as the community is still expanding its area through voluntary or forced annexations. However, once the suburb itself becomes surrounded by other incorporated places or makes a policy decision to stop further expansion, land saturation becomes possible. With land saturation comes stability. Some families settle in; others move out and are replaced by new residents much like themselves. The community has entered a period of little change. The politics of communities during this second phase of the suburban aging process may be described as follows (figure 3):

Hypothesis 19: The political differences in the first phase of the aging process between suburbs originating as vacant rural land (type 1 origin) and those originating from the massive suburbanization of small older incorporated places (type 2 origin) will tend to disappear some-

FIGURE 3

MERGING OF POLITICAL PATTERNS DURING THE FIRST TWO
PHASES OF SUBURBAN AGING PROCESS

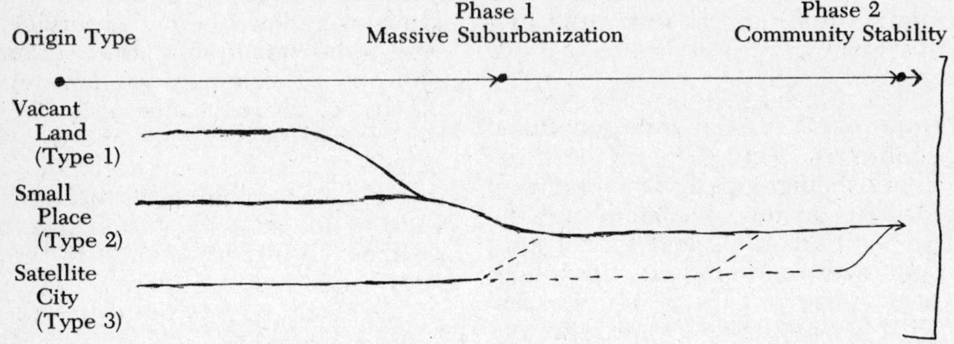

time before the full emergence of the second phase of the aging process.

Hypothesis 20: The political differences in the first phase of the aging process between suburbs originating as vacant rural land (type 1 origin) and those originating from the suburbanization of small, older, incorporated places (type 2 origin), on the one hand, and those originating from the suburbanization of larger satellite cities (type 3 origin) on the other, will tend to persist through the full period of the first phase of the aging process and well into, if not completely through, the second phase of the process.

Hypothesis 21: The politics of suburbs of type 3 origin will join the pattern of suburbs of type 1 and type 2 origins relatively early in the second phase of the aging process if the old original residents of the satellite city are relatively similar to the new residents who come to the city in the suburbanizing process.

Hypothesis 22: The politics of suburbs of type 3 origin will join the pattern of suburbs of type 1 and type 2 origins near, or at the end of, the second phase of the aging process if the old original residents of the satellite city are relatively *dissimilar* to the new residents who come to the city in the suburbanizing process.

Hypothesis 23: The politics of suburbs of type 3 origin, during that portion of the second phase of the aging process before they join the pattern of suburbs of type 1 and type 2 origins, will tend to continue as it was during the first phase of the aging process.

Hypothesis 24: The politics of suburbs of type 1 and type 2 origins will tend to be dominated more by issues focusing on questions of levels of city services and amenities and of city taxation and revenues in the second phase of the aging process than was the case in the first phase of the process.

Hypothesis 25: The political style of suburbs of type 1 and type 2 origins will tend to become more formal, more public, and less personal—and thus more like that of suburbs of type 3 origin—in the second phase of the suburban aging process.

Hypothesis 26: The most important difference between the politics of suburbs of type 1 and type 2 origins, on the one hand, and suburbs of type 3 origins on the other, will be the persistence of conflict between old and new residents in the latter and the absence of such conflict in the former.

During the second phase of the aging process, the politics of suburban communities of type 1 and type 2 origins tends to become more consistent with the stabilized life style of the people. The issue of community character has been resolved; now the problem is providing the governmental support systems for the people at a price which those same people are willing to pay. This often is not an easy task, especially if the dominant ideology of the people causes the community either to reject federal assistance or to be rejected for such assistance. In any case, the politics is clearly different from that of the first phase and also different from what will become the dominant style of the later phases in its evolution.

Phase 3 in the development of the suburban community, no matter what its circumstances of origin may have been, comes when the suburb experiences its first "invasion" of new residents of a qualitatively different people from those who arrived during the first phase and who later dominated the politics and life style of the community in the second phase. Once the invasion-succession process begins, community character once again becomes a central issue of local politics. Whether the particular manifestation is race, ethnicity or social class, the implications for suburban politics are much the same. Community preservation and change become the primary focus of attention. Indirectly, the battles may be fought over questions of zoning, crime, social services or quality of education in the local schools, but the ultimate concern continues to be community change or the prevention of such change. Probably this kind of change is inevitable in all suburbs; however, community character and community reaction to the threat of change can affect the rate and impact of these pressures.

Hypothesis 27: The dominant political issue in the third phase of suburban development will be community change.

Once community change gains momentum, it is only a matter of time before the suburb will pass from phase 3 to phase 4—from invasion to succession. Politically, the community will endure the conflicts for power and dominance between the old and the new residents, and in the long run the political style of the community will be modified to the character of the new. After these struggles have run their course, a new period of stability is likely to emerge, and services and taxation will again come to the fore. There is no necessary reason that a community will not experience a number of invasion-succession sequences throughout its history. Few American suburbs are old enough to have reached this phase, but logically there is no reason to believe that such sequences will not occur.

These *developmental factors* provide the foundations of suburban politics; they are the regular dynamic elements which structure the course of suburban politics generally. In addition to these, we suggested above a number of *descriptive factors* — economic base, residential class character, population size, and so forth—which also influence the politics of suburban communities. The impact of these various descriptive factors is both more difficult to access and different in kind from that of the developmental factors described. For the most part, the impact of the descriptive factors is to modify the basic pattern created by developmental factors. That is, developmental factors establish the essential character of suburban politics; descriptive factors modify or create deviations from the otherwise expected pattern.

Descriptive Factors Influencing Suburban Politics

The economic base and community character of a suburb must influence the politics of that community. In this context, suburbs can be classified into three types: (1) suburbs which are exclusively or overwhelmingly residential; (2) suburbs which derive a significant portion of their total assessed valuation from white-collar, office facilities; and (3) suburbs which derive a significant portion of their assessed valuation from manufacturing or commercial establishments. The reason for separating residential suburbs from the others is obvious. They must somehow pay for all of their services—police, fire, garbage, schools, and the like—from taxes levied against their own residents. The latter two types can use non-residential taxes to pay for the costs of governing.

The reason for segregating suburbs with office facilities from those containing large factories or commercial (shopping) centers may be less clear. Offices, while representing high assessed valuations, tend to make few demands on local government— except maybe those demands related to traffic movement and parking. Factories, especially, and shopping centers (perhaps to a lesser degree) both add significantly to the tax base of the community and make major demands for local governmental services. Furthermore, offices probably have little impact on community character or reputation; factories and shopping centers are likely to have considerable impact in these areas. Thus, for example, the politics of a residential suburb is more likely to be dominated by questions affecting the residential tax rate; by contrast, the politics of a community with a large manufacturing plant is more likely to be dominated by the "care and feeding" of the community's industrial benefactor and by issues focusing on the negative and positive aspects of that plant's presence in the community—jobs, tax base, pollution, traffic and noise, for example.

A second descriptive factor capable of influencing the politics of a suburban community is its political culture. Some might suggest that a relatively small city or suburb would not have a unique political culture distinct from the overall culture of the metropolitan area. Yet, students of suburbia recognize differences in community politics which cannot be attributed just to social class or racial differences. Ethnicity and religious distinctions—the bases for many cultural variations—have their impact in suburbia just as they do among the many neighborhoods of larger central cities. Whether one uses Wilson and Banfield's "public regarding" versus "private regarding" categories, or Elazar's "Moralist," "Individualist" and "Traditionalist" typology, or some other such as Alford's, cultural analysis[4] can make an important contribution to the study of suburban politics.

4. James Q. Wilson and Edward C. Banfield, "Public-Regardingness as a Value

Social class and racial composition also seem to be significant modifiers of the suburban political process. Williams and his colleagues have demonstrated attitudinal differences in the suburbs with regard to local government and political issues based on race and class.[5] Certainly these same factors are known to produce meaningful variations in levels of political participation, partisanship and voting behavior. Looking at the impact of class, in particular, on the typical flow of suburban politics as structured by metropolitan and community development, one may observe that a primary consequence of class is to affect the rate at which a community passes through the several phases of suburban aging. We suggest a curvilinear relationship something like that pictured in figure 4. Lower class areas—real slums and near-slums—tend to stay that way until there is some massive capital investment, either from the government or from some unique private source, to force renewal or rehabilitation. Working class areas, of course, are subject to racial and ethnic change; however, they also tend to contain many "self-made" people who cling tenaciously to their new-found possessions and real property. The middle class, by contrast, tends to have few roots in individual communities; at the same time, it has enough capital to seek better housing or neighborhoods when change

FIGURE 4

HYPOTHESIZED IMPACT OF CLASS ON RATE OF CHANGE IN THE SUBURBAN AGING PROCESS

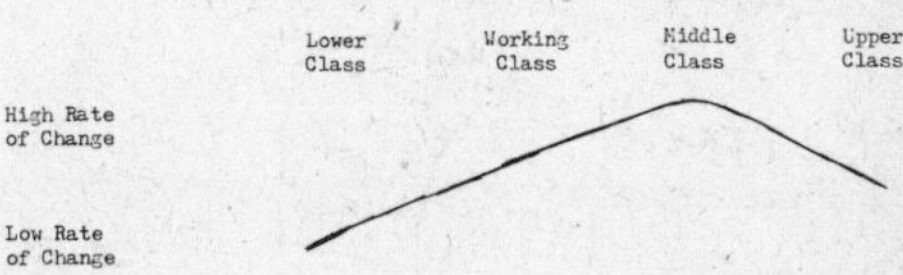

threatens. Finally, upper class areas —well-established areas with "class"—seem to preserve themselves even as aging takes its toll on housing stock and community facilities.

Community size is one descriptive factor which has been rather thoroughly researched, at least in the San Francisco Bay area. Eulau and Prewitt found suburb size to be directly related to such political variables as electoral accountability, city council decision structure, community governing style, and community self-image. By contrast, these same authors found that size was less important or even irrelevant as a variable affecting numerous public policy areas.[6]

The final descriptive factor worthy of note at this point concerns the physical location of the suburb within the evolving geographic structure of the metropolitan area. Obviously, geographic setting is directly related to our first developmental factor; that is, the metropolitan stage of development when the suburban community is founded or first experiences massive suburbanization. However, the two factors are not identical. Two suburban places might well incorporate at the same time in quite distinct geographic locations for very different reasons. An example is shown in figure 5. Here, the people

Premise in Voting Behavior," reprinted in Charles M. Bonjean et al., *Community Politics* (New York: The Free Press, 1971), pp. 125–135; Daniel J. Elazar, *American Federation* (New York: Crowell, 2nd ed., 1972); or Robert R. Alford, *Bureaucracy and Participation* (Chicago: Rand McNally, 1969).

5. Williams, *Suburban Differences*, pp. 211–238.

6. Eulau and Prewitt, *Labyrinths*.

FIGURE 5

IMPACT OF LOCATIONS ON SUBURBAN POLITICS

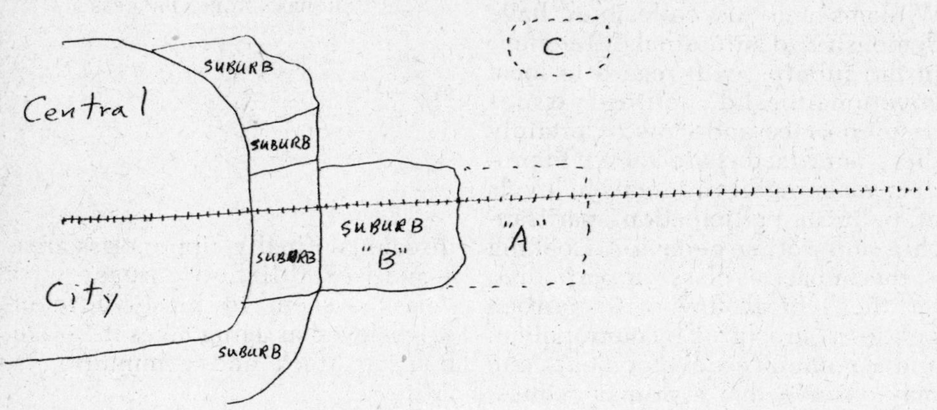

of location "A" may incorporate for fear of annexation by the already existing suburb "B." At the same time, the people of location "C" may also incorporate—not out of fear of annexation, for no one may want them at that time, but rather to provide needed municipal services and to gain access to necessary taxing authority under state law.

Thus, geographic location must be treated as a separate and distinct factor. The particular impact of this factor on suburban politics, on the other hand, is not so easy to specify. It is likely that the primary effect of location on the politics of individual suburbs falls in the areas of issues and rates of community change. Clearly, a suburb in the mainstream of metropolitan development will itself change with the pace of metropolitan change. Out-of-the-way places, by contrast, evolve at their own speed and may well remain fixed in an early phase of suburban development for an extraordinary length of time. Similarly, a suburb in the primary development flow of the metropolitan area usually has no choice about the question of growth. The people, the stores and the problems just keep coming. However, communities away from major transportation routes may have an option. Tax advantages, service rates, and chamber of commerce boosterism can make a difference. Or, from another perspective, systematically doing nothing in the hope that nothing will change also can work rather effectively.

SUMMARY AND IMPLICATIONS

Three developmental factors—stage of metropolitan development, circumstance of community origin, and phase in the community aging process—create the basic patterns of suburban politics. Descriptive factors—economic base, political culture, social class and racial composition, size and physical location—modify these basic patterns in complex but reasonably predictable ways. Thus, one can make sense of the politics of the many individual suburban communities.

After looking at the richness and variety of suburban politics, one may find it very easy to claim too much in its behalf, or even to suggest that suburban politics is the most important continuation of the small-town, democratic tradition of the agrarian nineteenth century in the urbanized world of the twentieth. On the other hand, it is also all too easy to damn suburban politics for its racism, its conservatism and its anti-metropolitan isolationism. There are elements of both extremes in the suburbs, but neither accurately characterizes suburbia.

For the most part, suburbanites, whether rich or poor, white or black, simply want to be left alone, to have secure economic (home) investments, and to ensure their family's safety. None of these are values to be taken lightly. In many ways, the politics of suburbia as analyzed and projected above emerges as a consequence of sincere people's seeking to achieve the goals of privacy, well-being and safety. Whether perceived accurately or not, the impact of suburbanization on community character, tax rates and community services, and community stability and change are seen as the public manifestations of the private values described above. Unfortunately, today such natural human goals must come into direct conflict with other equally appropriate goals such as equality and social justice. Thus, while the issues of suburban politics are inherently practical and down-to-earth, they are inevitably of broader consequence.

Given the emotional and intellectual climate of our times, there is a strong tendency to seek social justice without serious regard for what is being sacrificed along the way. Local self-government is seldom defended in the face of vigorous and accurate accusations of abuse. Yet, local self-government is a value unto itself—it can produce ennobling or degrading results, but self-government remains an inherent human value. Thus, economies of scale, fiscal responsibility and social justice ought to emerge from inter-suburban and city-suburban cooperation, not from artificially contrived mergers or bureaucratic schemes. However, inter-suburban cooperation is neither reasonably expected nor inevitable across the entire geographic area of the metropolis. Suburbs lying side by side, but in different phases of development, in distinctly different geographic juxtapositioning with regard to a major expressway, or comprised of significantly different kinds of people, may quite simply want nothing to do with each other. As long as new development, community aging, and intra-metropolitan population movements occur, suburbs will differ significantly and reflect these differences in their politics. Cooperation which makes good sense for one suburb may mean stagnation and community death to another. As a consequence, those seeking or needing such inter-suburban cooperation must recognize which communities are likely to share the same interests. While these places may not be obvious geographic partners, they will be strong interest partners. In some cases, physical separation makes cooperation impossible. More often, such cooperation is not impossible, but merely more costly or more awkward.

Some observers might argue that the difficulties of inter-suburban cooperation (and, of course, city-suburban cooperation) add even greater weight to the push for metropolitanism and regional government. Let us, at this point, put forth just a few words of caution. First, in many states, suburban representation in state legislatures is now strong enough—or soon will be

—to make state-imposed regional government politically unlikely. Second, international examples of success with metropolitanism—Toronto, London, or wherever—must take into account international differences in political culture, historic tradition, aggregate metropolitan size, and national political systems before realistic comparisons to the American scene make much sense.

Finally, those who advocate regional government must recognize that in many ways large city government in the United States is a type of regional government. If New York City government does not work, what makes us think that New York regional government will work any better? The answer is not simply the tax resources which have fled to the suburbs. If people have moved away from New York City and into self-governing suburban communities for reasons they still feel are valid—safety, a new home, governmental responsiveness, or the uglier manifestations of outright racism—we can be assured that merely extending the city's boundaries to include these people again will not solve the old center city's problems (unless, of course, we make these same suburban people both politically impotent and geographically immobile).

Today, many of what we call the city's problems are really the problems of aggregations of city residents. The city is not the cause of the problems, but at present it bears the financial responsibility and social consequences of these problems. Ultimately at fault are the national economic system and numerous national public policies. Cities cannot solve these problems, and neither will proposed regional governments. They must be tackled at a higher level.

Dilemmas of Suburbanization and Growth Controls

By James W. Hughes

ABSTRACT: The decentralization of every facet of American life and the shifting age contours of its population structure have increased the pressures for residential diversity in suburbia. As a reaction to these geographic and demographic forces, new attitudes toward community growth are synthesizing in the form of "growth controls"—attempts by suburban communities to limit the numbers and types of residents allowed within their borders. These reactions run counter to the new responsibilities that have accompanied the benefits of suburbanization. While their justification is embedded in a matrix of environmental and "quality of life" arguments, the complex set of motivations includes a powerful socioeconomic dimension having clear implications for the metropolitan region as a whole. Moreover, the myth of suburbia—of isolated family-raising environments—is being increasingly challenged by the reality of its participation in an urbanizing region, and growth controls may be interpreted as an attempt to preserve the older ideals. The overall issues emerging are not going to fade away quietly, and since they involve so many diverse and competing interest groups, they will not be resolved easily.

James W. Hughes is Associate Professor of Urban Planning and Policy Development at Livingston College, Rutgers University, and a Research Associate at the University's Center for Urban Policy Research. He is author of Urban Indicators, Metropolitan Evolution, and Public Policy, *co-author of* Urban Homesteading, *and editor of* Suburbanization Dynamics and the Future of the City *and* New Dimensions of Urban Planning: Growth Controls.

URBAN scholars suggested the inevitable decline of the city almost a decade ago in judicious and understated arguments:

The American city faces a crisis of function; . . . The concentration of businesses and jobs, the availability of neighborhood shopping districts and other service areas once made the central city a reasonably attractive and satisfactory place for living and working, particularly for low-income families or persons. These city advantages are less and less persuasive today. Innovations in transportation and communication are making centralness less and less essential. The telephone and the airplane have made wider and wider areas almost as accessible as the inner core of the great city. Jobs are relocated outward from the hard core of the city. As these changes become plainer and more visible to all eyes it becomes clear that we, as a society, are much better at building from scratch than we are at rebuilding . . . it was [once] fashionable to discuss the question of how to retain the white middle class in the central city. At the present the problem is more and more that of maintaining any middle class—be it black, white or any other hue.[1]

Although many contemporaries regarded such prophetic remarks as inordinately pessimistic, today, almost a decade since urban maladies and riots occupied the time and energy of a nervous capital, the notion of inevitable urban decline is common wisdom. No longer are the troubles of the cities given priority in the national agenda of concern. In fact, a number of government spokesmen have flatly declared that the urban crisis is over. This dramatic shift in outlook reflects the emerging belief that the city is not going to be rebuilt to its past glories, either

real or imagined. Stabilization and conservation are the current catchwords in describing urban policy; the last gasps of regeneration evolve into strategies for the maintenance and preservation of existing assets. The problems of the moment, or at least those which demand attention, are now to be found in the broad bands of suburban territories encircling our urban centers.

The degree to which we have become a suburban society was vividly underscored by the recent energy crisis—the dispersed patterns of jobs and residences were found to be inalterably dependent on highway transportation. The remaining public transportation networks, geared to declining job centers, were exposed as having little utility in tying together the new matrix of employment and residence places. But these concerns have also faded. With so much of present day America now congregated outside the city, suburbia will increasingly become the focus of public and private concern. Emerging as dominant public policy issues are the costs and benefits of continued growth and the techniques to harness development forces.

These issues emerge from a cyclical pattern of events. As the advantages of urban living declined in proportion to technological innovations and increased affluence, population movements to suburbia were stimulated. This led to a shifting spatial demand for what were once urban functions. Their resettlement in suburbia triggered a new round of residential demand which is running headlong into the desire of existing suburban residents to control and limit growth in their jurisdictions. This desire is extremely paradoxical; the diversity of urban

1. George Sternlieb, *The Tenement Landlord* (New Brunswick, N.J.: Rutgers University Press, 1966), p. xiii.

functions—employment, entertainment, and the like—is craved, yet without transforming the suburbs into cities.

In regard to this overall transformation, this article explores some of the emerging forces and the implications of the widespread resettlement process which has been set in motion. More specifically, it focuses on the growth control movement— that growing body of sentiment spurred, at least outwardly, by "quality of life" and environmental considerations that view continued growth and urbanization with increasing disdain.[2] The operationalization of this movement is reflected in both formal restrictions and gimmickry by local jurisdictions to limit the number and character of entering residents. Despite the elegant weaving of emerging environmental issues into a coherent fabric justifying limited growth, the related social rationales have received inadequate scrutiny, particularly in relation to the formal trends of metropolitan shifts and the changing demographic profiles of America's population.

This is not to say that the environmental justifications of slow growth mask irrational and hysterical motives for social exclusion; but the socioeconomic dimensions permeating the entire phenomenon are powerful forces having clear implications for the metropolitan region as a whole. It is to these concerns that this article is addressed.

The complex set of motivations underlying the growth control movement has been stimulated by the intersection of three dynamic trends —socioeconomic in character and national in scope—in suburbia; they are essential to the understanding of the growth control phenomenon.

THE BASIC TRENDLINES

The first major force serving to make suburbia the arena where crucial issues will be battled out is the spatial transformation of the metropolis—the overwhelming tendency for every aspect of social and economic life to resettle there. The critical mass of American society is now external to the city. The underlying dynamics have been sketched out in great detail by a number of observers;[3] the end results and most recent manifestations are revealed in table 1, which indicates that in 1974 the population of the suburban rings exceeded that of the central cities by a four to three margin, with the latter declining by 1.9 percent in the preceeding four-year period, while suburbia maintained a high growth rate of 8.4 percent.

Population shifts do not reveal the entire picture, however. Increasingly, those who live in suburbia also work there. For the 15 largest Standard Metropolitan Statistical Areas (SMSAs), the percentage of SMSA residents who work in suburbia increased from 37.0 percent

2. The scope of the growth control-managed growth discussion has been expanding greatly. For example, a recent edited compendium comprises three volumes and 1,750 pages [*see*, Randall W. Scott et al., eds., *Management and Control of Growth* (Washington, D.C.: Urban Land Institute, 1975)] and reflects a myriad of concerns and issues. We focus on one small dimension of the phenomenon—its potential impact on the trend toward suburban residential diversity.

3. For example, *see*, Louis H. Masotti and Jeffrey K. Hadden, eds., *The Urbanization of the Suburbs* (Beverly Hills, Calif.: Sage, 1973); and James W. Hughes, ed., *Suburbanization Dynamics and the Future of the City* (New Brunswick, N.J.: Rutgers University, Center for Urban Policy Research, 1974).

TABLE 1

POPULATION BY TYPE OF RESIDENCE: 1970 AND 1974

(in thousands)

TYPE OF RESIDENCE	1970	1974	1970–74 CHANGE	
			NUMBER	PERCENT
Metropolitan areas, total	137,058	142,043	4,985	3.6
Central cities	62,876	61,650	−1,226	−1.9
Suburban rings	74,182	80,394	6,212	8.4

SOURCE: Vincent P. Barabba, "Shifts of People and Jobs," in *Post-Industrial America: Metropolitan Decline and Interregional Job Shifts*, ed. George Sternlieb and James W. Hughes (New Brunswick, N.J.: Rutgers University, Center for Urban Policy Research, 1975).

NOTE: 1970 metropolitan area definition.

in 1960 to 47.6 percent in 1970,[4] a rate of increase which probably means that in 1975, suburban employment in these selected areas has achieved dominance. Furthermore, the vast Interstate Highway System, now nearing completion, transforms open country daily into corridor cities. As a result of these forces, the critical mass of American society is in suburbia.

As is discussed below, the image of suburbia still is wedded to outmoded myths—serene family-raising-only environments. However, the contours of America's population are changing unalterably, and they tend to conflict with this image. The compositional shifts are detailed in table 2, portending large impacts on the nation's housing markets. Despite the publicity of declining birth rates, those people who will require housing in the next 10 to 15 years have already been born. The major growth sector of the population—those persons born in the aftermath of World War II—has now graduated from campus protests and is rapidly evolving to household formation status. More often than not, their

4. Hughes, *Suburbanization Dynamics* p. 6.

TABLE 2

AGE STRUCTURE OF THE UNITED STATES

(in thousands)

AGE CATEGORY	1970	1980	1970–80 CHANGE	
			NUMBER	PERCENT
Total	204,897	224,132	19,253	9.4
Under 15	57,889	52,970	−4,919	−8.5
15 to 24	36,495	41,228	4,793	13.1
25 to 34	25,293	36,962	11,669	46.1
35 to 44	23,142	25,370	2,228	9.6
45 to 54	23,310	22,406	−904	−3.9
55 to 64	18,664	21,083	2,419	13.0
65 and over	20,084	24,051	3,967	19.7

SOURCE: U. S., Bureau of the Census, *Current Population Reports*, Series P-25, no. 519, (Washington, D.C.: Government Printing Office, 1973).

impact will not be a migratory phenomenon, since they represent for the most part the aging of the resident suburban population.

Nevertheless, this and other selected growth sectors of the population, in concert with a new consumer reality caused by emerging economic strictures, tend to foster what George Sternlieb has termed the "dissolution of the modular household."[5] Increasing in importance are relatively small-sized, adult-oriented households which are not in the process of rearing children. Their shelter needs are not of the detached, single-family home variety, but of smaller units typified by apartment, townhouse, and other higher density configurations, often of rental and condominium tenure. Their prime demand will not be felt in the older urban centers. However, these modes of residence tend to clash with the image of what the typical suburban residence should be, at least as perceived by many suburbanites.

As a consequence of, and as a reaction to, these geographic and demographic forces, there appears to be an emerging sentiment, gathering substantial momentum, to oppose any new growth which will tend to introduce change to an extant favorable situation. Pressures for increased density, new and perhaps different inhabitants, environmental alterations, and growing fiscal burdens—generated by the first two trends—have begun to mold new attitudes toward community growth. These urbanization pressures foster a "pull up the gang plank" mentality.

Often, these sentiments affect political responses, the most severe of which are growth control restrictions. While valid environmental, economic, and quality of life considerations underlie these feelings, equally important to their understanding is the substantial gap between the conventional image (or desired image) of suburbia and its new realities.

THE REALITY AND MYTH OF SUBURBIA

The gap between the reality and the myth of suburbia adds complexity to the discussion and delineation of the basic problems enveloping it.[6] "Suburbia" commonly evokes the traditional and romantic image of small residential bedroom hamlets, or nodes on commuter rail-lines, whose residents commute to, and are dependent on, nearby urban centers. However, the reality is one of broad, heterogeneous urbanizing regions, increasingly independent, where all the traditional activities once the sole province of the city can now be found. This evolution has radically altered the exclusive residential character of older suburbs and former rural areas and the future functions of the remaining urban centers. Yet with vigorous persistence, many suburban municipalities view themselves in the traditional mold, have little function beyond that of protecting a way of life they regard as unique, and have disregarded the new responsibilities that have accompanied the benefits of suburbanization. The myths, a part of the conventional American Dream, die hard.

5. For an elaboration of the concept, *see*, George Sternlieb, "The Future of Housing," in *New Dimensions in Urban Planning: Growth Controls*, ed. James W. Hughes (New Brunswick, N.J.: Center for Urban Policy Research, Rutgers University, 1974), p. 226.

6. Sternlieb, "Future of Housing."

Pressures for residential heterogeneity

As a by-product of economic decentralization, however, the residential structure of suburbia is experiencing substantial differentiation pressures, in which the traditional heterogeneity of the city—residential neighborhoods of unique social and economic characteristics—is transferred throughout the entire metropolitan domain. As the full spectrum of the nation's population and economic activities redistributes itself, an increasing demand is felt in suburbia for varied forms of shelter and residential environments. In some cases, they have been realized. As evidence, we have now the older suburbs that Sam Bass Warner once referred to as "street car" suburbs; the wealthy Scarsdales; the zones of black emergence, such as East Orange, New Jersey, where black communities are supplanting the former "elite"; blue collar communities; clusters of garden apartment developments; and elderly retirement enclaves.[7] These are but some of the types of suburban residential areas which are emerging in post-industrial society.

The bases of heterogeneity are quite different from those which served to create the once colorful urban neighborhoods (at least as envisioned by the current romanticizers of ethnicity) which were based very strongly along racial and ethnic lines. However, the Italian, Irish, Jewish and German urban communities have, to a large extent, been dispersed beyond the cities' bounds, only to resettle along new lines of separation. What do these new lines comprise?

A significant amount of empirical research in the fields of sociology and social geography has suggested several generalizable patterns of residential neighborhood and community types.[8] The results have consistently centered about three main variables of residential separation: socioeconomic status, stage in the family life cycle, and racial/ethnic status.

The most powerful of these is socioeconomic status, comprising a cluster of closely interrelated measures—income, education and occupation. Its significance is underscored by the characterization of many suburban areas as blue collar, middle class, exclusive, and so on.[9] As it always has been, one's address is a simple mechanism for symbolically expressing social status. In today's society, a person's social position is difficult to ascertain in day-to-day contact; making it known is not an insignificant matter. Thus "address" becomes an efficient social status indicator, one which is smoothly and unhesitantly elicited and communicated.[10] In terms of residential differentiation, this tends to reflect class lines at community or neighborhood boundaries, with higher classes attempting to protect

7. George Sternlieb, Robert W. Burchell, and James W. Hughes, "The Future of Housing and Urban Development," *Journal of Economics and Business* 27 (1974–1975), p. 100.

8. *See*, Brian J. L. Berry and Frank E. Hordon, *Geographic Perspectives on Urban Systems* (Englewood Cliffs, N.J.: Prentice-Hall, 1970) for reviews of the literature. The discussion here is along the framework provided by David Popenoe, "Urban Residential Differentiation: An Overview of Patterns, Trends, and Problems," in *The Community: Approaches and Applications*, ed. M. Effrat (New York: Free Press, 1974), pp. 33–56.

9. Popenoe, "Urban Residential Differentiation," p. 41.

10. Popenoe, "Urban Residential Differentiation," p. 42.

their status addresses by exclusion.[11] While this rationale may be the most obvious, it is certainly not the only one. However, in terms of illustrating a motivation for growth controls, it serves our purpose adequately. Its power is evident to anyone who has observed the battles to locate low and moderate income housing developments in middle class and affluent communities.

The second major variable can be expressed in terms of the rubric of stage in life cycle. Households go through a formation and maturation cycle not unlike a general aging process. The household cycle may begin when a single individual breaks away from his or her parents; the household may evolve to comprise a young married couple without children, then a family in the child-rearing years, followed by an aging couple whose children have grown; finally the household is dissolved with death of one or both of the marriage partners.

Each of these stages generates a demand for unique housing types and residential environments, and many communities and neighborhoods can clearly be distinguished in terms of their response to these needs, particularly those which cater to middle class households with school-aged children. As is evident from the age-specific growth sectors of America's population, it is those households not geared to school-aged children which now comprise or will comprise a significant portion of suburbia's housing demand. More than 80 percent of the growth in households between 1970 and 1973 constituted one- and two-person "non-modular" households— young unmarried individuals living away from their parents, young married couples without children, divorcees, "empty-nesters," and senior citizens.[12] Single-family units are often inappropriate for these consumers, who generally have limited space requirements or financial resources. However, the shelter options—townhouses, condominiums, and the like—are sometimes viewed with suspicion and growing hostility by those making suburban land use decisions.

Perhaps the most recognizable variable of residential differentiation in this country is race. If racial distinctions follow the general model established by ethnic status, then race will decline as a basis of residential differentiation as the economic status of the racial group in question rises.[13]

Nevertheless, all three of these variables—class, race, and stage in the family life cycle—should tend to distinguish local communities and neighborhoods throughout suburban areas, particularly if market pressures are eventually realized in housing starts. More specifically, they increasingly tend to define the housing types desired in suburbia and the growing emphasis on diversity. In essence, they represent the new reality of suburbia. Not only are the older pressures for accommodations to house low income and racial minority families in force, but they have been joined by another diverse element—the non-modular, adult-oriented household. Given the virtual impossibility of constructing unsubsidized low income housing and the difficulty of ensuring racial

11. Popenoe, "Urban Residential Differentiation."

12. Anthony Downs, "The Real Estate Outlook Through Mid-1976," *Real Estate Review* 5, no. 2 (Summer 1975), p. 27.
13. Popenoe, "Urban Residential Differentiation," p. 41.

integration, the non-modular household potentially has the most impact, since the market, if unrestricted, probably could satisfy this demand.

Implications: increasing scale

While these pressures portend a greater social diversity in suburbia, the former diversity of the central city tends toward uniformity, particularly in terms of race. An important consequence, discussed below, is the increasing isolation of the central city from the many suburbanizing activities which formerly made it an attractive place to live.

Moreover, these patterns of settlement in suburbia differ from the earlier urban counterparts in ways which are disturbing. Principally, the individual areas span a much larger geographic domain and are much more cut off from the greater region of which they are a part.[14] Moreover, some subareas, for reasons of geographic scale and poor accessibility, may be "functionally" isolated from both middle class areas and from the full range of opportunities which suburban living can bring.[15]

This phenomenon emerges from the fact that "the scale of suburban development combined with a pre-existing pattern of rural-originated local government jurisdictions causes many of these communities to fall under different local governments as well as into different geographic subareas."[16] In the older cities, these unique subcommunities fell under the same governmental jurisdiction. Thus "the post-indus-trial pattern helps to give local government in metropolitan areas a surprisingly benign character in the face of all of the problems it faces,"[17] because their concerns tend to be locally based. Local government structures are completely separate from one another, and local officials obviously decide who will live within their borders. Reconciliation between different subgroups could only take place at the metropolitan level, but unfortunately at this level there is no governmental apparatus at all.[18] This creates one of the real dilemmas of the growth control movement.

Underlying resistance

These patterns of and pressures for change are not operating unopposed. Despite the increased responsibility entailed by their new role as job centers, substantial resistance regarding additional residential growth is displayed by many local jurisdictions, which desire, for reasons of greater and lesser validity, to foster a singular socioeconomic milieu throughout the entire area under their political control. The multiplicity of local governments, the historic patterns of suburban development, and the personal preferences of its residents have fostered this situation.

The relentless drive of suburbanization in the post-World War II era was spearheaded by middle class families with school-aged children, now the dominant force in many suburban areas. Their choice of residence has been and still is greatly influenced by the educational systems serving the communities and

14. Popenoe, "Urban Residential Differentiation," p. 49.

15. Popenoe, "Urban Residential Differentiation."

16. Popenoe, "Urban Residential Differentiation," p. 50.

17. Popenoe, "Urban Residential Differentiation."

18. Popenoe, "Urban Residential Differentiation."

neighborhoods available to them.

Middle-class parents, and American citizens, generally, typically judge the quality of any school mainly in terms of the kinds of families who are predominant in its classrooms. . . . The widespread desire of middle-class parents to establish homogeneity in their own neighborhoods is a direct result of their value reinforcing objectives concerning the school experience of their children. . . .[19]

This form of behavior is operationalized by establishing residential homogeneity within a community or neighborhood, not only in terms of socioeconomic status, but also in terms of the family types allowed.[20] Garden apartments almost always housing families not in the process of child-rearing—but often perceived as being available to low income families with children, even if the units have only one or two bedrooms—are many times disdained. Moreover, the desire to maintain a high degree of predictability of public behavior patterns in suburban communities often evokes suspicion towards those who do not live in single-family dwellings.

This is but one example of the motivation underlying the tendency of households to favor not only communities housing those of similar social status, but also within the same stage in the family-raising cycle. This is not to say these motivations do not have validity and are inherently unjustified; viable neighborhoods and communities may be very fragile indeed. They simply suggest why elite suburbs tend to resist the pressures for new housing

not geared toward affluent family-raising households—not an insignificant impetus for growth controls.

To this point strong emphasis has been given to the residential socioeconomic component of suburban change and its significance in attempts to curb growth. These rationales are often underplayed. Yet, when they are stressed in the growth control discussion, attention is often directed to the social status and racial components. However, given changing population and household profiles, it is evident that the stage in life cycle, as a basis of residential demand and differentiation, will increasingly come to the fore. Nevertheless, the environmental and fiscal arguments ordinarily comprise such discourse. It is to these concerns that we now turn.

GROWTH CONTROLS: CONVENTIONAL RATIONALES

With the exception of the scale of the phenomena, these tendencies toward residential diversity are nothing new; however, they have gained increasing force in suburbia as growth pressures multiply, as the number of non-modular households grows larger, and as the critical mass of jobs and services located there provides a stronger rationale for more, and varied, residential developments. Likewise, resistance by the parties affected by impending change is not a novelty; but due to the fact that many suburban communities have inadequate mechanisms to control growth in rational fashion, there are fears that they will be overwhelmed and doomed to replicate the undesirable conditions that their residents left behind when they moved. In fact, these feelings may be even stronger among those who have made the suburban move

19. Anthony Downs, "Suburban Housing: A Program for Expanded Opportunities," *Real Estate Review* 1, no. 1 (Spring 1971), p. 4.

20. Downs, "Suburban Housing."

more than once, perhaps from a transitional inner suburb, rapidly changing as metropolitan expansion takes place, to more serene outer areas. Thus, a not irrational desire comes to the fore to protect their environment from the externalities of growth which have become visible in other areas of suburbia.

Concurrently, there appears to be a growing national ethic in America to challenge older notions of growth; this has been reflected in local sentiments toward limiting growth rates. Older planning platitudes to limit urban sprawl have been resuscitated in a new environmental guise. In fact, the surrounding rhetoric often has an elegance rarely seen in planning circles. Nevertheless, the fears center about a declining quality of life and the open space and environmental values which are endangered by growth processes. Accommodating further development is seen as a harbinger of negative changes— new and perhaps different residents, increasing densities, the disappearance of valued natural areas, and other environmental alterations. Moreover, the costs of new capital investments necessary to service new growth increments are not insignificant; these are often viewed as severe burdens on existing residents. Also, over-utilized water supply and sewage treatment systems, which often result from new growth, provide the potential for environmental hazards to public health. Add more cars, road congestion, increasing crime, and mounting solid waste problems, and a cycle of events is set in motion which appears to foreshadow the emergence of conditions once the sole province of the cities. All of these factors tend to congeal into a rational case for controls upon growth.

Consequently, it does not seem unreasonable to grant a community the right, within certain prescribed bounds, to plan its own development destiny.[21] In most cases, the operational document sketching out the future is a comprehensive plan; however, this statement of goals, as manifested in a picture of the future "end state" of the municipality, has no power to control the rate of development. It turns to zoning as the implementable device to regulate development patterns. However, this tool, a local exercise of a state's police power, is inadequate to the task: it must treat all parcels of land classified within a designated category in equal fashion, not being able to channel development along a desired time scheme or staging basis. Zoning cannot deny certain development on the grounds of prematurity (that is, if it is located in a remote and unserviced section of the municipality) if that request is in conformance with the zoning or the master plan. Thus, chaotic development patterns, leading to inadequate provision of public services and often increased property taxes, have not uncommonly occurred.

Consequently, managed growth schemes certainly appear to be needed if a satisfactory, environmentally sound land use configuration is to result. These ideally would take the form of mechanisms to time development and to channel it spatially through the phasing of a planned provision of required public facilities and services, backed by a financial commitment by the municipality. However, given the proclivity

21. Malcolm D. Rivkin, "Some Thoughts on Ramapo," *Zoning Digest* 24, no. 9 (1972), p. 305. The following discussion is based on Rivkin's analysis.

for a good portion of the sentiments of growth controls to be underlaid by the social rationale described above, which are borne out by court decisions examined below, it is of utmost importance that such efforts be constrained within strict tests of reasonableness.

Growth control mechanisms

These inadequacies have fostered a number of stop-gap attempts to limit rates of growth. Only those most worthy of note can be reviewed here. Each is devoid of criteria for holding down growth, and they can realistically be termed "gimmicks."[22] The most infamous is large lot zoning, the most traditional approach which, while under attack from the courts, permeates most of suburbia. A second favorite mechanism is the sewer moratorium, used by local and state governments in the absence of effective multigovernmental land use controls.[23] These usually have taken at least one of the five following forms:

1. a freeze of additional hookups of buildings to the sewer network;
2. a freeze on the extension of the sewer network to new developments;
3. a freeze on individual building permits;
4. a freeze on requests for new subdivisions; or
5. a refusal to rezone to higher density.

A third technique is termed by Malcom Rivkin as "trial by public hearing," whereby developers are subjected to the wrath of citizenry in the public arena, "allowing the furor of the non-growth advocates to prevent or defer developments, even if in accord with community plans."[24] Other ad hoc solutions reflecting local prejudices abound—direct building moratoria, requirements to have developers finance services, and population ceilings, to name a few.

However, realizing the deficiencies and shortcomings of these stop-gap solutions, more realistic management growth techniques have arisen in developing areas. These are based upon capital facilities plans using special permits issued only upon proven ability to tie into extant or shortly planned sewerage systems, drainage systems and other public facilities, all of which the sponsoring jurisdiction has made a financial and policy commitment to provide. This "staging of development" technique has manifested itself most visibly in Ramapo, New York, a suburb of New York City.

All of these techniques may be invalid for any one of a number of reasons, including:

1. *Violation of the "due process" clause.* This argument is based upon the premise that the landowner will be deprived of the reasonable use of his property.
2. *Outside the scope of the police power.* This argument is based upon the premise that the

22. Rivkin, "Some Thoughts on Ramapo," p. 305.

23. Michael R. Greenberg, "A Commentary on the Sewer Moratorium as a Piecemeal Remedy for Controlling Development," in *New Dimensions in Urban Planning: Growth Controls*, ed. James W. Hughes (New Brunswick, N.J.: Rutgers University, Center for Urban Policy Research, 1974), p. 189.

24. Rivkin, "Some Thoughts on Ramapo," p. 305.

"general welfare" requirement upon which all police power regulations are based prevents a locality from ignoring regional housing needs.

3. *Outside the power delegated in the enabling legislation.* This argument is based upon the premise that zoning powers delegated to municipalities by the state do not include the authority to exclude people from the jurisdiction.

4. *Violation of the equal protection clause.* This argument is based upon the premise that exclusionary land use laws tend to have the greatest impact upon racial minorities.

5. *Violation of the "right to travel."* This argument is based upon the premise that the constitutionally protected right to travel may not be restricted by a municipality's land use regulations.[25]

LEGAL DEVELOPMENTS

Ramapo

The most heartening boost to those advocates of managed growth is the now famous 1972 decision of *Golden* v. *Planning Board of the Town of Ramapo*, where the New York Court of Appeals upheld a staged development program.[26] The court believed that the "Ramapo plan" was not designed "to freeze population at present levels, but to maximize growth by the efficient use of land, and in so doing testify to this community's continuing role in population assimilation. In sum, Ramapo asks not that it be left alone, but only that it be allowed to prevent the kind of deterioration that has transformed well ordered and thriving residential communities into blighted ghettos with attendant hazards to health, security, and social stability—a danger not without substantial basis in fact."[27]

A key determinant in this decision was the nature of the capital improvements program prepared by the municipality, which the court viewed as demonstrating Ramapo's effort to accommodate growth and change. Operationally, the scheme prevents the construction of new housing unless the developer obtains a special permit, issued only upon the proven ability of specified community facilities to service the development at a minimal level. Their ultimate provision is scheduled in accordance with Ramapo's capital improvement program, which encompasses roads, parks, recreation areas, fire houses, sewerage and drainage systems. Scheduled over an 18-year period, new development is held in line with the municipal expansion of these facilities. Certain land not served by this expansion may not be developed for residential use; however, the reduced development potential and therefore the value of such lands is recognized and compensated for by reduced taxes.

While this does not appear unreasonable per se, there are certain key facets of the ordinance which tend to support our earlier reserva-

25. Jerome G. Rose, "Regulation of Population Growth and Distribution" in *New Dimensions in Urban Planning: Growth Controls*, ed. James W. Hughes (New Brunswick, N.J.: Rutgers University, Center for Urban Policy Research, 1974), p. 168. These principles were originally stated in Herbert Franklin, *Controlling Urban Growth—But for Whom?* (Washington, D.C.: Potomac Institute, 1973).

26. Rose, "Regulation of Population Growth."

27. Rose, "Regulation of Population Growth."

tions. First of all, the ordinance focuses specifically on housing development; nonresidential development is not encompassed by the scheme. Consequently, the municipality appears ready to accept the tax ratables associated with new industrial development and then, in theory, to delay the satisfaction of the potential housing needs of the associated employees some years hence until they can be accommodated by the expanding capital facilities. Adding further question is the fact that the plan does not establish any provision for housing other than single-family units—no townhouses, apartments, and the like. Surprisingly, apartment zones, previously permitted, were eliminated, and the only other type of housing allowed is elderly units in laboratory/office zones.

It is indeed unfortunate that this legal precedent demonstrated so little concern for the array of suburban housing needs as distinguished by varying social status and life cycle stages. It underscores the possible motivation to preserve homogeneity throughout the entire municipality—a single-family home community—and not only to avoid the undesirable side effects of rampant growth. Certainly, the quality of life is not indelibly linked to single-family units and to the family status of the potential residents allowed to settle within the community's borders.

Nevertheless, no matter how rational the scheme is at the local level, collective programs of this nature confront the metropolitan area with an irrational whole, with households not of a specified type left to find housing elsewhere. Indeed, "the spectre of chaos has been raised at the prospect of numerous jurisdictions within a metropolitan area adopting timing devices, each concerned with tamping down growth within its own boundary."[28] As past evidence suggests, communities are not going to behave as if there were a metropolitan ethos,[29] for if there is indeed an ethos, it is likely imbedded in the rationale described above. In the extreme, the potential side effects of every suburban district adopting a Ramapo ordinance could reduce the older exclusionary zoning problems to secondary status.

Petaluma

If growth control enthusiasts saw Ramapo as the first step in a series of precedents in justifying local growth control approaches, they were soon disheartened by a decision in the federal courts approximately one and a half years later in California. There the Federal District Court ruled in *Construction Industry Association of Sonoma County* v. *City of Petaluma* that a growth control ordinance implemented to preserve Petaluma's small town character by keeping newcomers out is basically unconstitutional, since it violates the constitutionally protected right to travel.[30]

Without elaborating on the details of the local technique, let us say that the procedure limited housing construction to 500 units per year, and within certain boundaries strict population ceilings were essentially im-

28. Rivkin, "Some Thoughts on Ramapo," p. 306.

29. Ibid.

30. Jerome G. Rose, "Recent Decisions on Population Growth Control," in *New Dimensions in Urban Planning: Growth Controls*, ed. James W. Hughes (New Brunswick, N.J.: Rutgers University, Center for Urban Policy Research, 1974), p. 180.

posed. Additionally, these actions were not in line with any capital facilities expansion program; in fact, it appears that certain public facilities were actually being intentionally restricted.

Specifically the court held "that a municipality capable of supporting a natural population expansion may not limit growth simply because it does not prefer to grow at the rate which would be dictated by prevailing market demand."[31] In basing its decision on the fundamental rights of travel, the court cited precedent cases.

The question posed is whether the township can stand in the way of the natural forces which send out growing population into hitherto undeveloped areas in search of a comfortable place to live. We have concluded not. A zoning ordinance whose primary purpose is to prevent the entrance of newcomers in order to avoid future burdens, economic or otherwise, upon the administration of public services and facilities cannot be held valid. . . .[32]

In other words, the city was trying to avoid the problems that accompany growth rather than to demonstrate that it was trying to do so in a rational controlled fashion. Moreover, as in Ramapo, only residential uses were subject to the growth control measures, thereby taking the form of a residential quota control system. The end result of these policies was the thwarting of basic demographic and market trends (as noted above), inevitably shifting the burden to other parts of the metropolis.

In this case, the court's decision emphasizes a point made by Norman Williams: in the history of land use controls, we are entering a period of increasing judicial review, with the court's realization that land use control regulations may have served non-legitimate purposes, may be a product of a parochial vision, may be unduly harsh with little compensating public benefit, or merely may be inept.[33] This trend of legal development is indeed fortunate, given the deficiencies of the managed growth schemes to date and their potential impact on suburbia.

CONCLUSIONS

As the pressures for suburban residential diversity grow increasingly stronger, the implementation of controlled growth schemes, even if they take the form of staged development geared to publicly provided services and facilities, is fraught with danger. At present, the approval and implementation of these plans is the province of local jurisdictions and therefore the responsibility of locally elected officials. However, even if the techniques are designed by an objective cadre of professionals, we should not lose sight of the fact that these local officials are the final decision makers. These officials are entangled in a web of local political forces and realistically must be viewed as continually running for re-election. Consequently, the sentiments of their local constituencies will weigh very heavily upon them. Moreover, theirs is a short range point of view, often limited to the scope of their jurisdiction, since there is little "payoff" for worrying about metropolitan problems.

When viewed at the local level, these officials' actions may be rational indeed; they may be attempt-

31. Rose, "Recent Decisions," p. 182.
32. Rose, "Recent Decisions."

33. Norman Williams, "The Future of Land Use Controls," in *Future Land Use*, ed. Robert W. Burchell and David Listokin (New Brunswick, N.J.: Rutgers University, Center for Urban Policy Research, 1975), p. 28.

ing to optimize their own fiscal, social and environmental position. However, their decision making matrix does not take into account the spillover costs that are incurred by surrounding municipalities. Consequently, when viewed from the scale of metropolis, this is an error of suboptimization of not insignificant proportions, since a multiplicity of localities, each striving to optimize their own position in similar fashion, may hinder the efficiency and performance of the whole.

Indeed, if we view their actions in terms of growth controls, municipalities attempting to pawn off growth to surrounding metropolitan jurisdictions can produce the following negative effects:

1. Those in need of housing, especially those who lack effective constituencies at the local level, may have their opportunities restricted. Moreover, a multiplicity of jurisdictions enacting growth controls could limit the basic metropolitan housing capacity—restricted supplies in the face of growing demand will make the available housing that much more expensive.

2. By being denied housing in specific areas, employment opportunities to the affected households may be reduced.

3. Surrounding municipalities may incur severe fiscal burdens if they have to bear the brunt of development. These burdens may translate into higher taxation levels, leading to growing inequities among political jurisdictions.

4. Those forced to settle in areas allowing or not preventing development may be subject to overloaded and inadequate community service facilities.

5. If certain areas tend to restrict their growth, one might suspect benefits to accrue to the housing markets of the older central cities. This is always a possibility; however, the probable result is an even greater dispersion of households throughout the metropolitan region. Increased distances between residence and workplace may result, adding additional cost burdens to those so affected. Moreover, such dispersion does not lend itself to any type of public transportation solution.

6. If increased dispersion is the end result of local growth control policies, the resultant land use patterns, when viewed from the metropolitan perspective, may be quite inefficient, generating fiscal burdens on the metropolitan area as a whole. One example is the cost of transportation and sewerage facilities to service more dispersed development.

7. The potential of increased commuting distances, which must be overcome by the automobile, can conceivably exacerbate the air quality objectives of the metropolitan area.

8. A more rigid suburban social pattern could result, with sharp lines drawn at municipal boundaries.

Given the potential severity of these effects, Herbert Franklin delineates the following criteria to evaluate the reasonableness of growth control ordinances: (1) is the program responsive to regional housing needs; (2) does the program provide for housing for employee households with existing or anticipated jobs in the jurisdiction; (3) does the program contain a real and sincere commitment for public investment to assimilate growth; (4) does the program apply only to residential development, or is commercial and industrial development coordinated with residential growth; and (5) does the program result in a tax effort that is reduced below the average for the metropolitan area?[34]

As should be evident, these criteria are metropolitan or regional in viewpoint. But motivations being what they are at the local level, jurisdictions will have to be prodded, and indeed, this has been the thrust of the recent Mount Laurel decision in New Jersey.[35] Even if prodded to meet these criteria, their reaction may be "how far must we go" rather than "how far can we go."

The growth control movement is not going to fade away quietly and, since it involves so many diverse and competing interest groups, it will not be resolved easily. It is

34. Franklin, *Controlling Urban Growth*, pp. 21–30.

35. *See*, Edward McCahill, "In Mount Laurel, Issues Are Not Black and White," *Planning* 41, no. 4 (May 1975), pp. 12–13, for a review of the decision.

wedded to a cycle of events giving rise to fundamental dilemmas. The myth of suburbia and the American Dream of a single-family home, although perpetuated by the media, are being challenged increasingly by the reality of an urbanizing suburbia and emerging economic strictures. People who have moved to suburbia in search of the ideal are discovering that the reality is, or soon will be, otherwise. Pressures for a more diverse suburbia press ever more heavily, and growth controls may be one attempt to preserve older premises. But whatever the interpretation of the phenomenon, its continued evolution is destined to be one of dominant public policy concerns in suburbia.

Amid this array of issues, it is somewhat paradoxical that the post-World War II baby crop, raised in the suburbs during an era of unprecedented affluence and subsequently engaged in the campus turmoil of the late 1960s, is now rapidly forming households. But not only are this generation's job prospects and economic advancement retarded by the current turn of events; they also find their shelter requirements shunned in a fashion once reserved for low income and minority racial groups.

The Urban-Suburban Investment-Disinvestment Process: Consequences for Older Neighborhoods

By CALVIN P. BRADFORD AND LEONARD S. RUBINOWITZ

ABSTRACT: The pattern of suburban growth and decline of older neighborhoods within metropolitan areas is often seen as inevitable. However, these processes are shaped, in a significant way, by a relatively small number of private sector actors, including institutional investors, developers and mortgage bankers. Because of their ideologies and their perception of the economic realities, these interests invest increasingly in large scale developments on the suburban fringe and choose not to invest in older urban and suburban neighborhoods. These investment decisions have significant negative impacts on these older, middle class neighborhoods which are struggling to remain viable. With the withdrawal of these traditional sources of real estate investment capital, such neighborhoods face a concentration of foreclosures and abandonment of housing. Because these investment decisions are so important to the future of older neighborhoods, it is appropriate that there be public intervention to assure that there is an adequate flow of capital into these neighborhoods. The approaches which might be used include regulation—that is, requiring the industry to change investment patterns without rewarding them for doing so—and subsidy—providing incentives for investors to provide capital for older neighborhoods.

Calvin P. Bradford is Assistant Professor of Urban Sciences, University of Illinois at Chicago Circle. He is also Co-Director of the Urban-Suburban Investment Study Group, Center for Urban Affairs, Northwestern University. Educated at Trinity College and Northwestern University, he is an Associate Editor of Urban Affairs Quarterly.

Leonard S. Rubinowitz is Associate Professor of Law and Urban Affairs, Northwestern University. He is also Co-Director of the Urban-Suburban Investment Study Group, Center for Urban Affairs, Northwestern University. Educated at the University of Wisconsin and Yale Law School, he is the author of Low-Income Housing: Suburban Strategies *and several articles related to housing and urban development. He has also served as Special Assistant to the Regional Administrator, U.S. Department of Housing and Urban Development in Chicago.*

THE pattern of decaying older cities and development of the suburban fringe areas is becoming so familiar that it is often seen as the "normal" course of events for metropolitan areas. The fact that the suburban portions of the major metropolitan areas grew rapidly in the last decade, while the central cities, as a whole, actually lost population, is one of the most publicized findings of the last census.

Some social scientists suggest that the city is becoming the "reservation" of the poor and the blacks, while those who have money escape from the reservation to the security of the suburbs. Some residential neighborhoods of older cities, which only a few years ago were viable, now lie abandoned. This is in sharp contrast to the major concern for the overcrowded conditions of older neighborhoods which dominated the minds of social planners in the 1960s.

Both the growth of suburban areas and the decay of older neighborhoods have been explained by economic or social models of neighborhood change. The economic theory is known as the "filtering" or "trickle down" model. In *Opening Up the Suburbs*, Anthony Downs summarizes this model as follows:

Existing housing units are vacated by households with rising incomes who move to more modern and hence more desirable new units. These new units are out of the reach of low income households. . . . Relatively lower income families unable to afford the increasing costs of maintaining the older units replace the higher income groups who have moved out. Over time, as successively lower income groups come to occupy the structures, the buildings fall into disrepair and deterioration sets in.[1]

Due to the fact that buildings of the same age and type are concentrated together, this deterioration becomes a neighborhood phenomenon. Then the "trickle down" process results in "critical mass" effects of the "concentration of poverty."[2] This trickle down phenomenon is seen as the efficient way in which the natural market provides housing for low income families.[3]

An alternative to this model is the sociologist's "human ecology" model of neighborhood change. In this model, different social groups "invade" the neighborhoods, or areas of other groups; they "compete" with them for control of the area. After the struggle, there is a "succession" as one group replaces the other. This model is basically a social version of the trickle down model in that it, too, defines the neighborhood change where "invasion" and "succession" lead to a neighborhood's falling into the hands of a

1. Anthony Downs, *Opening up the Suburbs: An Urban Strategy for America* (New Haven, Conn.: Yale University Press, 1973), pp. 2–6.
2. Downs, *Opening up the Suburbs*, p. 9.
3. Downs, *Opening up the Suburbs*, p. 202.

poorer, less self-sufficient group until it becomes a slum.

In these models, the trend of central city decay and suburban boom are seen as "natural" economic or social forces. As so-called natural forces, they seem to be removed from the control of policy interventions. Members of the real estate investment and development industry are seen as actors who respond to these trends. They are not seen as creating or shaping these trends.

THE INVESTMENT-DISINVESTMENT MODEL

The thesis of this article is that these trends are not inevitable, but are in an important way the result of identifiable private and public investment decisions, made by identifiable public actors and members of the real estate investment and development industry.[4] These decisions can be made otherwise, with different consequences for older neighborhoods. While there is no Napoleon who sits in a position of control over the fate of a neighborhood, there is enough control by, and integration of, the investment and development actors of the real estate industry that their decisions go beyond a response and actually shape that market.

The focus here is on the impact of institutional investors, developers and other members of the real estate industry—the primary private sector actors in this process. The decisions of these actors with regard to suburban development appeal to people's preferences rather than to any basic need for a "decent home and a suitable living environment," which is the goal articulated by Congress for all Americans. These actors seek to encourage people to move out of those decent homes and suitable living environments in the city or older suburbs to "preferred" homes and environments in the fringe suburbs.

These investment decisions have highly significant consequences for older middle class neighborhoods in the central cities and nearby suburbs. These areas are left without an adequate supply of conventional mortgage credit and must rely on federally insured loans. As these loans are concentrated in older neighborhoods, the neighborhoods tend to decline. In short, the private investor's decision to invest in the growing suburbs and disinvest from the older neighborhoods decreases the chances for those neighborhoods to remain viable.

The purpose here is to examine the role of the investors, developers and related real estate industry actors in the processes of metropolitan growth and neighborhood change. The first question to be addressed is how these actors have become able to shape these processes rather than simply respond to them. Second, the impacts of these actors' investment decisions on suburbia and older neighborhoods are examined. Finally, this article looks at the implications for public policy of the investment-disinvestment thesis.

The issues described above are addressed with regard to housing and neighborhoods only. While much

---

4. Darel Grothaus, a creator and the other Co-Director of the Urban-Suburban Investment Study Group, is responsible for the development of much of this model. Without his work over the last three years, both in observation of, and data collection related to, the real estate development process and the mortgage banking industry, and in conceptualizing the linkages between suburban growth and the decline of viable older neighborhoods, this article could not have been written.

of the analysis applies, in somewhat modified form, to commercial and industrial development, lack of space requires this narrower focus. Similarly, although public investment—roads, water and sewer facilities, for example—are an important part of the picture, as are subsidies, tax laws and the regulation of institutional investors, the analysis is confined to private investment decisions.

The critical areas of concern here are newly developing suburban areas and older, viable neighborhoods in the central city and older suburbs. The private investment decisions in these areas are an important determinant of whether the older neighborhoods stabilize as viable communities or decline.

For the neighborhoods that are faced with massive deterioration and/or abandonment, either the disinvestment process is too far along for private investors to take useful initiatives unilaterally, or the process has not progressed far enough, to the point that private actors can assemble and acquire land cheaply for redevelopment purposes.

INVESTOR-DEVELOPER COMPLEX —THE DEVELOPER

A relatively small number of investors, developers and other actors influence the processes of metropolitan growth and decay in a significant way. Some actors pull people from existing areas to the suburban fringe. Looking first at these actors, we begin with the developer.

Every developer borrows money to finance his developments. How much he can borrow depends upon the income, or profit, expected from what he plans to build, *not upon the cost* of the development. It used to be quite common for the costs to be so low that his loan would surpass them. Today, however, the costs of materials, labor, land and money have increased much faster than the projected increases in income or profits. Developers have responded to this squeeze in three ways.

First, developers have tried to counter these increased costs by moving from single-family detached houses to multifamily units, where clustering and common-wall construction reduce costs. In the last 10 years, the greatest change in the construction of homes has been the shift from 80 percent single family homes to 55 percent multifamily units in new construction.

The second response by developers to increased costs is the Planned Unit Development (PUD). This allows the builder to meet only density per acre requirements and to cluster, or combine, the units or uses in ways which reduce construction costs and increase income. Such flexibility may also reduce the costs of roads, sewers and excavation.

The third way in which developers have increased profits is to increase the scale of their operations. Thus, there has been a marked increase in the size of developments and developers. In 1968, *Professional Builder* (the official magazine of the home building trades) found only 55 builders who built more than 400 units a year. But in their survey of builders in 1973, they found 419 such developers. They note that builders with more than $10 million in gross sales continue to increase their share of the housing and light construction market. In total, they account for more than 26 percent of all new housing units built in the United States last year (623,537 units). "[These giants] . . . although numbering less than one-half of one percent of the nation's approximate 100,000 active builders in housing and light construction, are the influentials in the industry."[5]

Investor-Developer Complex —The Investor

All of these responses to the cost squeeze—multifamily construction, PUDs and increased scale—have forced developers to become more dependent upon larger institutional investors for their financing. These institutions make the individual home mortgages for tract developments or the mortgages on the entire project for multifamily developments. Developers must secure a commitment from a lender either to make these individual home mortgages or to take the single mortgage on the entire development.

As the scale of developments increases, developers must turn from the many local banks and savings and loan associations to larger sources of capital, most frequently life insurance companies. Regulations on the amount of money a bank or savings institution may invest in a single venture increasingly necessitate this process.

The trend toward multifamily rental units also forces the developer to go beyond the local savings and loan associations for permanent financing, since regulations require them to invest primarily in single-family home loans. Mixing commercial, industrial and residential uses has a similar effect.

As developers gravitate toward larger institutional lenders, such as major banks and life insurance companies, they find that they must compete with alternative investments, as these investors are not restricted to real estate investments. Thus, they must present these lenders with developments which are profitable enough to compete with alternative investments, such as stocks or corporate bonds.

Since these very large institutional investors operate on a national scale, they must have some kind of local agent to link them with developers. A separate set of actors called mortgage bankers act as correspondents for these investors, informing local developers of the commitments these investors are willing to make and the terms and conditions of these investments. Mortgage bankers then bring to the investors those developments which they feel will be most appealing. The mortgage bankers' profits are based on the fees they get for placing and servicing these investments. Thus, they must effectively transmit the values of the investors to developers.

Institutional investors often perceive themselves as simply responding to the proposals that come to them from developers; but the anticipated response of these investors is firmly fixed in the minds of those who bring them proposals. Developers know what kinds of projects investors are willing to finance— the kinds of locations, the price range of the housing, and sometimes even the building materials and color of roofing required. In some cases, the control of the investors has reached the point where insurance companies actually own the development corporation.

This increased concern among developers for the requirements of money is evident at seminars offered at major conventions of builders. Nothing compares to the turnout for

5. "Annual Report of Housing Giants," *Professional Builder and Apartment Business* (July 1973), p. 67.

such seminars as "Packaging both Equity and Debt Financing," "10 Steps to a Quick Mortgage Commitment," or "How to Sell 'The Deal' to Investors."[6] On the display floor, the "Economic Contact" booths are frequently busier than the displays for cost-saving building materials.

IMPACT OF THE INVESTOR-DEVELOPER COMPLEX ON OLDER NEIGHBORHOODS

This investor-developer complex has important impacts on the older areas. First, the increased size of developments and the need for large tracts of open land encourages developers to look to urban fringe areas for development. Second, costs of development have risen so high that developers are building for the upper one-fourth of the income groups. This is not a "market of need," but a market where developers are seeking to define what kinds of buildings, with what kinds of amenities, will attract people already in adequate housing into a new development. It is, as one major study of housing needs in the next decade terms it, a "market of preference."[7] The market is generally devoid of large families and poor and minority groups. These groups of people are left to their own resources in the older neighborhoods.

The investor-developer complex is shifting a finite source of real estate investment capital out of older areas and placing it in urban fringe areas. It is facilitating the redistribution of significant numbers of people by controlling the development of large parcels of land and designing them for only the wealthier members of our society. This puts added stress on the older neighborhoods.

DISINVESTMENT COMPLEX

At the same time that the investor-developer complex attracts people who live in decent housing in older neighborhoods out to the periphery, other actors operate in ways which undermine the ability of older neighborhoods to remain viable. These conventional lenders who withdraw their resources and the FHA-backed lenders who fill the void are the disinvestment complex.

The practices of the Federal Housing Administration (FHA) and those who participate in the federal programs, particularly mortgage bankers and realtors, have led to the abandonment of large numbers of homes and the rapid decline of neighborhoods. In many cases, these neighborhoods have been characterized by physically sound structures but an inadequate supply of conventional loan funds for home purchases and home improvements. When the conventional lenders—those making loans which are not federally insured—refuse to make loans in an area, or "redline" it, the FHA lenders move in to fill the gap. In the last decade, it has been the departure of conventional sources and the influx of FHA loans that has spelled out the decline of many urban neighborhoods.

Older neighborhoods are in a different relationship with investors than are newer areas on the suburban fringe. As indicated above, a rela-

6. Apartment Builder/Developer Conference and Exposition, sponsored by *Apartment Construction News* (29, 30 April and 1 May 1974, and 28, 29, 30 April 1975).

7. David Birch, *America's Housing Needs: 1970–1980* (Cambridge: Joint Center for Urban Studies, Massachusetts Institute of Technology and Harvard University). *See,* especially, "The Influence of Consumer Preference on Housing Markets," pp. 5-1 to 5-71.

tively small number of investors and developers accounts for a significant proportion of housing development in the growing areas. In the older areas, whatever investment takes place—usually purchase or repair of a home or apartment building, and occasionally development or redevelopment of an area—takes place on a small scale. Each property owner or purchaser must negotiate for the purchase, maintenance or rehabilitation of his own property with the available sources of capital.

For the neighborhood as a whole to secure adequate credit, individual owners must be successful in dealing with the multiplicity of conventional sources of mortgages and home improvement loans, primarily savings and loan associations and commercial banks. But these investors have the opportunity to invest in new properties on the suburban fringe or in older homes. Their choice is made more simple by the fact that larger institutional investors are making major investments on the fringe, which will enhance the value of smaller investments made by savings and loan associations in frontier suburban areas.

The decisions of conventional lenders are also facilitated by appraisers, who act as communicators of the perceived values of neighborhoods. An appraisal is needed before an institution will finance a home loan or apartment sale, so the appraiser is in a central role to influence the lender's decision. Appraisers are trained to assume that older neighborhoods inevitably decline, even if they are presently viable middle income areas.[8] Lenders are then inclined to accept this negative view of older neighborhoods and to restrict or terminate their lending there.

For single-family homes, the crucial actors are the savings and loan associations. Their decisions are critical since they financed approximately one-half of all single-family home loans in the first half of the 1970s. Savings and loan associations may choose not to make loans in older, middle class, viable neighborhoods—even if they are located in those neighborhoods, their deposits come primarily from that area, and they have outstanding mortgages in that area to protect.

When neighborhoods are thus "redlined," the only resource for buyers or owners seeking loans is FHA-insured loans. These loans are insured by the federal government, so that if the borrower defaults, the lender is protected against loss by the federal government. The major actor in this process is the mortgage banker. In addition to acting as part of the investor-developer complex in the suburbs by placing investments for institutional investors there, mortgage bankers originate about 75 percent of all FHA-insured, single-family loans. These loans are predominantly in older neighborhoods.

Because of the insurance, the FHA lender does not have the same incentive as the conventional lender to exercise care in assessing the risks involved in lending money on a

---

8. American Institute of Real Estate Appraisers, *The Appraisal of Real Estate*, 5th ed. (Chicago: American Institute of Real Estate Appraisers, 1967). *See*, especially, "Neighborhood Analysis," pp. 81–100. For a graphic presentation of "neighborhood age patterns," *see*, "Impact of Urban Forces Upon Property Values" and "Value Analysis of Neighborhood Characteristics," in Alfred A. Ring, *The Valuation of Real Estate* (Englewood Cliffs, N.J.: Prentice-Hall, 1970), pp. 55–92.

particular house to a particular buyer. In addition to this structural problem, there have been serious administrative abuses. Since FHA began insuring large numbers of mortgages in older neighborhoods in the late 1960s, there has been maladministration and fraud in these programs. The result has been a high level of foreclosure and abandonment in neighborhoods where FHA loans are concentrated, generally the "redlined" neighborhoods. Because the concentration of FHA loans takes place in neighborhoods where conventional lenders have withdrawn their resources, this process is referred to as "disinvestment."

The concentration of FHA loans and the attendant problems threaten the viability of neighborhoods. Even if the foreclosure rate in FHA programs were at its same high level but the loans were scattered randomly throughout metropolitan areas, no individual neighborhood would be endangered.

With regard to the multifamily buildings in older neighborhoods, the traditional source of mortgage money has been life insurance companies. Like savings and loan associations, however, insurance companies have decided not to continue to invest in older neighborhoods and are investing instead in new suburban developments. This decision by insurance companies makes it increasingly difficult for buyers of apartment buildings in older areas to secure mortgages. They must often secure financing at higher interest rates and with shorter terms than were previously available. With the increased cost of financing these transactions, the rents in the buildings are increased while the quality is not. The result

is that the more affluent, mobile tenants look elsewhere for housing.

In short, both in single-family and multifamily housing, older neighborhoods are at a serious financial disadvantage compared to newly developing suburban areas. Older communities are without major institutional investments to help increase, or even to maintain, their desirability and value. Local lenders, as well, have tended to choose to invest in suburban areas, forsaking the communities from which they receive a large share of their deposits. The neighborhoods are then left in the hands of mortgage bankers and other lenders who use FHA mortgage insurance programs. The result is the concentration of foreclosures and abandonments, which dot these communities and blight the area. Thus, as conventional investors remove their financial resources from older communities, these communities suffer the burden of trying to survive while depending on investors who have no risk, and thus no stake, in the economic future of the neighborhood.

The investor-developer complex and the disinvestment complex constitute a single, interrelated metropolitan investment-disinvestment complex. The decisions of this complex have important negative consequences for older central city and suburban neighborhoods and communities.

The investment-disinvestment complex has made these decisions based on a combination of ideology and perceptions of economic realities. The ideology views suburban growth as inevitable and desirable. On the other side of this ideological coin is the belief that older neighborhoods inevitably decline and die.

The prevalent economic perception of the investment-disinvestment complex is that profits are to be made on the suburban fringe by building for the upper quarter of the market. On the other hand, older neighborhoods are seen as unacceptably risky investments. In short, the ideology and the economic analysis are mutually supportive, and both serve to justify the decisions of these actors to the public.

PUBLIC POLICY IMPLICATIONS

Given the negative consequences for older neighborhoods that flow from the investment-disinvestment complex's actualizing its ideological and economic values, it is appropriate to ask how a more socially constructive set of investment decisions could be brought about. For example, what forms of public intervention in the private investment processes would be appropriate and effective to assure an adequate flow of capital into older neighborhoods?

The approaches to public intervention might be categorized into regulatory and subsidy strategies. Regulatory approaches would require private interests to behave differently, without rewarding them for doing so. In this case, regulatory strategies would require that private decision makers, individually or collectively, make sufficient credit available in older neighborhoods. This kind of approach would be based on an assumption that these actors have a perception of economic realities that is, at least in part, inaccurate. It would assume not only that shifting investments from the suburban fringe to the older neighborhoods would permit private actors to continue to make "reasonable" profits, but also that they

should be required to do so because of the important public policy impacts of the location of their investments. Since this type of major shift in investment practices has not been tried (except for the FHA process, which has the problems described above), the risks and profits involved are not yet known.

At the local, state and federal levels, regulatory strategies are being considered and, to a limited extent, implemented. Many of these are directed at prohibiting "redlining," so that financial institutions cannot refuse to issue mortgages or home improvement loans because of the age or other aspects of the neighborhood which are not related to demonstrable risks. Other ideas include mandatory pooling by institutional investors to make resources available to older neighborhoods.

Since the investment-disinvestment complex has not yet borne the burden of demonstrating that it is economically infeasible to invest in ways that maintain older neighborhoods rather than bringing about or accelerating their decline, public regulation seems to be an appropriate starting point. Such regulation would demonstrate the extent to which the industry could continue to make reasonable profits while serving the public interest.

If regulatory efforts indicated that there were unreasonably high risks and low profits for investors in providing necessary capital in older neighborhoods, this would indicate that some form of public subsidy might be necessary. Such an incentive system, perhaps in combination with a regulatory strategy, would make it financially feasible to put additional resources into older neighborhoods, if it was not profitable otherwise. A variety of governmental subsidies could be considered, from providing tax incentives to depositing governmental funds in financial institutions which make capital available in older neighborhoods.

Any incentive approach should carefully avoid the mistakes of the past and the present, such as those that are characteristic of the structure and administration of the FHA mortgage insurance programs. The loans which are made with governmental inducements must be quality loans which will enhance the viability of older neighborhoods.

CONCLUSION

The investors involved in the investor-developer and disinvestment complexes are the same. Thus, the investment-disinvestment complex is a single entity. On one side, it builds to suit the preferences of people who do not *need* housing. On the other side, conventional lenders, acting on the assumption that older viable neighborhoods are on their way to blight, withdraw their resources and initiate a self-fulfilling prophecy. The growth of suburban areas and the decay of older neighborhoods are interrelated —one cannot gain without a loss to the other.

Racial Segregation: The Persisting Dilemma

By KARL E. TAEUBER

ABSTRACT: Although moderate to high social and economic heterogeneity are typical of suburbs as well as central cities, the black population has become highly segregated residentially. This segregation has little economic base, but is based primarily on racial discrimination. The military images used to describe black "invasion" of neighborhoods and white "flight" from central cities express racial conflict and distort our perception of metropolitan trends. As a one-in-eight minority nationally, blacks are not numerous enough to "take over" many central cities. The high concentration of blacks in a couple dozen cities ensures that blacks will remain a small minority in 200 other metropolitan areas. Demographic data since 1970 indicate a reversal of the centuries-long process of increasing metropolitan concentration and a sharp diminution in the flow of black migrants to large cities. To date, there is no evidence of sharp shifts in the residential isolation of blacks. Black suburbanization in some metropolitan areas has followed the central city pattern of segregation. The altered demographic circumstances of the 1970s and 1980s hold out prospects for change, but those prospects depend on the nation's efforts to reduce continuing discrimination in the sale and rental of housing.

Karl E. Taeuber is Professor of Sociology and Fellow of the Institute for Research on Poverty, University of Wisconsin. Educated at Yale, Harvard and the University of Chicago, he is co-author of Negroes in Cities: Residential Segregation and Neighborhood Change, Migration in the United States, *and numerous articles on migration and black population distribution. He has served as chairman of his department and the Population Research Committee of the National Institute of Child Health and Human Development and on the boards of directors of the Social Science Research Council and the Population Association of America.*

This paper is one in a series, "Studies in Racial Segregation," supported by funds granted to the Institute for Research on Poverty at the University of Wisconsin by the Department of Health, Education, and Welfare pursuant to the provisions of the Economic Opportunity Act of 1964. Conclusions and interpretations are the sole responsibility of the author.

THE National Advisory Commission on Civil Disorders, appointed by President Johnson in response to the ghetto riots of the mid-1960s, reported in early 1968 its basic conclusion: "Our nation is moving toward two societies, one black, one white—separate and unequal."[1] The image of "two societies" took root in people's minds in a way that the commission's recommendations for action never could. Translated into geographic terms, this image now dominates the nation's perception of central city and suburbs: a black core surrounded by a white noose.

For decades scholars and the public have used battlefield imagery to describe residential patterns of blacks and whites. Early in this century, as black populations grew in the cities, the so-called colored were said to be threatening and invading white neighborhoods. During my childhood in World War II, a "blockbuster" was a bomb of awesome destructive power; in college in the 1950s I learned that a "block-buster" was an unscrupulous character who dared to sell or rent to Negroes in white areas. In the years since the Kerner Commission report, the imagery has become that of defeat and panic, of white flight to the suburbs in fear of blackening central cities.

This racial battlefield imagery of cities and suburbs is, like the other city-suburban imagery, a gross exaggeration that nevertheless blinds the national perception to reality. Racial conflict is a prominent aspect of the American metropolitan scene, but the two-society image is too narrow a perspective. A survey of certain census data on population distribution and migration can broaden the perspective and provide a glimpse of both the uniformities of racial residential patterns throughout the nation and of the diversities in scale and character of the problems posed by these patterns in individual metropolitan areas.

THE BLACKENING OF CENTRAL CITIES

What did the 1970 census reveal about the so-called blackening of central cities? In the 243 metropolitan areas, blacks composed a majority of the population in only three central cities. These three cities—Washington, Newark and Atlanta—are each severely underbounded with respect to the spread of urbanization around them. (Washington had 26 percent of the metropolitan area's population; Newark, 21 percent; and Atlanta, 36 percent.) In the total metropolitan population of these three places, blacks were outnumbered three or four to one.

In only 12 other metropolitan areas did blacks in 1970 compose between 40 and 50 percent of the central city population. Four of these 12 were Southern cities in which the black percentage either declined or increased only slightly during the 1960s: Birmingham, Alabama; Charleston, South Carolina; Pine Bluff, Arkansas; and Richmond, Virginia. The other eight cities experienced rapid increases in percentage of blacks during the 1960s, and most will probably have black majorities by the time of the 1980 census. These eight, in declining order of city size, are Detroit, Balti-

1. National Advisory Commission on Civil Disorders *Report* (New York: Bantam Books, 1968), p. 1.

more, St. Louis and New Orleans, among the nation's large cities, and Savannah, Wilmington, Augusta and Atlantic City among the medium-size cities.

A few central cities other than these eight may experience such rapid white out-movement and black increase during the 1970s that they, too, will have black majorities by 1980. But in 211 of the 243 central cities, whites outnumbered blacks more than two to one in 1970. Many of the 32 cities in which blacks composed more than one-third of the 1970 population were medium-size Southern cities from which blacks were fleeing as fast as whites in the 1960s. In other medium-size cities whites were moving in, not out, and at a faster rate than blacks.

About one of every eight persons in the United States is Negro (according to census classification). A minority group, outnumbered seven to one, cannot "take over" all of the nation's central cities. Indeed, more than half of the nation's black population already lives in central cities of metropolitan areas. Black urbanization in the future cannot continue at the former pace. There are not enough blacks left in the rural South to provide a continuing large flow into the cities.

Although 198 of the 243 metropolitan areas experienced an increase during the 1960s in the percentage of blacks in the central city, there is no typical metropolitan area. Black population in New York City increased by more than half a million. In Provo-Orem, Utah, the black central city population increased from 18 to 28 persons. There are prevailing patterns of racial population change, but the specific pattern in each metropolitan area takes on a unique size and shape.

BLACK SUBURBANIZATION

Variety is the prominent feature of patterns of black suburbanization among the nation's metropolitan areas. In 1970 there were 70 million whites living in the suburbs (census definition) and 3.4 million blacks. Blacks composed about five percent of all suburban residents; but this aggregate figure of five percent is a misleading indication of the general pattern. In most of the old South, blacks lived in towns and villages and throughout the countryside. As metropolitan areas grew, they incorporated within their domain the pre-existing pattern of racial enclaves. Despite the exclusion of blacks from most of the new suburban housing of the past 50 years, in many of the South's metropolitan areas blacks compose from 10 to 40 percent of the suburban population. In every Northern metropolitan area and in some Southern areas, blacks compose less than 10 percent of the suburban population and often only a miniscule proportion.

During the 1950s and 1960s more blacks moved out of many Southern metropolitan areas than moved in; this was true of suburbs as well as central cities. The huge flow of black population to Northern central cities drew heavily from Southern urban blacks as well as from blacks in the rural hinterlands. With rapid white suburbanization in these Southern metropolitan areas, the percentage that blacks composed of the suburban population often fell.

In the Northern metropolitan areas, racial patterns of suburbanization varied. In many areas with rapid suburbanization of whites, the number of blacks has shown a sharp percentage increase. Some observers have seen in these demographic figures the harbinger of a new era of extensive black suburbanization. Caution is warranted, however, whenever one looks at percentage change data from a small base population. Between 1960 and 1970 the white suburban population in the Boston metropolitan area increased only 11 percent, while the black suburban population increased 53 percent. Numerically, however, the white suburbanization greatly outweighed the black: the white suburban population increased by 200,000, from 1.9 million to 2.1 million; the black suburban increase was less than 8,000, from 15,000 to 22,000. The *rate* of black suburbanization was greater, to be sure, and the percentage that blacks composed of Boston's suburban population did increase—from less than one percent to just over one percent. If this is the harbinger of a new era of black suburbanization, it is obvious that the old era will be with us for a long time before being ushered out.

Another kind of evidence shows that the black suburbanization currently occurring in a number of large metropolitan areas, whatever its numerical scale, is following the essential dynamics of the old era rather than ushering in a new era of race relations. This evidence pertains to the location of black suburbanites and the character of their new communities. Consider Chicago, for example, where the quantity of black suburbanization has been rather large. In the two decades from 1950 to 1970, the black suburban population in the Chicago area increased by 85,000 persons (from a 1950 base of 44,000). Nearly two-thirds of this increase occurred in nine old industrial suburbs (such as Joliet, Waukegan and Chicago Heights), each of which was experiencing the same kind of blacks-replacing-whites in segregated neigh-

borhoods that occurs in central cities. Another one-fourth of the black suburban increase occurred in five "black suburbs" (such as Robbins and East Chicago Heights), small communities or neighborhoods in which new housing developments had been marketed directly to black families. The Chicago suburban territory, aside from these 14 communities, was home to more than 3 million whites in 1970, but it made room for a black increase of fewer than 10,000 persons during the 20-year period.

ECONOMICS OR DISCRIMINATION?

The residential segregation of blacks from whites within central cities and the exclusion of blacks from suburbs are often assumed to be a reflection of the relatively poorer economic circumstances of blacks. In fact, although metropolitan areas have both wealthier and poorer neighborhoods, most residential neighborhoods throughout the metropolis have housing that rents or sells for a wide range of prices. Thus, the first premise of the poverty interpretation of racial residential patterns is only a half-truth. The residential distribution of persons among neighborhoods in the metropolis is only in small part a function of housing costs, family income or other economic factors.

The second premise of the poverty interpretation of housing segregation is that blacks are poorer than whites. This is again only a partial truth. If the entire distribution of families by income is considered, rather than just average incomes, a considerable overlap is seen among races. Many wealthy and middle income black families have greater economic resources than do millions of poor white families.

The conclusion from the two premises of the poverty interpretation of residential segregation is that the residential locations of blacks and whites differ because of economic differences. The reality, alas, is not so simple. Sociologists and economists have devised various statistical techniques for assessing the influence of economic factors on the differential residential location of black and white households, but they have not reached any consensus beyond agreement that other factors are important. I have contributed to the esoteric literature on this topic, but I am more impressed by the results of common sense and simple statistics. Common sense and open eyes reveal that rich blacks do not live interspersed with rich whites. Poor whites do not live interspersed with poor blacks. Racial residential segregation exists to far too high a degree in all American cities for economic factors to be the primary cause. Simple statistics offer surprising confirmation. In Chicago in 1960, the average rent paid by white tenants was $88 a month; the average rent paid by black tenants was $88 a month. Black renters were highly segregated from white renters despite their obvious ability to pay as much.

But suburbanization is different, is it not? Granted that patterns of housing segregation in the central city are not primarily economic in origin, is it not true that economic factors play a more important role in suburban locations? Consider data for 29 of the nation's largest metropolitan areas.[2] Among white families with incomes of $5,000 to $6,999 (not a very good income even by 1969 standards), the proportion who lived in the suburbs was greater in every case than the suburban proportion among black families with incomes of $15,000 to $24,900. Consider also a specific metropolis. In Detroit in 1970, more than half of the white families in each income level, from very poor to very rich, lived in the suburbs. Among blacks, only one-tenth of the families at each income level (including very rich) lived in the suburbs.

I have concluded from my own research and a review of the work of others that the prime cause of residential segregation by race has been discrimination, both public and private.[3] Racial discrimination was influential in developing the racially segregated pattern of American cities. In recent years, despite court rulings and legislation clearly outlawing virtually all types of racial discrimination in housing, past patterns persist, and every investigation uncovers evidence that old impediments to free choice of residence by blacks continue. I refer specifically to practices such as:

1. racially motivated site selection and tenant assignment policies in public housing;
2. racially motivated site selection, financing, sales, and rental policies of other types of government subsidized housing, such as Federal Housing Administration and Veterans Administration insurance programs;
3. racially motivated site selection, relocation policies and practices, and redevelopment policies in urban renewal programs;

2. Albert I. Hermalin and Reynolds Farley, "The Potential for Residential Integration in Cities and Suburbs: Implications for the Busing Controversy," *American Sociological Review* 38 (October 1973), pp. 595–610.

3. This paragraph is taken from Karl E. Taeuber, "Demographic Perspectives on Housing and School Segregation," WAYNE LAW REVIEW 31 (March 1975), pp. 840–841.

4. zoning and annexation policies that foster racial segregation;
5. restrictive covenants attached to housing deeds;
6. policies of financial institutions that discourage prospective developers of racially integrated private housing;
7. policies of financial institutions that allocate mortgage funds and rehabilitation loans to blacks only if they live in predominantly black areas;
8. practices of the real estate industry such as (a) limiting the access of black brokers to realty associations and multiple listing services; (b) refusals by white realtors to cobroke on transactions that would foster racial integration; (c) blockbusting, panic selling, and racial steering; (d) racially identifying vacancies, either overtly or by nominally benign codes (advertising housing according to racially identifiable schools or other neighborhood identifiers); (e) refusing to show houses or apartments or refusing to encourage blacks to consider housing in white neighborhoods; (f) reprimanding or penalizing brokers and salesmen who act to facilitate racial integration; and
9. racially discriminatory practices by individual homeowners and landlords.

Mass Migration to Metropolis

A century ago the black population in the United States was predominantly a rural agricultural one because the South of which blacks were a part was itself a rural agricultural region. As the South slowly urbanized, blacks participated. Southern cities, together with their outlying suburbs, grew with a pattern of separate housing for blacks. A slow northward movement of black population that had been occurring in the first half-century after the emancipation of slaves accelerated during the 1910–20 decade. Continuing for the next half-century and a few years beyond, the flow of blacks to Northern cities was truly a mass migration. Between 1920 and 1930 in Georgia and between 1940 and 1950 in Mississippi, nearly half of the young black males reaching adulthood left their states. In 1920, 1930 and 1950, in Michigan, Illinois and New York, from one-third to more than one-half of the young adult blacks enumerated in the census had moved to those states within the preceding 10 years.

The mass migration northward drew blacks from all over the South, from cities as well as villages and tenant farms. The Northern destinations, by contrast, were few in number. Of all Northern blacks in 1970, two-thirds lived in seven metropolitan areas containing more than 300,000 blacks each (New York, Chicago, Philadelphia, Detroit, St. Louis, Newark and Cleveland). In the West, two-thirds of the blacks lived in Los Angeles or San Francisco. In the South, only five metropolitan areas contained more than 300,000 blacks each, and the 16 containing more than 100,000 blacks included only one-third of the region's total black population.

End of an Era?

Any mass migration carries within itself the seeds of its own destruction. As youth move from one region to another, they transfer future natural increase from the place of origin to the place of destination. This demographic fact of life ensures that new generations will be born and raised in the destination places and that the supply of future migrants from the place of origin will be depleted. In addition, any mass migration is cause and effect of massive social and economic transformations at origin and destination.

During the half-century of massive black migration, the character of the migration was continually changing. By the time national attention was focused on the so-called urban crisis following the Watts riots of 1965, Northern black populations were increasingly Northern-born and Northern-raised. Northern blacks who migrated from the South were increasingly from the urban South. For blacks, as for whites, long distance migration was a feature of a metropolitan industrial economy in which those persons with greater education and marketable skills moved for economic benefit and for a better life. The poor and poorly educated rural blacks who were still being displaced from agriculture were far more likely to move a few miles to a Southern town or city than to take off directly for a Northern metropolis.

The steady aggregation of Americans, white and black, into metropolitan areas is a mass migration that must come to an end sometime. This migration has ebbed and flowed with economic circumstances—as in the slowdown during the depression of the 1930s—but at least until 1970 it was a continuing feature of American demographic history. No one foresaw the sudden cessation of this steady population concentration, but cessation is what appears to have happened since 1970. From 1970 to 1974, metropolitan areas lost migrants to nonmetropolitan territories. Analysts first thought that the results might simply reflect a spilling over

of metropolitan expansion beyond the current boundaries of metropolitan areas. Further investigation revealed, however, that the population in counties adjacent to metropolitan areas was growing less rapidly than the population in nonmetropolitan counties not adjacent to any metropolitan area.

The national shift away from an ever-greater piling up of population in metropolitan areas has been matched by an extraordinarily sharp decline in black metropolitan movement. During the early 1970s there was still a slow rate of net in-movement of blacks to metropolitan areas, but it hardly compared to the rapid pace of the 1950s and 1960s. It is the nation's largest metropolitan areas that have experienced the sharpest shift in total migration rates, and it is these areas that in the past were most attractive to black migrants. As the black population has become increasingly urban, and as young blacks have become increasingly well educated, the character of black migration has increasingly resembled that of white migration. During recent decades white migration to central cities declined and then reversed, first in the largest cities and more recently in many of the medium-size centers. Already in the 1960s, blacks displayed a net out-movement from some central cities, and it should not have surprised us so much that this trend would gain momentum in the 1970s.

PERSISTING SEGREGATION

Recent information on population redistribution of both whites and blacks during the 1970s has surprised demographers and other social scientists. The sharp changes in fundamental long term trends were not anticipated and have not yet been investigated. It is difficult to change long-accustomed perceptions, and many observers suspect (or hope) that the latest demographic shifts are a temporary response to the unusual economic circumstances of the early 1970s. Taking cognizance of the fact that no trend continues forever, I am much less skeptical of the new information. We may well be entering a new era in American population distribution.

The identification of eras is an analytical distinction imposed on a continuous reality. The trends of population concentration in metropolitan places and dispersal within metropolitan areas have not suddenly been obliterated; rather, the magnitude of the former has declined, and we do not yet know how the pace of suburbanization has been and will be affected. Thus it is extraordinarily difficult to assess the future of black suburbanization.

In the early decades of the twentieth century, as the so-called Great Migration of blacks to Northern cities accelerated, the black newcomers to the cities behaved much like other newcomers of those times. Negro migrants repeated the behavior of Italian and Polish migrants and other ethnic groups in settling initially in certain downtown areas of inexpensive housing accessible to public transportation. As numbers grew, ethnic colonies spread. With time, increasing numbers of the group became familiar with the ways of the city, with how to get along economically, and with other residential choices that might be more pleasant than crowded central neighborhoods. From the beginning of mass concentration of each successive European ethnic group in New York, Chicago, Detroit and other great cities, some members of the group were moving elsewhere in the city, sometimes establishing secondary colonies, sometimes settling into ethnically heterogeneous neighborhoods. Many of the children and grandchildren, natives of America and of the city, exercised even wider ranges of choice of residence. Statistical measures of the degree of segregation of each major European ethnic group document declining segregation as time passed.[4]

For blacks, however, residential patterns took a different twist. The mechanisms of racial discrimination identified above were deliberately devised and elaborated to control the dispersal of blacks and to produce a more "orderly" channeling of rapidly growing black populations. Statistical measures document increasing segregation of blacks.[5] The residential segregation between blacks and whites increased well beyond the levels characteristic of turn-of-the-century ethnic group segregation in Northern cities. Some Southern cities that grew to prominence after the Civil War also experienced their first large influx of black population during this period, and their residential patterns developed similarly to those in the North. In some older Southern cities, where a large black population was present ever since the days of slavery, a more dispersed racial residential pattern survived for many decades. But even in those cities, such as Charleston, South Carolina, with its traditional pattern of backyard and alley dwellings for blacks, the modern national style of separate residential areas eventually took

4. Stanley Lieberson, *Ethnic Patterns in American Cities* (New York: Free Press of Glencoe, 1963).

5. Karl E. Taeuber and Alma F. Taeuber, *Negroes in Cities: Residential Segregation and Neighborhood Change* (Chicago: Aldine, 1965).

over. Urban renewal in the 1950s largely completed the task of racially modernizing these cities.

During the 1950s in the North, and during the 1960s in both Northern and Southern cities, the intensity of residential segregation of blacks and whites diminished somewhat from its peak levels.[6] These declines were too small to reflect or presage a new liberalism in race relations. Rather they arose, I believe, from the large scale of the white out-movement from central cities and from the simultaneous rapid increase in the numbers of black families (native Americans all and many second or third generation urbanites) who did not like the ghettos and who pursued as best they could—within the confines of a discriminatory housing market—the standard American dream of a decent home and a decent neighborhood in which to raise one's children.

The slight diminution in the degree of racial residential segregation within the central cities occurred during a period of rapid increase in white suburban populations. The 1970 census was the first to provide data for individual city blocks throughout the urbanized area, and hence for 1970 it is possible to calculate area-wide segregation indexes of the same sort described above for central cities. Among 40 of 44 Northern metropolitan areas, the segregation index for the total urbanized area is greater than that for the central city alone. Among Southern metropolitan areas, with their historical pattern of suburban black enclaves, the area index is higher in 27 of 44 cases.

These statistical data document the severity of the two-society pattern of increasingly black central cities and white suburbs. Until there is a much more even distribution of blacks and whites among central cities and suburbs, segregation indexes for metropolitan areas cannot fall. The evidence presented above indicates that black suburbanization to date, while numerically greater than ever before, remains a minor pattern in black population redistribution. Suburbia shows no signs of quickly becoming for blacks, as for whites, the primary destination of migrants. The evidence further shows that the suburbanization to date has occurred with the same racially discriminatory channeling of black residents into selected localities that characterizes central cities.

The lowered birth rate in the United States and the lowered rate at which whites and blacks are moving into metropolitan areas should sharply reduce population pressure on urban and suburban housing. Older and less desirable housing seems increasingly likely to be abandoned, as happened in the 1950s and 1960s even with growing populations. Reduction of central city densities should occur, and a potential exists for greatly increased black suburbanization. With black populations growing more slowly, and with blacks interested in the full spectrum of metropolitan residential neighborhoods, there could be rapid residential desegregation without the population pressures that in the past led so often to immediate resegregation. This pattern could develop, but there is no evidence yet that it will. Racial segregation persists in suburban housing because racial discrimination persists in suburbia.

Whether these patterns change depends not only on whether we

6. Annemette Sørensen, Karl E. Taeuber, and Leslie J. Hollingsworth, Jr., "Indexes of Racial Residential Segregation for 109 Cities in the United States, 1940 to 1970," *Sociological Focus* 8 (April 1975), pp. 125–142.

develop the will and devise the means to enforce existing nation-wide laws against all types of housing discrimination; change in the racial patterns of housing also depends on what happens to segregation in schooling and employment. It has become somewhat fashionable to recognize these linkages only to use them as an excuse. Segregated schools are said to depend on segregated housing, which depends on black poverty, which depends on occupational discrimination, which depends on earlier discrimination in Southern schooling, which depends on antebellum social institutions. This kind of logic rests on a specious reading of social science evidence. There is indeed a certain "unity of the Negro problem," as Gunnar Myrdal noted more than 30 years ago, but that unity may be expressed in the present tense, not only as a historical residue of slavery:

Behind the barrier of common discrimination, there is unity and close interrelation between the Negro's political power; his civil rights; his employment opportunities; his standards of housing, nutrition and clothing; his health, manners, and law observance; his ideals and ideologies. The unity is largely the result of cumulative causation binding them all together in a system and tying them to white discrimination.[7]

7. Gunnar Myrdal, *An American Dilemma: The Negro Problem and Modern Democracy* (New York: Harper & Brothers, 1944), p. 77.

Metropolitan School Desegregation: Practical Remedy or Impractical Ideal?

By EVERETT F. CATALDO, MICHAEL GILES, AND DOUGLAS S. GATLIN

ABSTRACT: School desegregation has become an increasingly important issue in non–Southern metropolitan areas. The absence of significant residential desegregation in the suburbs and the concentration of the black population in central cities make effective school desegregation difficult, if not impossible, without consolidated planning for the entire metropolitan region. Cross-busing between central cities and suburbs may raise stiff resistance among white parents whose children would be transferred to city schools. An analysis of areawide desegregation in Duval County, Florida, suggests that suburban diffusion of the white population does not in itself constitute a barrier to consolidated planning. A judicious application of desegregation plan features for the entire metropolitan region can produce satisfactory and equitable results.

The authors are associated with Florida Atlantic University. Everett F. Cataldo is Director of the Institute of Behavioral Research and Associate Professor of Political Science. Michael Giles is Associate Professor of Political Science. Douglas S. Gatlin is Professor of Political Science and Department Chairman. The authors received their advanced degrees from Ohio State University, University of Kentucky and University of North Carolina, respectively.

This article was prepared with the support of Research Applied to National Needs, Division of Advanced Productivity Research and Technology, National Science Foundation, Washington, D. C. The views expressed herein are those of the researchers and should not be ascribed as views of the National Science Foundation.

S CHOOL desegregation has become one of the nation's most salient social and political problems. Once a Southern regional issue, the desegregation controversy has spilled far beyond the boundaries of the old Confederacy, and will be played out, inevitably, in the nation's major metropolitan regions.

Achieving school desegregation in the South was, of course, largely a matter of enforcing the law. *Brown v. Board of Education* outlawed *de jure* segregation. At the time, all Southern states operated dual school systems, patently and undeniably. Outside the South, school segregation has also existed, but it was long thought to be based on residential segregation and not legal action. Increasingly, however, suits have been brought against non–Southern school districts, and the courts have scrutinized the legal actions of state and local authorities. As decisions affecting Denver, Detroit and Boston have shown, non–Southern school districts have been far less innocent of operating Southern-style, dual school systems than was formerly presumed.

SCHOOL DESEGREGATION IN THE SOUTH

The first 10 years after the *Brown* decision were characterized by delay, obstruction and little real progress. By the 1964–65 school year, only 2.2 percent of black elementary and secondary school students in 11 Southern states attended schools with whites.[1] However, passage of the Civil Rights Act of 1964 and the Elementary and Secondary Education Act of 1965, along with increasingly tougher stances by federal courts, brought greater pressure to bear on recalcitrant school districts.[2] With both the judicial and executive branches of government joined in concerted effort, substantial progress began to be made. By 1966, 14 percent of Southern black school children attended predominantly white schools. This figure rose slightly to 18 percent by 1968, and then jumped dramatically to 40 percent by 1970.[3] By 1972, the South led the nation in school desegregation, with more than 46 percent of its black school children attending predominantly white schools. For the border and north/west states, the comparable figures were 32 percent and 28 percent respectively.[4]

Overall, the Southern experience with desegregation should be judged a qualified success at least. To be sure, the number of private schools in the South, which was never great, mushroomed and became havens for white escapists as public schools desegregated. A *New York Times* survey reported that 700 all-white private schools were established in Southern states from 1965 to 1970— 300 of them in 1970 alone when desegregation finally came to holdout districts in the deep South.[5] By the school year 1971–72, Southern segregation academies enrolled an estimated 500,000 white students. These are impressive figures, but the half-million represented only five percent of all Southern white

1. U.S., Commission on Civil Rights, *Twenty Years after Brown: Equality of Educational Opportunity* (Washington, D.C., March 1975), p. 10.

2. U.S., Commission on Civil Rights, *Twenty Years after Brown.*

3. U.S., Commission on Civil Rights, *Twenty Years after Brown*, p. 48.

4. U.S., Commission on Civil Rights, *Twenty Years after Brown.*

5. *New York Times*, 29 August 1971.

school children.[6] It would be a mistake to assume, then, that desegregated school districts throughout the South are awash in a tide of white rejection and resegregation.

Conspicuous deviations from the aggregate trends have occurred, however. For example, a suit to desegregate Atlanta's public schools was initiated in 1958, when the schools were 70 percent white and 30 percent black. By 1971, after desegregation had occurred, Atlanta's school system had become 70 percent black and 30 percent white, a classic case of resegregation.[7]

In choosing a paradigm for desegregation results outside the South, most observers would choose the Atlanta example over the general Southern trend. Much of the South is nonmetropolitan, and many blacks live outside the central cities. While most Southern school districts have been declared unitary, a majority of them cover medium- to small-sized cities and towns and rural areas where the logistics of desegregation are relatively easy, where suburban mobility is not possible, and where many whites cannot easily afford the high costs of private schools for their children. Outside the South, the vast majority of blacks live in large central cities. It is precisely in major metropolitan centers that the logistics of desegregation may be most difficult, suburban mobility is high, and white wealth can most easily facilitate the establishment of private schools.

SUBURBAN DIFFUSION

Of course, in the Atlanta case and others like it, it is hard to distinguish between white flight from the schools and white flight from the cities. That may not be necessary, however. Both may occur simultaneously in mutual reinforcement, producing a common result: city schools become increasingly black, suburban schools virtually all-white.

Census figures show that white flight from the cities continued unabated from 1960 to 1970. By contrast, black migration into the suburbs was very small and represented mostly an extension of the city ghetto to nearby municipalities. Thus, metropolitan fragmentation and suburban diffusion have left central cities and their suburbs stratified by race. The absence of any appreciable residential desegregation, when coupled with school districts that are mostly contiguous with municipal boundaries, renders school desegregation in metropolitan areas nearly a physical impossibility. Many proponents of desegregation have argued that this situation, in and of itself, constitutes a denial of equal educational opportunities; many have concluded that the only effective remedy is consolidated desegregation planning over entire metropolitan regions, affecting central cities and suburbs alike.[8] Residential preferences thus would not exclusively determine school assignments, and the racial stratification between central cities and suburbs would be broken, at least insofar as education is concerned.

Suits for consolidated desegregation have already been brought and approved by federal district judges in two prominent cases involving

6. *New York Times*, 2 September 1972.

7. John Beckler, "Has School Integration in the South Gone as Far as It Can Go?" *School Management* 15 (October 1971), p. 2.

8. *Hearings before the Select Committee on Equal Educational Opportunity*, U.S. Senate, 92nd Cong., 1st sess., pp. 10445, 10466, 10469–10476.

the Richmond and Detroit metropolitan areas. In both cases, the United States Supreme Court refused to sanction consolidation. However, both times four justices voted affirmatively, and in the Detroit case a fifth justice indicated an inter-district remedy would be appropriate where it could be shown that state authorities had acted to deny equal educational opportunities.[9] Possibly, then, the last word on the subject has not been heard.

METROPOLITAN SCHOOL DESEGREGATION

Can metropolitan areawide desegregation work? Since 1971, the authors have been studying parental reactions to school desegregation in eight Florida school districts, including Duval County, the country's sixty-fourth largest metropolitan region and Florida's most heavily industrialized one. Although city-county consolidation has occurred, extending the city services of Jacksonville throughout the county, the area retains many of its traditional physical patterns and social mores. The old city of Jacksonville is clearly defined, bounded by the St. Johns River and the Seaboard Coastline Railroad. It has a large central business district, heavy industry, a large wharf area and numerous tenements. The white population in the old city continues to decline; population growth is occurring only in the suburbs, which are virtually all-white. The school district is countywide, as are all others in Florida. Prior to desegregation, almost all of the black schools were in the central city.

9. *Bradley* v. *School Board of City of Richmond*, 462 F. 2d 1058, 1061; *Milliken* v. *Bradley*, 42 U.S.L.W. 5249 (U.S., 25 July 1975).

The field work for our project was conducted during the school year 1972–73, halfway through a two-year, court-ordered plan to desegregate schools throughout the county. At the time, Duval County had the twentieth largest school district in the nation, with more than 100,000 students. Approximately 67 percent of the students were white, and 33 percent were black. The county desegregation plan provided for transferring blacks from the city to suburban schools and whites from the suburbs to city schools. Students were also transferred between suburban schools to achieve satisfactory racial balances. Employing pairing and clustering of schools, modified feeder patterns, and rezoning of attendance districts, as well as cross-busing, the plan resulted in substantial desegregation. For the school year 1972–73, 77 percent of the black students attended predominantly (more than 50 percent) white schools. Of the remaining black students, only 14 percent were in schools 80 percent black or more.

Interviews with white parents were conducted in the spring of 1973 by National Analysts, Inc., of Philadelphia. Official school district records were used to select samples of both complying and rejecting parents. Compliers were defined as parents whose children attended desegregated public schools in the county in both 1971–72 and 1972–73. Rejecters were parents whose children had attended county public schools in 1971–72 but were withdrawn from their assigned public schools for 1972–73 and placed in local private schools. Random selection procedures were used, but rejecters were over-sampled. The results reported herein are based on a procedure weighting compliers and rejecters proportionate to their estimated distribution in the population. Random procedures were used to select the male or female parent within the household.

Our analysis focuses on two groups of white parents: (1) those whose children were assigned to suburban schools in 1971–72 but were transferred to city schools for 1972–73; and (2) those whose children were assigned to suburban schools in both 1971–72 and 1972–73.

Liberal racial orientations are associated with higher social status.[10] This suggests that suburbanites might not resist the transfer of some black students into suburban schools. The transfer of their children to central city schools, however, may be another matter entirely. After all, a preference for suburban housing is often a preference also for suburban schools. Their jobs aside, suburbanites are thought to feel physically and psychologically separated from the central city. The stronger these feelings, the greater the potential barrier to effective metropolitan school desegregation. We would expect, therefore, that parents whose children are transferred from suburban schools to central city schools would be more likely to reject than parents whose children remain in suburban schools. There is a small but statistically significant difference between the two groups ($p < .001$), but not in the expected direction. The "suburb-suburb" group is more likely to reject (5.1 percent) than the "suburb-city" group (3.0 percent).

Perhaps the effects of school location are obscured by other factors.

Suburb-city transfers often involve busing, but the suburb-suburb transfers of the Duval plan also involved busing. Previous analysis of the eight-county data suggests that the onset of busing in combination with a school transfer may have some effect on parental reactions.[11] Table 1 compares rejection rates between the suburb-city and suburb-suburb groups, distinguishing between those whose children experienced the onset of busing between 1971–72 and 1972–73 and those whose children did not (that is, their children were already bused in 1971–72, or they were not scheduled for busing in either 1971–72 or 1972–73).[12]

A fairly sharp increase in the rejection rate accompanies the onset of busing, but only for the suburb-suburb group. For the suburb-city group the rejection rate for those who experience the onset of busing is nearly identical to the rate for those who do not.

Thus far, the expected resistance to desegregation by suburban parents with children transferred to city schools has not been confirmed by the data. Neither by itself nor in combination with the onset of busing does the suburb-city transfer contribute appreciably to rejection. Another important factor remains to be considered—percent black in the assigned public schools. The authors have previously found that the rejection rate increases significantly

10. *See*, for example, Hubert M. Blalock, *Toward a Theory of Minority Group Relations* (New York: John Wiley and Son, 1967); Seymour M. Lipset, *Political Man* (New York: Doubleday, 1960).

11. Wen-Fu P. Shih, Everett F. Cataldo, Michael W. Giles, and Douglas S. Gatlin, "The Impact of School Desegregation Plan Features on White Rejection," from the 1974 Social Statistics Section (Proceedings of the *American Statistical Association*), pp. 436–439; Michael W. Giles, Douglas S. Gatlin, and Everett F. Cataldo, "The Impact of Busing on White Flight," *Social Science Quarterly* 55 (September 1974), pp. 493–501.

12. Busing status was obtained from items on the interview schedule.

TABLE 1

REJECTION RATES BY BUSING

	SUBURBAN SCHOOLS 1971–72, CITY SCHOOLS 1972–73	SUBURBAN SCHOOLS IN BOTH 1971–72 AND 1972–73
Not bused 1971–72 and 1972–73, or bused both years	2.5%	3.7%
Not bused 1971–72, bused 1972–73	3.0%	11.2%

when a threshold of 30 percent black is crossed.[13] Table 2 compares rejection rates under three conditions of the percent black variable. Under the first condition, the 30 percent black threshold is not reached for the assigned public school in either 1971–72 or 1972–73. Under the second condition, the threshold is crossed from 29 percent black or less in the assigned school for 1971–72 to 30 percent black or more in the school for 1972–73. Under the third condition, the assigned school is 30 percent black or more in both years.[14]

As can be seen from table 2, the threshold effect is clear for the suburb-suburb group. The rejection rate is extremely low under the first condition, rises when the threshold is crossed, and then drops. For the suburb-city group there is a linear trend in the rejection rate. Crossing the 30 percent black threshold has considerable effect, but the highest rejection rate is for those whose children are transferred from suburban schools 30 percent black and more to city schools also 30 percent black and more.

In table 3, the busing variable is controlled by the percent black variable. The data clearly confirm that the suburb-city group reacts to school transfers not in terms of the onset of busing, but in terms of percent black. When the assigned schools are less than 30 percent black in both years, the rejection rates are infinitesimal, both for those who experience the onset of busing and for those who do not. When the threshold is crossed from schools less than 30 percent black in 1971–72 to schools 30 percent black or more in 1972–73, the rejection rates rise, but they are uniform within both categories of the busing variable. When the transfer is from suburban schools 30 percent black or more to city schools also 30 percent black or more, those who experience the onset of busing are actually less likely to reject than those who do not. Clearly then, percent black, and not busing, is the controlling factor in rejection decisions for parents whose children are transferred from suburban schools to city schools.

The effects of percent black can also be observed for the suburb-suburb group. For those with children in schools 30 percent black or more in both years, the onset of busing does not contribute to rejection. Among parents whose children cross the 30 percent black threshold between school years, those who also experience the onset of busing are only slightly more likely to reject. For parents with

13. Michael W. Giles, Everett F. Cataldo, and Douglas S. Gatlin, "White Flight and Percent Black: The Tipping Point Re-examined," *Social Science Quarterly* 56 (June 1975), pp. 85–92.

14. School assignments and percent black were obtained from official school district records.

TABLE 2

REJECTION RATES BY PERCENT BLACK IN ASSIGNED PUBLIC SCHOOLS

	SUBURBAN SCHOOLS 1971–72, CITY SCHOOLS 1972–73	SUBURBAN SCHOOLS IN BOTH 1971–72 and 1972–73
29% black or less 1971–72 and 1972–73	0.3%	1.4%
29% black or less 1971–72, 30% black or more 1972–73	8.6%	11.8%
30% black or more 1971–72 and 1972–73	15.5%	4.1%

children in schools below the threshold both years, the onset of busing does appear to contribute to rejection. However, the number of cases in that particular cell are insufficient to support a firm conclusion. The suburb-suburb group may be influenced somewhat by the onset of busing. The suburb-city group certainly is not.

CONCLUSION

Suburbanization does not appear to be a barrier to consolidated desegregation planning in metropolitan areas. Parents with children reassigned from suburban schools to city schools were less likely to reject than parents whose children remained in suburban schools. Even the onset of busing in combination with the transfer had no appreciable effect. The reactions of both the suburb-suburb group and the suburb-city group were conditioned by percent black in the schools, but in a somewhat different fashion. The effect of crossing the 30 percent black threshold between school years increased rejection for both groups. For the suburb-suburb group, however, once the threshold was crossed, the rejection rate declined considerably. By contrast, the suburb-city group was even more likely

TABLE 3

REJECTION RATES BY PERCENT BLACK AND BUSING

	SUBURBAN SCHOOLS 1971–72, CITY SCHOOLS 1972–73	SUBURBAN SCHOOLS IN BOTH 1971–72 and 1972–73
29% black or less both years and		
(a) Not bused or bused both years	0.9%	1.1%
(b) Not bused 1971–72, bused 1972–73	0.1%	15.2%
29% black or less 1971–72, 30% black or more 1972–73 and		
(a) Not bused or bused in both years	9.3%	9.2%
(b) Not bused 1971–72, bused 1972–73	8.2%	13.9%
30% black or more in both years and		
(a) Not bused or bused in both years	21.1%	4.4%
(b) Not bused 1971–72, bused 1972–73	12.1%	1.9%

to reject when the assigned schools for both years were 30 percent black or more than when the suburban school was 29 percent black or less and the city school was 30 percent black or more.

This pattern, coupled with the absence of busing effects, suggests that metropolitan areawide school desegregation may be facilitated by even more cross-busing between suburbs and cities, rather than less. This would reduce further the black ratio in city schools, making them more acceptable to suburban whites. The black percent in suburban schools would increase, however, and could produce higher rejection among suburbanites whose children remain there, particularly if the 30 percent black threshold is crossed. Our data suggest however, that once this initial effect is felt, rejection will decline and may stabilize at a low level.

In metropolitan regions where blacks constitute less than 30 percent of the students, our data suggest that consolidated school desegregation may be very effective, provided that racial balances are equalized throughout the schools. When percent black in the schools was 29 or less in both years, the rejection rates for both the suburb-city and suburb-suburb groups were extremely low.

Our study indicates that areawide planning can be a practical approach to desegregating schools in metropolitan areas. Metropolitan fragmentation and suburbanization are not, in and of themselves, insurmountable obstacles. To be sure, some white flight will occur, but it appears to be related mostly to percent black in the schools—a problem whether desegregation takes place within or across municipal boundaries. Furthermore, white rejection can be contained by the judicious application of desegregation plan features. Desegregation planners in metropolitan areas outside the South apparently can benefit from a careful assessment of the Southern experience with school desegregation.

Aging Suburbs and Black Homeownership

By George Sternlieb and Robert W. Lake

ABSTRACT: The 30 years since rapid post-World War II suburban residential development began have seen an increasing diversification in the characteristics of the suburbs. The principal dimensions of diversification include the age of housing, age of the population, and distance from the central city. Since suburbanization proceeded outward from the central city, the signs of this aging process are most pronounced in the inner suburbs, with densities and an aging population. As first-round suburbanites progress through the life cycle, their housing preferences can be expected to change, resulting in a large supply of older housing on the market. The primary source of demand for these units in the inner suburbs appears to be the upwardly mobile black middle class seeking to leave the central city. While black suburbanization is increasing in some localities, however, black demand appears to be below the level expected based on income. In suburban home purchase, the availability of equity associated with previous homeownership may be a better index of buying power than current income. Historical limitations on black homeownership thus continue to limit black suburban home purchases. Public policy initiatives are needed to counteract these trends, facilitate middle class black migration, and contribute to the viability of the inner suburbs.

George Sternlieb is Director, Center for Urban Policy Research, and Professor of Urban Planning and Policy Development, Rutgers University. He has been a frequent, invited witness before several congressional committees and national commissions on urban problems and has served as a consultant at the federal, state and local levels. He is the author of Residential Abandonment: The Tenement Landlord Revisited, The Ecology of Welfare, Housing Development and Municipal Costs, *and numerous other books, monographs and articles pertaining to urban housing and related issues.*

Robert W. Lake is a Research Associate, Center for Urban Policy Research, a faculty member of the Department of Urban Planning at Rutgers University, and a doctoral candidate in urban geography at the University of Chicago. His research is in the field of urban housing, residential satisfaction, and community attitudes towards change. He has written articles on racial and ethnic patterns in cities.

COLLECTIVE nouns are useful only as they provide effective mental holds on aggregated phenomena. Their value is in direct proportion to the degree to which the implied grouping can predict either the behavior or the characteristics of the units placed under their rubric. The so-called information explosion of recent years has seen an enormous increase in the ranks of conventionally used but non-informative collective phrases. The terms *liberal* or *conservative*, *Republican* or *Democrat*, for example, have faltered substantially in the utility provided by their mental shorthand, although not, unfortunately, in the frequency of their use. The words simply do not allow prediction: it becomes increasingly difficult to forecast on the basis of these collective labels how one will vote or act on any of a variety of crucial issues.

The parallel holds true when the subject of discussion is the term *suburbia*. In popular usage, the word evokes a relatively narrow set of images, ranging perhaps from tract developments to stately homes, with a common denominator of lawns and greenery. Secondarily, the term implies a vision of early morning commuter throngs of white collar workers bound for offices in the central city. The suburban label has surprising vitality, for while the image has continued unaltered, the realities behind it—that is, the types of suburbs—have diversified substantially, certainly well beyond the ability of a single word to encompass usefully.

The notion of suburban diversity is hardly a new one. Even before the post-World War II suburban explosion, for example, Harris utilized observations in 140 metropolitan districts throughout the country to delineate a fivefold suburban typology, largely differentiating between "dormitory" and various types of industrial suburbs. Somewhat more recently, Schnore distinguished functionally between industrial and residential suburbs, the former representing a decentralization of production and the latter a decentralization of consumption.[1] The traditional literature on the suburbs, then, points to differences between residential and other types of suburban communities and thus demonstrates the heterogeneity inherent in the term.

Beyond this general bifurcation of suburban types, however, recent evidence suggests the need to recognize the proliferation of different types of residential suburbs as well. In the mid-1970s, the original Levittown is approaching its thirtieth year, and suburban residential construction proliferates over an area extending in places for more than a hundred miles from the central city.

Massive suburban residential development can thus be seen to extend substantially both back in time and outward over space. As a result, residential suburbs have become markedly differentiated by both age and location. Due to the interaction of these dimensions of time and space in the development of the suburbs, American society today contains suburban residential communities that are widely differentiated in functional terms. The bases of this diversification include such crucial factors as the age (and thus size, style and condition) of housing; the age (stage in the life

1. Chauncy D. Harris, "Suburbs," *American Journal of Sociology* 49 (July 1943), pp. 1–13; Leo F. Schnore, "The Functions of Metropolitan Suburbs," *American Journal of Sociology* 61 (March 1959), pp. 453–458.

cycle) of the population; and the distance from (and orientation to) the central city.

This article aims to examine this new reality of suburbia and some of the functions it plays in our society. To a large extent, many of these functions constitute new roles for the suburbs, perhaps mirroring the loss of functions associated with the demise of the central city, which we have discussed elsewhere.[2] We are concerned here with the evolution of roles associated with the aging of the inner ring suburbs. Our point of departure is the changing parameters of supply and demand for housing in these aging suburbs. These patterns in turn are seen to influence the turnover and succession of population in these areas.

Specifically, we focus on the evolving role of inner suburban areas as the zone of emergence, the place of first homeownership for blacks and other minorities seeking to escape the trauma of the central city. The thesis of our discussion is that the inner ring of older suburbs plays this important role for the current generation of middle class aspirants. While this role in itself may be a traditional suburban function, the fact that for the first time the emerging suburbanites are black, coupled with current realities of racial segregation, implies that the suburbs for the first time are becoming the locus of racial residential conflict and change.

It is our belief that new forms of suburban development are evolving which represent a resegregation of racial categories. The upwardly mobile black middle class, aspiring to homeownership and anxious to leave the central cities, provides a source of demand for the older housing of the inner-ring suburbs. At the same time, the new generation white ethnics perceive their inner-city areas to be increasingly threatened, the inner suburbs too subject to central city problems, and the middle ring of affluent suburbs too expensive. As a result, preliminary evidence indicates that this group is vaulting out to the far reaches of suburbia, especially to areas where land prices are still low and suburbanizing industrial activity provides nearby jobs. In the discussion which follows, we utilize examples from the New York–New Jersey region to examine the impact of several components of this multifaceted process on the evolving characteristics of suburbia.

EVOLUTION OF THE INNER SUBURBS

More than a quarter-century has elapsed since the beginning of the major postwar suburban housing boom. Since suburbanization generally proceeded outward from the central city, the signs of this aging process are most pronounced—and have their greatest impact—in the inner suburbs.

The evolution of suburbia implies a twofold, interrelated process: the aging of the resident population and the aging of the housing stock. The interaction of these two sets of forces can be demonstrated, utilizing data for the 15 municipalities of Nassau and Suffolk Counties on Long Island as an illustration.

Suburbanization on Long Island has proceeded in a linear manner eastward from New York City, sequentially reaching each of the municipalities arrayed along the narrow, 100-mile expanse of the island. Age

2. George Sternlieb, "The City as Sandbox," *Public Interest* 25 (Fall 1971), pp. 14–21.

of suburbanization is thus almost perfectly correlated with distance from the central city; as of this writing, the wave of massive residential construction has reached, and is now concentrated in, Brookhaven Township, some 60 miles from New York City. East of Brookhaven Township, Long Island is still largely a sparsely developed agricultural and resort area inhabited by a long term resident population.

The relationship between age of development and age of population is demonstrated by the data in figure 1. Here, the number of housing units per acre is utilized as a measure of the duration of development, on the assumption that higher density represents a longer period of construction and in-filling of vacant parcels.

The dashed line in figure 1 portrays housing density per acre for the 15 Long Island municipalities arranged by distance from New York City. Clearly, the inner ring of older suburbs exhibits the highest densities, and density decreases with distance from the central city. This trend line continues eastward to the Town of Brookhaven—the edge of suburbanization. Beyond the suburban frontier, in the exurban fringe of eastern Suffolk County, housing densities remain stable at a very low level.

The data on median age of the population can be interpreted against this backdrop of successive suburban development. The solid line in figure 1, representing the median age of the population, exhibits an almost perfectly monotonic negative relationship with distance from the central city, as far as Brookhaven Township. The five municipalities of the inner-ring Nassau County suburbs had an average 1970 median age of population of 31.8 years; in contrast, the average median age of the population in 1970 of the five intermediate-ring municipalities of western Suffolk County was 25.1 years. In other words, within the built-up portion of the Long Island suburbs, the closer to the central city, the older the population. The suburban boundary, marked by the stabilization of housing densities east of Brookhaven Township, is reflected in the sharp increase in median age of the population: the average 1970 median age for the five eastern Suffolk County municipalities was 37.6 years.

In summary, the graph of median age of the population roughly parallels the graph of housing density per acre as one traverses suburbia from the central city limits to the suburban fringe. The inner suburbs reflect their earlier development with a higher median age of the resident population.

To the extent that generalization is possible on the basis of the Long Island data, the inner suburbs are clearly characterized by relatively high density development and an aging population. Residents of these areas, representing the first round of postwar suburbanites, are now reaching a stage in the life cycle in which their housing needs are likely to change substantially. As families age and children move away, these residents will increasingly begin the search for smaller units requiring less maintenance. Concomitantly, aging of the housing stock, increasing maintenance costs, and changes in taste for housing styles will spur the decision to move away from these first suburban residences.

To summarize the discussion thus far, two interrelated components of the suburban aging process can be identified. First, housing once new —the housing which provided the basis for the suburban stereotype—

FIGURE 1

HOUSING DENSITY AND MEDIAN AGE OF POPULATION

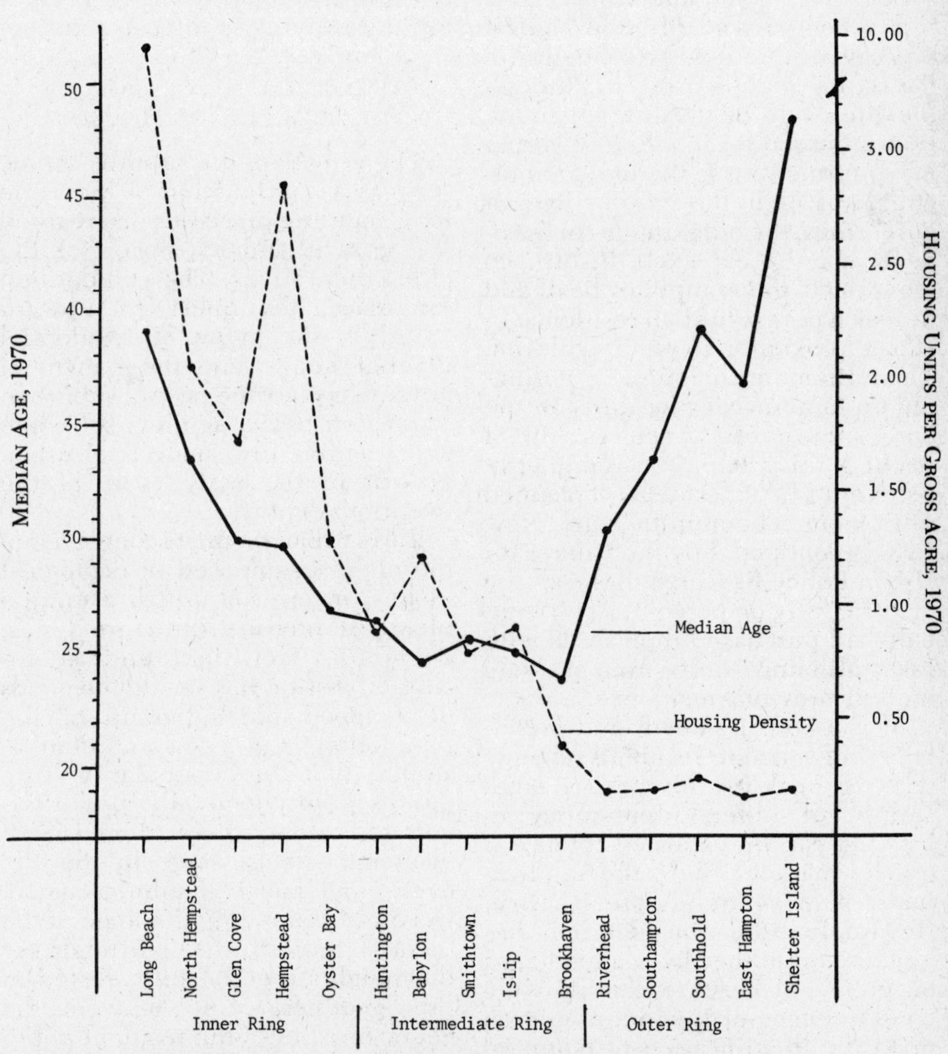

LONG ISLAND MUNICIPALITIES, BY DISTANCE FROM NEW YORK CITY

SOURCE: Nassau-Suffolk Regional Planning Board, *U.S. Census 1970*, vol. 3, *Age*, and vol. 4, *Housing Inventory*.

is now no longer so. Aging of the housing stock implies increasing maintenance costs, loss of the "new home" mystique, and changes in the perceived attractiveness of units associated with changing tastes in housing design. Secondly, the resident population of the inner suburbs has seen the passage of a generation. The concomitant changes in the life cycle stage of this population are expressed in changing housing needs associated with decreasing family size and preferences for a different set of services and amenities.

A second round of suburbanization can be identified associated with the aging and progression through the life cycle of these first-generation suburbanites. As their offspring move further out to the more affordable housing in the intermediate or outer rings, the older inner-ring residents may be expected, in turn, to move out of their emptying nests and to seek a new suburban residence in closer proximity to their children. The retirement communities springing up in numerous locations in the outer suburbs can be seen as a direct result of this trend. For example, in a survey of 1,033 residents of planned retirement communities in New Jersey, conducted by the Center for Urban Policy Research in the spring of 1975, fully 88 percent of respondents had purchased their units with cash, utilizing equity from the sale of their previous residence.

As the housing needs and preferences of current residents change with the passing of time, a large supply of older, inner-suburban housing can be expected to appear on the market. While the implications of these trends are massive, seemingly little consideration has been given, either by academicians or policy makers, to the possible consequences of this out-migration or to the identification of potential sources of demand for this older suburban housing.

Continued lack of attention to the evidence provided by even imperfect data, however, will result in the simple extension from the inner city to the inner suburbs of the problems associated with out-migration and the inability to sustain an adequate level of demand for housing. As the suburbs become urbanized, the traditional urban processes of residential turnover and succession are becoming operant in the suburbs, a trend deserving of intense scrutiny.

RESIDENTIAL SUCCESSION AND THE DEMAND FOR HOUSING

The growth of the suburbs can be seen as a continuation of the same long-standing processes that marked the growth and expansion of the cities themselves. The competition for space, the quest for upward mobility, the aging of residential neighborhoods, and the growth of new areas mark the pace of suburban expansion today, as they did when first identified by analysts of urban growth in the early years of the twentieth century.

Early urban theorists conceived of the city as composed of ecological niches, in each of which a unique blend of physical structure types, economic facilities, and socio-cultural institutions served the needs of a specifiable subgroup of the population.[3] Later research demonstrated that these population subgroups could generally be differentiated along three dimensions: economic status, stage in the life cycle, and racial or ethnic characteristics.[4] Extending the logic of the theorists a step further, one might say that neighborhood stability rested on the "goodness of fit" between the characteristics of the resident population and characteristics of the residential setting. A change in the quality of housing in an area, for

3. See, for instance, Robert E. Park, Ernest W. Burgess, and Roderick D. Mackenzie, *The City* (Chicago: University of Chicago Press, 1925).

4. Eshref Shevky and Wendell Bell, *Social Area Analysis* (Palo Alto, Calif.: Stanford University Press, 1955); Brian J. L. Berry, ed., "Comparative Factorial Ecology," special issue, *Economic Geography* 47 (June 1971).

instance, might signal a reduction in the perceived utility of the housing stock for the resident population. Correspondingly, a change in the resident population's housing requirements would have the same effect.

The theory of urban growth developed by Park and others proposed that such resulting disharmony would be resolved through the process of residential succession. A growing mismatch between residents' housing needs and an area's housing characteristics engenders out-migration in search of an improved residential setting. Arrival of a replacement population, for whom the extant housing is perceived to be more suitable in terms of condition, price, location, and so forth, completes the succession process.

Extension of this mode of analysis to the inner suburbs is straightforward. Changing housing needs of first generation suburbanites, coupled with the changing characteristics of their housing as discussed earlier, are likely to engender a substantial out-migration to retirement communities or smaller homes elsewhere in suburbia. The principal question which arises, therefore, pertains to the source of demand for the housing in the inner suburbs being vacated by first-round whites as their housing needs and preferences change.

Preliminary evidence suggests that a principal potential source of demand for older housing in the inner suburbs appears to be concentrated among upwardly mobile blacks and other minority groups who, for the first time, are moving out of the central city in substantial numbers. A few statistics on black suburbanization illustrate the broad dynamics of this process.

The Census Bureau reports that numerous areas recorded rapid gains in the size of the black suburban population between 1960 and 1970. For example, the black population in the suburbs of Los Angeles increased by 105 percent between 1960 and 1970, and by 453 percent in Cleveland. The black population in the suburbs of Washington, D.C., doubled over the decade, increasing from 84,000 to 166,000.[5] In a recent analysis of 1960 to 1970 trends in metropolitan areas in the East, North and West, Connolly was able to identify 24 suburban communities in which the black population increased by more than 100 percent over the decade and exceeded 10 percent of the total 1970 population. On the basis of national data, Farley concluded that the black suburban population increased during the sixties and at a faster rate than during the fifties.[6]

A similar overall trend is evidenced by data on the changing distribution of the black population in New Jersey metropolitan areas. As one of the most urbanized states,[7] New

5. U.S., Bureau of the Census, Census of Population and Housing: 1970, *General Demographic Trends for Metropolitan Areas, 1960 to 1970.* Final Report PHC (2)-1 United States (Washington, D.C.: Government Printing Office, 1971); Eunice S. Grier, *Black Suburbanization in Metropolitan Washington,* report no. 1, "Characteristics of Black Suburbanites" (Washington, D.C.: Washington Center for Metropolitan Studies, 1973), p. i.

6. Harold X. Connolly, "Black Movement into the Suburbs: Suburbs Doubling Their Black Populations during the 1960's," *Urban Affairs Quarterly* 9 (September 1973), pp. 91–111; Reynolds Farley, "The Changing Distribution of Negroes within Metropolitan Areas: The Emergence of Black Suburbs," *American Journal of Sociology* 75 (January 1970), pp. 512–529.

7. *See,* for instance, Gary Gappert and Harold M. Rose, eds., *The Social Economy of Cities,* vol. 9, Urban Affairs Annual Reviews (Beverly Hills, Calif.: Sage Publica-

TABLE 1

RATES OF CHANGE, TOTAL AND METROPOLITAN POPULATION, UNITED STATES, NORTHEAST REGION, AND NEW JERSEY, 1960 TO 1970

AREA	PERCENT CHANGE 1960 TO 1970
UNITED STATES	
Total population	13.3
Metropolitan areas	16.6
Inside central cities	5.3
Suburbs*	28.2
Black population	20.1
Metropolitan areas	31.9
Inside central cities	32.6
Suburbs*	29.2
NORTHEAST REGION	
Black population	43.4
Metropolitan areas	44.3
Inside central cities	44.6
Suburbs*	42.7
NEW JERSEY	
Black population	45.9
Metropolitan areas	51.3
Inside central cities	49.8
Suburbs*	53.0

SOURCE: U.S., Bureau of the Census, Census of Population and Housing, 1970, *General Demographic Trends for Metropolitan Areas, 1960 to 1970*, Final Report PHC(2)-1 United States, tables 1 and 5.

* Suburbs are defined as the non-central city portions of metropolitan areas.

Jersey may provide a portent of urbanization elsewhere in the country.

As indicated in table 1, the growth rate of the total black population in the Northeast region exceeded the growth rate for the United States black population as a whole (43.4 percent versus 20.1 percent). The growth rate of the total black population for the state of New Jersey exceeded, in turn, the rate for the region (45.9 percent versus 43.4 percent). Furthermore, the black population in New Jersey suburbs grew at a faster rate than the black population in the state as a whole (53.0 percent versus 45.9 percent). Finally,

tions, 1975), pp. 43–44, for a discussion of New Jersey's ranking in several measures of urbanization.

and perhaps most significantly, the suburban black population in the state grew at a faster rate than the black population in the central cities of the state (53.0 percent versus 49.8 percent). This last finding represents a reversal of the trend found at both the regional and national levels, where central city black growth outpaced suburban black population increases between 1960 and 1970. In New Jersey, in other words, the black population in the suburbs grew faster than the black population in the state's central cities; faster than the black population in the Northeast region's cities or suburbs or in the region itself; and at almost twice the rate of black population increase in the suburbs of the country as a whole.

These data might be seen as an indication of increasing black suburbanization. Indeed, some observers have indicated the potential for such a trend. At the beginning of the decade, for instance, Bernard Frieden noted that "in the next decade, the opportunities for black people to move to suburbia will be better than they have been for a long time. During the 1970's, an increasing stock of older suburban housing is likely to be available at prices that many black families can afford."[8]

The black population of suburbia is undoubtedly increasing. Further evidence on the New Jersey case compiled by the Center for Urban Policy Research indicates that the black population of the suburbs is also becoming increasingly middle class.[9] Considering occupational characteristics, in 1970 a larger proportion of the suburban black population of New Jersey's Standard Metropolitan Statistical Areas (SMSAs) was employed in white collar occupations than was the black population of central cities. Perhaps more significantly, the decade of the sixties witnessed a significant convergence in the occupational composition of white and black populations in the suburbs, with the proportion of black population employed in white collar occupations much closer in 1970 to the proportion of white population employed in such occupations than it was in 1960. Finally, while the pattern of black population growth in the suburbs is evidenced in numerous instances where the ghetto has extended to the city limits and is simply continuing its expansion in the inner suburbs, evidence from case studies in New Jersey metropolitan areas indicates that the movement of middle class black families to inner suburban "zones of emergence" is clearly not restricted to the process of ghetto expansion.

Nonetheless, despite the overall patterns, the data on increasing black suburbanization are at best contradictory and must be interpreted with considerable caution. Nationwide, between 1960 and 1970 the black population in the suburbs increased at about the same rate as the white—29.2 percent and 27.5 percent respectively. As a result, the black proportion of the suburban population for the nation remained at a stable 5 percent level over the decade. Similarly, the proportion of the black population living in the suburbs remained relatively unchanged, at roughly 15 percent at both the beginning and the end of the decade.

LIMITATIONS ON EFFECTIVE DEMAND: A LEGACY OF PAST PATTERNS

Evidence from a number of sources indicates that, despite an increasing rate of black surburbanization in some localities, a serious discrepancy exists between the actual and potential scales of black suburbanization.

Although Frieden claims that "the income levels of black families match the cost of housing in the suburbs well enough to permit substantial movement there, and there are

8. Bernard J. Frieden, "Blacks in Suburbia: The Myth of Better Opportunities," in Resources for the Future, *Minority Perspectives*, no. 2 in a series on the Governance of Metropolitan Regions (Washington, D.C.: Resources for the Future, 1972), p. 32.

9. George Sternlieb and Robert W. Lake, "Middle Class Black Suburbanization in the Zone of Emergence," unpublished manuscript (New Brunswick, N.J.: Center for Urban Policy Research, 1975).

signs that this movement is now under way,"[10] other analysts suggest that actual rates of black suburbanization are far below expected rates calculated on the basis of black income. Utilizing data on the 29 largest urbanized areas for the period 1950 to 1970, for instance, Hermalin and Farley found that at all income levels and at all levels of housing value, blacks are overrepresented in the central cities and underrepresented in the suburbs. They also found that increases in black family income were not reflected in proportionate increases in the size of the black suburban population. They concluded that "the increasing income of blacks has done little to reduce their concentration in central cities . . . . In all areas, blacks in the higher income categories are less represented in suburbia than are whites in middle or low income brackets. . . . Apparently a low income white family can obtain a suburban home or apartment more readily than a high income black family."[11] Identical findings have been reported in case studies of Los Angeles and Philadelphia.[12]

These and related findings suggest that, to the extent that income levels reflect potential demand, the full potential of black demand for housing in the suburbs has not been actualized to date. While the data indicate that the black population which *is* moving to the suburbs is increasingly middle class, the bulk of the black population of all class and income levels remains concentrated in the central cities. By implication, however, this central city black population constitutes a reservoir of potential demand for housing in the inner suburbs as it is vacated by first-round suburbanites. A significant policy question is posed in the need to identify means by which this potential demand can be fully realized.

The attempt at amelioration, of course, requires the identification of causes. Three possible explanations for limitations on home purchases by blacks in the suburbs come to mind.

First, blacks may be refraining from purchasing homes in the suburbs due to a preference for residence in the central city and/or an antipathy to suburban residence. While this may, in fact, explain some portion of the residential distribution of the black population, it seems unlikely to be an overwhelming cause. Middle class black dissatisfaction with the quality of housing, schools and services in the inner city appears to be commensurate with that expressed by whites, with the exception that the white middle class has been able to express its dissatisfaction through migration to the suburbs.

A more viable explanation for the extent to which increases in black family income have failed to generate increased black suburbanization is found in an examination of past patterns of black homeownership. In the case of a suburban home purchase, family income per se may be an inadequate measure of purchasing power. Instead, effective demand is likely to be more dependent on the availability of equity associated with

10. Frieden, "Blacks in Suburbia," p. 35.

11. Albert I. Hermalin and Reynolds Farley, "The Potential for Residential Integration in Cities and Suburbs: Implications for the Busing Controversy," *American Sociological Review* 38 (October 1973), p. 601.

12. Francine F. Rabinowitz, *Minorities in Suburbs: The Los Angeles Experience* (Working paper no. 31, Joint Center for Urban Studies of M.I.T. and Harvard, March 1975); Phoebe H. Cottingham, "Black Income and Metropolitan Residential Dispersion," *Urban Affairs Quarterly* 10 (March 1975), pp. 273–296.

previous homeownership. Limitations on current black suburbanization, then, can be seen at least in part as a legacy of past restrictions on black homeownership.

Differences between black and white households in the availability of equity for the purchase of a new home are revealed by a survey conducted in the spring of 1971 by the Center for Urban Policy Research, which elicited data on the characteristics of 270 recent home-buyers in four New Jersey suburban communities. The four communities differ widely in terms of total population, size and growth of the black population, housing density, distance from the central city, and related measures. In all four communities, recent home purchases by both black and white households could be identified. Of the total sample of respondents, 161 were white and 109 were black.

Considering the communities as a combined sample, close to 40 percent of the white households, but only 28 percent of the black households, had owned their previous housing units. Black home-buyers, in other words, were less likely than their white counterparts to be able to draw upon stored equity in a previous home to finance the purchase of a suburban home. In a smaller follow-up survey of the original respondents, conducted in the spring of 1975, 74 percent of the black homeowners interviewed reported that they had drawn on savings for their downpayment; only 20 percent had been able to utilize equity from the sale of property or other investments for this purpose.

A further complication arises when the location of black homeownership is considered. Even those few blacks who do own are less likely than whites to be able to realize the equity on their homes. Traditional patterns of central city residential segregation indicate that the homes owned by blacks are located in those sections of the city in which resale is highly problematic. The inability to attract buyers for central city homes in black neighborhoods effectively minimizes the likelihood that even the small proportion of blacks who do own will be able to realize a return on their investment which, in turn, could provide the downpayment on a suburban home.

The disparities between levels of demand for suburban housing as expected on the basis of black income and occupational characteristics, and actual demand, as expressed by growth of the suburban black population, can be explained in part, therefore, by white-black discrepancies in the availability of equity based on previous homeownership. In the case of a home purchase, effective demand is more likely to be a function of available equity and financing terms than simply a function of current income. Differences between potential and actual demand noted in the research cited above indicate the extent to which historical limitations on black homeownership are limiting the effective demand for housing in the inner suburbs, which are being vacated by whites in the normal course of residential transition.

This historical legacy can be seen as part of a larger pattern of white discrimination against black homeownership, which itself constitutes a third factor overtly limiting the movement of blacks to the suburbs. The extension to the suburbs of central city practices of residential discrimination can be expected in light of continued white antipathy to integration. Nonetheless, such attempts to limit the suburbanization of the black middle class are likely to be self-defeating. To the extent that this group constitutes an important source of potential demand for housing in the inner suburbs, failure to capitalize on this demand will inevitably make continued viability of these communities highly problematic. The traditional function of the inner suburbs as a zone of emergence for the upwardly mobile attempting to leave the central city cannot be disavowed simply because the current generation of out-migrants is black. Assimilation of the upwardly mobile black middle class may indeed constitute the major new role of the inner suburbs.

CONCLUSIONS

Past restrictions on black home-ownership, as well as present discriminatory practices, contribute to significant limitations on the suburbanization of the black population. These constraints are likely to place limits on the effective demand for housing in the inner suburbs. Given the extension to the suburbs of traditional urban processes of residential mobility with progression through the life cycle, such artificial limits on demand are likely to have severely adverse effects on older suburban residential communities. A simple projection of these trends suggests that the inner suburbs can expect to be confronted with increasing vacancy rates, deterioration of older housing, and an extension of central city housing problems in the not too distant future.

This scenario is admittedly a projection based on anticipated demographic changes which are likely to affect the inner suburbs in the near future. A reorientation of public policy prior to substantial problem formation can significantly forestall the extension to the inner suburbs of inner city problems.

A basic policy objective must aim at reducing the barriers of discrimination which limit the access of the middle class black population to suburban housing, since it is this group that offers promise of maintaining the viability of the inner suburbs. Within this context, the major thrust of policy must serve to bolster the effective purchasing power of the black middle class. Specifically, an attempt should be made to extend the availability of long term, low-interest mortgages to this group and to minimize downpayment requirements in order to offset the effects of historical limitations on equity formation within the black community.

Recent policy initiatives at the federal level reveal little appreciation of the problems discussed here. For example, the recently approved federal program of tax rebates for purchasers of *new* homes continues the traditional focus of federal subsidy of white suburbanites purchasing new housing at the suburban fringes. While lauded as a boost for a lagging construction industry, such a policy is conspicuously inadequate in ameliorating the problems of the inner suburbs—the area perhaps most in need of enlightened policy intervention.

Similarly, an effort is required to encourage homeownership in the central city by minority group members, as the first step in the equity accumulation pattern required for the suburban move. This path too, however, is fraught with difficulty. It introduces substantial questions to which continued research must be addressed. To the degree that current central city minority group residents may themselves be the last wave of in-migrants to the city, their capacity to recapture the equity represented by paid-down mortgages may be sadly lacking.[13] There is little anticipation of a new wave of home buyers to "take them out." The same restraints are even more likely to prevent central city homeowners from capitalizing on the potential of inflationary increases in value derived from their home purchases. Thus it is possible that homeownership in the central city may increasingly prove to be a poor form of savings. Even if this legacy of past trends can be overcome, will home purchase in the inner suburbs serve as an effective form of forced savings for newcomers, or are the suburbs doomed to replicate the patterns of the central city? We have yet to see an adequate focus on the zone of emergence in the inner suburbs to provide the data needed to shape policy.

13. *See*, for instance, George Sternlieb and Robert W. Burchell, *Residential Abandonment: The Tenement Landlord Revisited* (New Brunswick, N.J.: Center for Urban Policy Research, 1973) for a discussion of the uncertainty of equity recapture in declining areas.

Suburbanization of Ethnics of Color

By William J. Siembieda

ABSTRACT: The suburbanization of ethnics of color made slow progress during the 1960s. The nation continued its long term trend towards dual societies. Only one major metropolitan area, Los Angeles, was able to double the number of ethnics of color (blacks and Mexican-Americans) living outside the central city. However, the central city still became blacker, browner and poorer. The ethnics of color who migrated to the suburbs were middle class and had a high propensity toward homeownership. Rises in real income, an available housing supply, a lessening of discrimination practices and an economically differentiated metropolitan area are variables that help explain the Los Angeles experience. Ethnics of color did not suburbanize in a random manner. They tended to locate in selected suburban communities, forming flows to the southern and eastern sections of Los Angeles County. Most lived in segregated suburban neighborhoods. The goal of an integrated society is still far in the future.

William J. Siembieda is on the faculty of the Urban and Rural Studies Program, The Third College, University of California, San Diego. He holds degrees in City and Regional Planning and Economics from the University of California, Berkeley. He has previously taught at Tuskegee Institute and Shaw University. He was a National Urban Fellow with the National League of Cities, U.S. Conference of Mayors, and is presently preparing a book on the suburbanization of ethnics of color with Francine Rabinovitz, Department of Political Science, University of California, Los Angeles.

FOR THE better part of this century, the United States has been decentralizing its population and economic activities. The causes of this decentralization can be traced to changes in production processes, technology, rising middle and working class affluence, and shifts in general residential location. Shifts in residential location have become apparent over the last two decades in the form of social preference due to desires to exit from deteriorating central city life.[1] This social preference, exhibited mostly by middle class whites, resulted in dual societies in this country: one white, residing largely in the suburbs, and one of ethnics of color and the poor, residing primarily in the central cities and adjacent older industrial suburbs.

The dysfunctional social consequences of these dual societies have been well documented in the findings of the National Advisory Commission on Civil Disorders (Kerner Commission) and the President's Commission on Urban Housing (Kaiser Commission). These commissions told us what was already known: if existing patterns of segregation remained unaltered, the duality of societal separation would result in continued strife and disharmony. Outlining the changing nature of employment location, the commissions pointed out that more manufacturing and retail jobs are located outside the central cities. This results in further difficulties for ethnics of color and the poor in obtaining access to and information about employment.

In the late 1960s, the commissions called for an opening up of the suburbs and a substantial dispersion of ethnics of color in an attempt to achieve an integrated society. We still await this occurrence.

A recent report of the United States Civil Rights Commission states, "Despite a plethora of far reaching remedial legislation, a dual housing market continues today in most metropolitan areas across the United States."[2] The commission cites lack of adequate legal enforcement by federal agencies, lip service by local authorities, and lack of resolve by others involved in suburban development as perpetuating the systematic exclusion of minorities and low income families. The larger, older metropolitan areas continue to become the territories of ethnics of color and the poor.

The Housing and Community Development Act of 1974 recognizes the dual society problem. It is the first legislation to make deconcentration of the poor and disadvantaged from the central cities an objective. The assumptions of this objective are that there are distinct benefits for the poor and disadvantaged to be gained from deconcentration.[3] A clear case for this remains to be made.

1. Brian J. L. Berry and Yehoshua S. Cohen, "The Decentralization of Commerce and Industry: The Restructing of Metropolitan America," in Louis H. Masotti and Jeffrey K. Hadden, eds., *The Urbanization of the Suburbs* (Beverly Hills, Calif.: Sage Publishing, 1973), p. 453.

2. U.S., Commission on Civil Rights, *Equal Opportunity in Suburbia* (Washington, D.C., July 1974), p. 64.

3. An opposing case has been made that desegregation will harm rather than help the plight of the black urban poor. Rather than desegregation, the opposing argument calls for group solidarity by the poor and the black. Remaining in the central city allows for the greatest amount of political strength. Deconcentration will drain off human resources, especially among the educated and upwardly mobile. *See*, Frances Fox Piven and Richard

PROGRESS TOWARDS DECONCENTRATION IN LOS ANGELES

Deconcentration of ethnics of color on a national scale progressed slowly over the past decade. Most large metropolitan areas show slight percentage increases. The exception has been Los Angeles. Between 1960 and 1970, Los Angeles more than doubled the number of blacks and Mexican-Americans residing in communities outside the central city; it houses more ethnics of color than any other major metropolitan area in the country.[4]

Why has Los Angeles achieved a higher rate of deconcentration than other major areas? A simple explanation would be that a higher proportion of ethnics of color had the income available to make the suburban move. This explanation follows the general policy perspective held by the Nixon administration towards integration of the suburbs. Labeled "income policy," it relies on rises in real income of ethnics of color as the prime lever for prying their way out of the central city and away from its problems.[5] In essence, the suburbanization of ethnics of color would proceed at a pace related to their economic and occupational rise.[6]

This policy rests on two general assumptions, based on class and a suburbanization tendency. The class assumption is that the economically and upwardly mobile middle class seek out middle class settlement. The suburbanization assumption is that ethnics of color will suburbanize in a manner similar to their white counterparts when and if the resources for this move become available. There is some evidence in the Los Angeles experience to support this view, although income and class alone cannot explain variables in social behavior such as race prejudice, changing housing markets and kinship networks.

A second possible contributing factor in Los Angeles' ability to accommodate deconcentration is that it is historically and structurally unlike many Eastern and Southern cities. It is younger; developed on a basis of lower densities; has never experienced large immigrations of first generation European stock; has a longer history of assimilation of Asian and Mexican populations; contains less differentiation between city and suburb; and has a highly decentralized pattern of employment location. That is, the cost of suburban location, viewed as the discrimination premium paid by ethnics of color, is lower in economic and psychological terms in Los Angeles than in other major cities in the country. The premium is the addition to the cost of residential location—either in dollar or psychosocial terms—paid by ethnics of color in relation to the cost of resi-

---

A. Cloward, "The Case Against Desegregation," *Social Work* 12, no. 1 (January 1967), pp. 12–21.

4. Due to Los Angeles' extensive economic decentralization and lack of a central core in the traditional central city sense, there are problems in determining what is a "true" suburb. The problem of suburban definition exists throughout the country. No good solution has been found. With this in mind, the standard census definitions have been used. Mexican-American as used here includes all Spanish-surnamed, Spanish-speaking, and foreign-born people of Hispanic heritage. The overwhelming majority of Spanish heritage people in Los Angeles are of Mexican decent.

5. Francine F. Rabinovitz, "Minorities in Suburbs: The Los Angeles Experience," *Joint Center for Urban Studies—Harvard-MIT*, 1975, p. 2.

6. Nathan Glaser, "On Opening up the Suburbs," *Public Interest* 37 (Fall 1974), p. 106.

dential location paid by whites.[7] When this premium is high, the rate and spatial extent of residential mobility is low, and the tendency is for expansion of the ghetto to take place solely on its periphery. When the premium is low, residential mobility increases, with the middle class leading the migration along the paths of least resistance. The lower the discrimination premium, the more rapid the deconcentration. With the premium at zero, perfect freedom of choice would exist. However, the premium almost never reaches this point.

A third explanation is that of housing supply. Ethnics of color are dealing with an expanding housing market that responds to their pent-up demand. Faced with a declining white demand in certain submarkets of the metropolitan area, owners and builders have grown more amenable to selling and renting to ethnics of color. This explanation rests on a form of "filtering" process in which echnics of color can improve their housing status only in periods of excess supply.[8]

A fourth explanation of the Los Angeles experience rests on the notion that the deconcentration of ethnics of color is a result of normal migration to areas where there already existed some enclaves of non-white settlement. The new immigrants go to locations where inroads toward integration have already been made. In this case, the migrants would be following the ethnic pioneers of earlier years.

The Watts riots of 1965 cannot be ignored as a possible reason for changes in the way the people of Los Angeles relate to the black situation and to ethnics of color in general. The riots and civil rights legislation contributed to the acceptability of ethnics of color in suburban locations. Change occurs more rapidly under conditions of crisis. The burning of Watts certainly contributed to the atmosphere of change in Los Angeles.

THE CHANGING SUBURBS

In order to explain how each of the above contributed to the Los Angeles experience and thereby help to draw appropriate policy recommendations, this article examines what has happened in a group of Los Angeles communities. The cities examined are Los Angeles, Alhambra, Carson, Compton, El Monte, Inglewood, Pasadena and Pomona. Each had black or Mexican-American populations equal to or exceeding the 1970 county average (see table 1).

In 1960, only the cities of Los Angeles, Compton and Pasadena equaled or exceeded the county average for blacks. The city of Los Angeles contained more than 70 percent of the entire black population in the county, with Compton and Pasadena accounting for most of the remainder.[9] In 1960, there was a clear pattern of black ghettoization in Los Angeles. By 1970, the situa-

---

7. John F. Kain, "Effect of Housing Market Segregation on Urban Development," in Jon Pynoos et al, eds., *Housing Urban America* (Chicago: Aldine, 1973), p. 258.

8. Filtering only operates to a minimally acceptable level during large increases in supply, and even then its effect on helping the poor improve shelter is limited. *See,* Bernard J. Frieden, "Urban Housing: Old Policies and New Realities," in David M. Gordon, ed., *Problems in Political Economy: An Urban Perspective* (Lexington, Mass.: D. C. Heath, 1971), pp. 380–385.

9. Compton, being directly adjacent to the Watts section of the city of Los Angeles, can be functionally considered an extension of Watts. Its separate municipal status allows for more local control but also imposes heavy burdens on the residents due to its limited tax base.

TABLE 1

POPULATION AND INCOME CHARACTERISTICS FOR THE LOS ANGELES SMSA AND SELECTED COMMUNITIES, 1960–1970

	1960						1970					
	Total Population	Median Family Income	Percent Negro Population	Negro Median Family Income	Percent Spanish Surnames Population	Spanish Median Family Income	Total Population	Median Family Income	Percent Negro Population	Negro Median Family Income	Percent Spanish Surname Population	Median Spanish Family Income
Los Angeles	6,038,777	7,646	8	5,165	10	5,762	7,032,075	10,972	11	7,573	18	9,062
Los Angeles City	2,479,015	6,896	14	5,050	10	5,564	2,816,061	10.535	18	7,200	19	8,211
Alhambra	54,807	6,020	§	*	5	6,494	62,125	11,004	‡	*	18	10,105
Carson†	38,059	6,568	§	—	9	5,750	71,150	11,948	12	13,474	20	10,925
Compton	71,812	6,256	39	5,887	9	5,838	78,611	8,729	71	8,688	13	8,271
El Monte	13,163	5,655	§	—	**	—	69,837	8,981	‡	—	31	8,093
Inglewood	63,390	6,618	§	—	7	—	89,985	10,892	11	12,291	12	9,934
Pasadena	116,407	6,922	13	4,821	4	4,821	113,327	10,825	16	6,932	11	9,693
Pomona	67,157	6,585	1	4,594	9	4,594	87,384	10,014	12	7,708	16	8,354

SOURCE: U.S., Bureau of the Census, *Characteristics of the Population*, 1960–1970.
* Not reported in Census.
† Unincorporated in 1960. Figures indicate Census tracts which correspond to 1968 incorporation.
‡ Less than 1 percent.
§ Less than 5 percent of the Census sample. All percentages rounded to nearest whole number.
** Not reported in 1960 Census, *Characteristics of the Population with Spanish Surnames*. All percentages rounded to the nearest whole numbers.

tion in Los Angeles County had changed substantially. The cities of Los Angeles, Compton, Pasadena, Carson, Inglewood and Pomona equaled or exceeded the county average. Between 1960 and 1970, Compton became the black spillover city of Los Angeles. It experienced large scale white flight beginning in the 1950s, and in 1970 it was almost totally occupied by ethnics of color —71 percent black, 13 percent Mexican-Americans.

In 1960, only Los Angeles equaled or exceeded the county mean for Mexican-Americans, although Carson, Compton and Pomona fell just below the mean. By 1970, Alhambra, Carson and El Monte also exceeded the countywide mean, with Pomona close behind. The share of the county's Mexican-American population in Los Angeles increased slightly over the 1960 to 1970 period, from 41 percent to 42 percent of the county total. The distribution of the Mexican-American population was quite even, with no city containing less than 11 percent in 1970.

INCOME CHANGES AND MOBILITY

The Nixon administration's integration policy relied on economic advancement through the market process, in addition to normal enforcement of civil rights legislation, to open up the suburbs. In Los Angeles the income experience for blacks was very mixed, with a slight decrease in the gap between black and white incomes for the metropolitan area (see table 1). In 1960, black median family income was 67 percent of that of the metropolitan area, rising to 69 percent in 1970. In Los Angeles, the gap between white and black family incomes widened. For blacks and Mexican-Americans, the poorer members of

these races remained in the central city.

Why has this gap widened? To some extent it widened because middle income blacks moved out. There were marked income increases in Carson and Inglewood, where black income exceeded that of whites. It is safe to say that both Carson and Inglewood received the majority of their middle income black residents from Los Angeles. Three facts support this view: (1) in 1960, neither Carson or Inglewood had any black population per se; (2) in 1960, Los Angeles and Pasadena housed more than 80 percent of the blacks in the county; and (3) the data on black mobility patterns reveals that 51 percent of Carson's blacks and 61 percent of Inglewood's blacks lived in the same county but not the same city in 1965.

The widening of the income gap for blacks in Pasadena indicates that factors similar to those operating in Los Angeles were at work. The black population expanded slowly from 13 percent in 1960 to 16 percent in 1970. Yet the black residents were poorer in 1970, in relation to the city as a whole, than they were in 1960. Contrast Pasadena to Pomona, where the black income gap closed and there was a substantial increase in the number of blacks in Pomona who had lived within the same county in 1965. With the exception of Pasadena, black family income in all of the cities examined exceeded that for blacks living in Los Angeles.

The Mexican-American experience is somewhat different. On a countywide basis the income gap decreased, but it widened for those living in the city of Los Angeles (see table 1). As with blacks, the poorer Mexican-Americans lived in the central city. In the outlying cities they held their own and improved their income status—with the exceptions of Alhambra, where there was a decrease from 107 percent to 91 percent of the median. Alhambra, like Carson and Inglewood, had substantial Mexican-American in-migration, with 46 percent of the population living in the same county in 1965. Mexican-American mobility was widespread throughout the metropolitan area, with at least 37 percent of the population not residing in the same house in the same city in 1965.

The income data supports the fact that middle income ethnics of color are suburbanizing faster than their poorer brothers, with the blacks doing so at a higher rate than Mexican-Americans. To some extent, income alone buys an exit visa from the ghetto in Los Angeles. However, the income policy does not say anything about the extent of integration that takes place within the suburban communities.

Suburban Housing Availability

The success of any deconcentration or integration policy rests on housing availability. Two factors contribute to availability. First is the absence of discriminatory practices by the sellers and/or financial institutions which control mortgage lending. Second is the ability to pay the generally higher costs of suburban location.[10] Because suburban cities usually contain more single-family than multiple units, one measure of how well ethnics of color fare is to examine their levels of owner-occu-

pancy as related to the city in which they reside and to the metropolitan area.

Using the owner-occupancy index, we find that blacks in Los Angeles have made substantial progress towards housing parity in some suburban communities. With the exceptions of El Monte and Alhambra, which are less than one percent black, Carson, Inglewood, Pomona, Pasadena and Compton exceed Los Angeles in the percentage of black owner-occupancy (see table 2). The ratios between black and nonblack median housing values approximate the ratios between black and nonblack median family income. This indicates similar expenditure patterns for housing in the suburbs by blacks and nonblacks. The high owner-occupancy figures for Compton approach the percentage ratio of the black population, indicating little absentee ownership.

Of particular interest are Inglewood, Carson and Pomona, which have black populations approximating the countywide average and extremely high levels of black owner-occupancy. Home purchasing seems to be the primary objective for suburbanizing blacks in these communities. This seems to be particularly true in Inglewood and Pomona where the high percentage of black homeownership shows a clear preference for owner-occupancy over rental.

Although a general case can be made that ethnics of color were less discriminated against in the Los Angeles housing market and that fairer treatment was given them during this period, there are other factors which shed some light on the cases of Inglewood, Pomona and Carson. Inglewood is an older, lower-middle income, residential suburb, and is not far from existing middle

---

10. Central city contract rents are lower due to the age and condition of the housing inventory. In 1970 the median contract rent for the city of Los Angeles was $70 per month, while for the county as a whole it was $81 per month.

TABLE 2

Home Ownership and Home Value Los Angeles and Selected Communities, 1970

	Median Owner Value ($) for City	Percent Owner Occupied All Units	Negro					Spanish Surname			
			Percent Population	Median Owner Value ($)	Value as % of All	Owner Occupied as % of Negro Population		Percent Population	Median Owner Value ($)	Value as a % of All	Owner Occupied as % of Population
Los Angeles Long Beach SMSA	24,300	48.5	11.0	18,900	77.7	37.6		18	21,200	87	41.2
Los Angeles	26,700	40.9	18.0	18,500	69.2	31.8		19	21,800	81	31.2
Alhambra	23,500	46.6	0.3	20,000	85.1	13.4		18	24,000	102	41.6
Carson	25,700	75.0	12.0	30,000	116.7	85.7		20	24,800	96	68.9
Compton	18,000	57.8	71.0	18,100	100.5	60.7		13	16,800	93	46.5
El Monte	19,700	43.5	0.2	—	—	12.1		31	19,000	96	34.8
Inglewood	25,000	36.0	11.0	28,800	115.2	74.3		12	25.300	101	24.2
Pasadena	26,300	43.6	16.0	17,900	68.0	35.7		11	22,800	86	33.6
Pomona	17,200	56.6	12.0	16,400	95.3	63.0		16	15,800	91	48.9

Source: U.S., Bureau of the Census, *Housing Characteristics: California*, 1970.

class black communities in the city of Los Angeles. It can be reached from Watts in less than a 30-minute drive. It has a middle-aged white population and moderately priced homes and is close to the Los Angeles airport. Some white flight, lower resistance to ethnics of color, and general situation of changing life cycle for older residents explain why this housing market became available to middle income blacks.

The case of Pomona is somewhat different. Its housing stock expanded rapidly during the late 1950s, with a substantial amount of Veterans Administration (VA) and Federal Housing Administration (FHA) residences built to accommodate the large demand in that period. In part, Pomona had an overbuilt housing market and large numbers of VA and FHA mortgage defaults. Faced with diminishing demand on the part of whites for housing in this area and an oversupply of housing, it appears that the only remaining market was ethnics of color. A buyers' housing market in Pomona contributed to the ability of ethnics of color to leave the central city.

The evidence on improvements in Mexican-American housing status is mixed. Although Mexican-Americans approximate the owner-occupancy of blacks in Los Angeles, they do not fare as well in the suburban communities (see table 2). In no city do they equal the average level of owner-occupancy. This disparity cannot be explained by income alone, since median income is higher for Mexican-Americans than for blacks in Los Angeles, Pasadena and Pomona, and almost equal in Compton.

A more realistic explanation has been given by Grebler and Moore, whose study of the Mexican-American revealed that, due to larger family size, a higher percentage of income was spent on non-housing items, with less left for housing.[11] Family incomes do not appear to be high enough to meet family needs and pay off a mortgage at the same time. When Mexican-Americans do reside in owner-occupied housing in the suburbs, the value of these units is extremely close to the median, indicating that it is the middle class Mexican-Americans with higher than average income who have the capacity for homeownership. What was said above of the housing market conditions for blacks also holds true for Mexican-Americans—migration streams have developed along two finger patterns: one to the south, extending almost to Long Beach, and one to the east, extending through Pomona.

LENDER BEHAVIOR AND DECONCENTRATION

If lenders do not make home loans, people do not buy houses. The actions of the lending institutions affect both whites and ethnics of color, although in different ways. One factor that may have helped to open up the suburban housing market was that lenders changed their behavior regarding loans to ethnics of color during the 1960s. Lenders became more receptive to ethnics of color and made more loans to dual wage-earner households. The Watts riots may have influenced this form of lender behavior. Since a much higher percentage of nonwhite families have dual wage-earners, the acceptance of both incomes in determining loan eligibility is crucial in the lending decision.

There is little data about the actual behavior of mortgage lenders;

11. Leo Grebler, Joan W. Moore, and Ralph Guzman, *The Mexican-American* (New York: Free Press, 1970).

however, recent reports by the Center for New Corporate Priorities and the Western Center on Law and Poverty are instructive.[12] Using information on lending practices of state-chartered savings and loan associations, they found that red-lining ocurred in a large number of Los Angeles cities. Red-lining is the practice of refusing to make loans in certain areas without regard to an applicant's worthiness or the condition of the property. The higher the percentage of ethnics of color in any particular census tract, the higher the incidence of red-lining.

Red-lining was also correlated with home value and closely associated with the availability of FHA-insured loans. Shifts from conventional to FHA financing between 1968 and 1974 coincide quite closely with changing neighborhood racial composition. In areas such as Pomona, nearly no conventional loans were made during the study period. The difficulty in securing conventional loans has two effects: it lowers home prices so they do not go beyond the FHA limits; and it precludes or makes more difficult the sale of older homes not eligible under FHA regulations.

If the above evidence holds true for other lending institutions, particularly federally chartered savings and loan associations, we are likely to see a downgrading of red-lined residential areas and a general lowering of home values. The effects of this in the short run will be to increase the supply of lower-cost housing in selected suburban neighborhoods. The neighborhoods are likely to experience in-migration of ethnics of color and to produce new segregated areas. The new residents will be lower-income working class persons seeking their first home.

SEGREGATION AND NEIGHBORHOOD STABILITY

Has the move to suburbia helped improve the welfare of ethnics of color? The questions of segregation within suburban communities, neighborhood stability, and quality of life remain unanswered. In all of the communities where inroads have been made in opening up the suburbs, substantial segregation still exists. Ethnics of color in these communities generally reside in only a few census tracts. Some of the segregation may come about by choice. People with similar tastes, incomes, cultural backgrounds, social preferences, and skin color desire to live close to one another. However, segregated neighborhoods still do not achieve the objective of an integrated society. Segregation in suburbia for ethnics of color still appears to be a matter of necessity rather than choice.

Little is known about the stability of neighborhoods within these suburbs, especially those directly adjacent to ones populated by ethnics of color. Past evidence has shown that most transition occurs on the periphery of mixed neighborhoods. Will there be major neighborhood transition over the next decade, or will the middle class characteristics of suburbanizing ethnics of color be enough to achieve some sort of stability within these cities? Glaser believes the problem is now one of

12. Center for New Corporate Priorities, *Where the Money Is: Mortgage Lending, Los Angeles County* (Los Angeles, 1975); and Jonathan Leher-Graiwer and Cary D. Lower, *Conventional Red-lining: The Tip of the Iceberg* (Los Angeles: Western Center on Law and Poverty, 16 June 1975).

class, not race.[13] I do not think the evidence exists, at least based on the Los Angeles experience, to support this view.

If some of these suburbs turn majority lower and middle class ethnic, as has happened to Compton, what will this mean? Surely no resemblance to integration will have occurred. Will the quality of life be improved by living in segregated suburbs? Inevitably, some of the problems of the central cities will slowly but surely move to the suburbs, be they white or integrated. The manner in which suburban communities and the nation as a whole will handle these problems should immediately become part of our national urban policy agenda.

13. Glaser, "On Opening up the Suburbs," p. 107.

Administration Hara-Kiri: Implementation of the Urban Growth and New Community Development Act

By Helene V. Smookler

ABSTRACT: New communities have been offered as an alternative to suburban sprawl. Through economies of scale and a "clean-slate" development approach, a more attractive and innovative environment can be produced. The federal government became involved through the 1968 Housing Act. In order to insure the attainment of social goals, loan guarantees and grants were made available to developers. In 1970 the act was strengthened by making public developers eligible and increasing the number of grants. Now, seven years after the passage of the original act, the program appears to be a failure. Despite promises of 10 federally guaranteed new communities a year, only 14 have received commitments thus far. All of these communities are behind in their development schedules, and most are near financial collapse. While the federally guaranteed new communities were hard hit by the economic recession, most of the blame for the current crisis can be placed on the Republican administration's implementation of the program. Categorical grants were suspended, other funds were impounded by the Office of Management and Budget, and there was little intra- or inter-agency cooperation or coordination. Due to lack of political support, the prospects for the program appear dim.

Helene V. Smookler is an Assistant Professor of Political Science at Wellesley College. She has published several articles on new communities and recently completed a two-year study on the potential for socioeconomic integration in new communities.

WHEN the Urban Growth and New Community Development Act was passed in 1968, it was heralded as one of the landmark pieces of legislation on urban affairs of this generation. Many persons interested in housing and urban development saw in the federal legislation some seeds of hope for producing an alternative to monotonous and inadequately serviced suburban sprawl. This optimism was given some credibility by the stated provisions of the 1970 act, which have the appearance of coming from the bottom of Pandora's box. Also, the legislation was passed in the "heady days of the 1960s when some thought it might be possible to produce managed solutions to the problems of housing the poor and revitalizing the cities."[1] The new communities program was seen as having the potential for becoming:

A major instrument of national urban growth policy—magnetizing trend growth into highly attractive new cities, carefully programmed to meet and harmonize the differing needs of a fully representative population for housing, employment, commercial and recreational facilities, community services and transportation.[2]

Congress shared this enthusiasm, predicting that, beginning in 1969–70, 10 new communities a year would receive funding under the act.[3]

Now, seven years after the passage of the original act, the Department of Housing and Urban Development (HUD) announces that it is no longer accepting loan applications so that it can prevent the financial collapse of the 14 new communities which have received federal commitments. The euphoric optimism of a few years ago stands in sharp contrast to the obituaries being written on these communities.[4] What happened in the interim? Why were so few communities funded? Were the goals of the legislation unrealistic? Did the program fall victim to the vicissitudes of the economy, or is it only possible to do good deeds in an expanding economy? Or did the federal administration garrote a program it never really wanted to succeed?

On the surface it would appear that much of the blame would have to be put on lack of governmental support. Even though new communities suffered from the downturn in the economy, the very existence of federal financial support should have prevented failure.

LEGISLATIVE INTENT

Although by the mid-1960s nearly 100 large scale developments were being planned or were under construction in this country, not all met the criteria for designation as a new community: scale of development— usually 1,000 or more acres, with a minimum population of 10,000; unity of planning and development, with the site owned or controlled by a unified management; comprehensive

1. David E. Blum, "Problems and Progress in the HUD New Communities Processing System," *Systems Building News*, July 1973, p. 40.

2. Blum, "Problems and Progress."

3. *Housing and Urban Development Legislation of 1969*, Senate Report 91-392 to accompany S. 2864, 90th Cong., 1969, pp. 22–24.

4. *See*, for example, "New Towns in Trouble," *Time*, 24 March 1975, pp. 70–71; Scott Jacobs, "New Towns Go to Seed, Default," *Chicago Sun-Times*, 24 November 1974; "New Towns' Future Shock," *Newsweek*, 24 February 1975; "Can New Towns Survive the Economic Crunch?" *Business Week*, 10 February 1975, pp. 43–44.

planning, with facilities and services provided at an early stage of development; and a degree of self-sufficiency through commercial facilities and industry which provide job opportunities. Many proponents of new communities also included the desirability of social balance in their conceptualization. This goal developed out of the perception of the new community as a microcosm of a city. Integration could be facilitated in new communities because they were being developed primarily on the fringes of metropolitan areas, where there are few existing neighborhoods with entrenched social or political prejudices, such as exclusionary zoning.

Although the financial projections for these communities suggest their long term profitability, the development of a new community involves extraordinary land acquisition costs.[5] High acquisition and development costs not only involve large initial capital formation, but also high carrying costs. This requires enormous amounts of cash to meet the principal and interest payments, real estate taxes, management and other capital expenditures. This severe cash flow pressure is aggravated by the gestation period of 15 to 20 years from initiation to achieving a positive cash flow. Also, in order to compete with existing developments, new communities must create extensive physical infrastructures of utilities and community services.

Those lobbying for federal involvement to assist new community developers felt that unaided, private entrepreneurs would not satisfy any kind of national commitment to build new communities of the right kinds,

in the right places and at the right time. Support for the New Communities Act grew out of the belief that "the private sector simply does not think of problems of design and resource allocation in terms of social need"[6] and that social objectives are neither profitable nor entirely feasible in the open market system. Thus, the following provision was critical for passage:

An adequate range of housing and a variety of housing types for both sale and rental for people of all incomes, ages and family composition, including a substantial amount for people of low and moderate income, during each major phase of residential development.[7]

PROVISIONS OF THE ACT

The prime mechanism for achieving the grandiose objectives of the New Communities Act (see figure 1) is the loan guarantee. Under the 1968 act, developers could receive loan guarantees up to $50 million for any one project. This made it possible for a developer to tap the corporate bond market and borrow money at lower interest. Only interest on the debt need be paid during the first 10 years of the maximum 20-year development period.

These rates and terms provide the developer with large amounts of front-end cash needed to buy land, provide infrastructure, and construct facilities for schools, shops and parks. Developers were also eligible to receive loans to cover interest charges during the early years.

5. In the early 1960s, land acquisition cost for Columbia was $22 million; Reston, $12 million; and Laguna Niguel, $6 million.

6. Michael Harrington, "Housing and the Public Sector," *Architectural Forum* 134, no. 4 (May 1971), p. 33.

7. U.S., Department of Housing and Urban Development, Office of the Secretary, "Assistance for New Communities, Notice of Proposed Rule Making," *Federal Register* 36, no. 148 (31 July 1971), p. 14208.

FIGURE 1

OBJECTIVES OF THE URBAN GROWTH AND NEW COMMUNITY ACT OF 1970

(1) Encourage the orderly development of well-planned, diversified, and economically sound new communities, including major additions to existing communities, and to do so in a manner that will rely to the maximum extent on private enterprise;

(2) Strengthen the capacity of State and local governments to deal with local problems;

(3) Preserve and enhance both the natural and urban environment;

(4) Increase for all persons, particularly members of minority groups, the available choices of locations for living and working;

(5) Encourage the fullest utilization of the economic potential of older central cities, smaller towns, and rural communities;

(6) Assist in the efficient production of a steady supply of residential, commercial, and industrial building sites at reasonable cost;

(7) Increase the capability of all segments of the homebuilding industry, including both small and large producers, to utilize improved technology in producing the large volume of well-designed, inexpensive housing needed to accommodate population growth;

(8) Help create neighborhoods designed for easier access between the places where people live and the places where they work and find recreation;

(9) Encourage desirable innovation in meeting domestic problems whether physical, economic, or social; and

(10) Improve the organizational capacity of the Federal government to carry out programs of assistance for the development of new communities and the revitalization of the Nation's urban areas.

SOURCE: "Draft Regulations, Urban Growth and New Community Development Act of 1970," enacted by Title VII, Housing and Urban Development Act of 1970, Public Law 91-609, *Federal Register*, 36 F.R., 14205-14, 31 July 1971.

Funds were authorized to cover three-fourths of planning costs and for supplementary grants for water and sewer, open space and beautification during initial development period. The act recognized four kinds of new towns as being eligible for assistance: free standing, the satellite, the "add-on" (built onto the nucleus of a small existing town), and the new-town-in-town. The last form was included in order to gain support for the legislation from the nation's mayors.

The 1970 act provided a significantly expanded program of assistance. The new program, Title VII, raised the ceiling on loan guarantees to $500 million (the $50 million limit per development remained), and the program was extended to public developers. Title VII also increased the number of grants for which developers were eligible to 14. These include mass transportation, highways, airports, recreation, open space, beautification, water and sewer facilities, and other public works.

IMPLEMENTATION

Despite the sanguine expectations, only two communities had been funded by the time Title VII was passed. In addition, the Nixon administration opposed the 1970 bill on grounds that it was inflationary. There is much irony in this opposition. The New Communities Act was the first federal statute to focus directly on the needs of the private developer. It is also in line with the philosophy of self-reliance, local initiative, and keeping federal expenditures to a minimum. HUD guarantees private loans in return for the right to exercise control over the projects. The developers must also pay fees which are kept in a revolving fund for covering the government's risk on the loans and "any other program expenditure, including administrative and non-administrative expenses."[8]

Originally, developers were attracted by Title VII's cornucopia, and although only 3 communities had received guarantees or commitments for guarantees by mid-1970 (see table 1), there were more than 70 applications waiting for approval. Four years later, a total of 15 communities had received commitments,[9] and only one or two applications were pending.

Financial strangulation

To undertake a program of the scope and complexity of new towns requires the strong commitment and backing of government at all levels. The most widespread developer complaint is that the administration has shown blatant disregard for a strong congressional mandate and that the program has never really been implemented.[10] Ten adverse budget decisions have been made by the Office of Management and Budget (OMB), and HUD has failed to take advantage of authority provided by the law (see table 2).

The public service grants were never funded. The supplementary grants for physical infrastructure, which had been important in attracting developers, were terminated in July 1973. Although the administration requested no appropriation for the grant program for assistance for innovative planning—environmental, social and technological advancement—Congress appropriated $5 million. This small appropriation was impounded by OMB.[11]

In testimony submitted to the Senate Appropriations Committee, former general manager of the New Communities Administration (NCA) in HUD Alberto F. Trevino, Jr., explained that the Section 715 planning grants were discontinued because they were "undesirable." He rationalized that new communities would be receiving benefits not available to other communities.[12]

Administrative morass

Other administrative and substantive problems have had significant impact on the program. The average processing time for applications was often more than three years. This has had a discouraging effect on developers. Both uncertainty and delay in processing time can cause considerable hardship in obtaining and securing temporary financing and in retaining options. The cost to developers in interest can run as high as $10,000 per day. Reasons for the delay appear to center around inadequate staffing of NCA. Since the original act was passed, there have been complaints about shortage of staff, high turnover, lack of experienced specialists, poor office

8. U.S., HUD, "Assistance for New Communities," Sec. 717.

9. Beckett New Town, N.J., received a commitment for $35.5 million in October 1973. The developers, however, decided not to accept it.

10. *See*, "Oversight Hearings on HUD New Communities Program," *Hearings before the Subcommittee on Housing, Committee on Banking and Currency*, House of Representatives, 93rd Cong., 1st sess., 30–31 May 1973.

11. For a legislative history of Title IV and Title VII and an analysis of early implementation, *see*, Francine F. Rabinovitz and Helene V. Smookler, "Rhetoric Versus Performance: The National Politics and Administration of U.S. New-Community Development Legislation," in *New Towns— Why and For Whom?*, ed. Harvey Perloff and Neil Sandberg (New York: Praeger, 1973), pp. 90–114.

12. Reported in the League of New Community Developers' *Newsletter*, June 1974.

TABLE 1
Projects Approved by HUD as of August 1974

	Location	Date of HUD Commitment	Date of Project Agreement	Guarantees Committed	Acres	Projected Dwelling Units	Projected Population	Development Period (Years)
Projects Guaranteed:								
Jonathan, Minnesota (S)	20 miles southwest of Minneapolis	2/70	10/70	$21.0	8,194	15,000	50,000	20
St. Charles Communities, Maryland (S)	25 miles southeast of Washington, D.C.	6/70	12/70	24.0	7,408	25,000	75,000	20
Park Forest South, Illinois (S)	30 miles south of Chicago	6/70	3/71	30.0	8,163	37,000	110,000	15
Flower Mound, Texas (S)	20 miles northwest of Dallas	12/70	10/71	18.0	6,156	18,000	64,000	20
Maumelle, Arkansas (S)	12 miles northwest of Little Rock	12/70	12/71	7.5	5,319	14,000	45,000	20
Cedar-Riverside, Minnesota (NTIT)	Downtown Minneapolis	6/71	12/71	24.0	101	13,000	30,000	20
Riverton, New York (S)	10 miles south of Rochester	12/71	5/72	12.0	2,437	8,000	26,000	16
The Woodlands, Texas (S)	30 miles north of Houston	4/72	8/72	50.0	17,000	47,000	150,000	20
Gananda, New York (S)	12 miles east of Rochester	4/72	12/72	22.0	4,733	17,000	56,000	20
Newfields, Ohio (S)	7 miles northwest of Dayton	10/73	11/73	32.0	4,032	13,000	40,000	20
San Antonio Ranch, Texas (S)	20 miles northwest of San Antonio	2/72	—	18.0	9,318	29,000	88,000	30

TABLE 1 (*Continued*)

	Location	Date of HUD Commitment	Date of Project Agreement	Guarantees Committed	Acres	Projected Dwelling Units	Projected Population	Development Peroid (Years)
Soul City, North Carolina (FS)	45 miles north of Raleigh	6/72	—	14.0	5,180	13,000	44,000	20
Harbison, South Carolina (S)	8 miles northwest of Columbia	10/72	—	13.0	1,740	6,000	23,000	20
Shenandoah, Georgia (S)	35 miles south of Atlanta	2/73	—	40.0	7,200	23,000	70,000	20
Projects without Guarantees*								
Radisson, New York (S)	12 miles northwest of Syracuse	—	—	—	2,670	5,000	18,000	20
Roosevelt Island, New York (NTIT)	East River between Manhattan and Queens	—	—	—	143	5,000	18,000	7

Source: Compiled from New Communities Administration data.

* State Land Development Agency Projects. Obligations will not be guaranteed by HUD, but project is eligible for other program benefits. Subject to Review.

    S = Satellite new community
NTIT = New-town-in-town
  FS = Free-standing new community

TABLE 2

GUARANTEES, LOANS, GRANTS, AND OTHER ASSISTANCE AUTHORIZED BY TITLE VII
(in millions)

AUTHORIZING SECTION	PURPOSE	AUTHORIZED BY CONGRESS	REQUESTED BY HUD	APPROPRIATED BY CONGRESS	COMMITTED
713	Authority to guarantee obligations issued by private or public developers	$50 single; $740.5 total	—	—	$325.5
713	Interest differential grants	as necessary	0	0	0
714	Interest loans	$20 single; $240 total	0	0	0
715	Public service grants	as necessary	0	0	0
718	Supplementary grants for public facilities[1]	$36(71); $66(72); $66(73)[2]	$30	$25	22.8
719	Technical assistance	as necessary	0	0	0
720	Special planning assistance	$10[4]	0	(3)	0
735	701 75-percent planning grants to states and regions for development of rational urban growth patterns, including new communities	as necessary[5]	0	0	0

SOURCE: *Oversight Hearings on the HUD New Communities Program before the Subcommittee on Housing of the Committee on Banking and Currency*, House of Representatives, 93rd Cong., 1st sess., 30-31 May 1973 (Washington: Government Printing Office, 1973), p. 76, and updated by the New Communities Administration, May 1974.

[1] Federal programs eligible for supplementary grants include: highways, mass transit, airports, hospitals, libraries, parks and open space, sewer and water, neighborhood facilities, wastewater treatment plants, and certain other educational facilities, plus public works in areas of high unemployment and in rural areas.

[2] After 1973 as necessary (1974 and after). Funds to remain available until appropriated and expended.

[3] Includes $17,500,000 appropriated in fiscal year 1972 or fiscal year 1973 which was also available for special planning assistance.

[4] Funds to remain available until appropriated and expended.

[5] While no 75-percent grants as authorized under 735 have been made, ⅔ planning grants under 701 have been made which have benefited Newfields, Ohio; Flower Mound, Tex.; Soul City, N.C.; Riverton, N.Y.; Cedar-Riverside, Minn.; Park Forest South, Ill.; and St. Charles communities Maryland. Also, the state of New Jersey has received a grant to develop statewide policies for new communities.

management, and tangled lines of authority.

After five years, there are still no final regulations or handbooks setting the ground rules. This has resulted in ad hoc review of applications and virtually no monitoring of projects.

NCA admits experiencing problems in staffing and processing of applications. It places most of the blame, however, on the unprecedented scope and complexity of the program and the necessity of involving all levels of government and the private sector. Furthermore, NCA calls attention to the fact that "new ground is being broken in virtually every subject matter."[13] NCA denies that its difficulties are caused by legislative goals that are "too vague or [too] numerous," and claims it is hamstrung by the fact that "most of the original provisions of the Act designed to achieve these goals have never been funded," and also because a few of the objectives are so sweeping that they are incapable of achievement— for example reversal of migration trends.[14]

Status of the Program

By the fall of 1974, 12 of the new communities had issued bonds for $252 million in federally guaranteed debentures. However, all of the new communities are behind in their development schedules.

As table 1 shows, the satellite new community has been the overwhelming financial response of de-

velopers. Yet only two of these, Park Forest South and Jonathan, have significant populations, with approximately 4,000 and 1,500 persons respectively. Development of Cedar-Riverside, the only new-town-in-town, has been held up by an environmental suit and, like Soul City, it is being accused of mismanagement of funds.[15]

Financial crisis

As stated above, an enormous amount of capital is needed to develop a new town. It has been estimated that a community with a projected population of 70,000 requires a minimum of $700 million in mortgage loans for 20,000 units; another $400 million is required for capital outlay, public services and buildings; and an additional $400 million is needed for industrial and commercial development.[16]

Section 712(2) of Title VII says that a new community is eligible for assistance only if the HUD secretary determines that the program will be economically feasible in terms of economic base or potential for economic growth. Judgment was faulty. At the moment, most of the federally guaranteed new communities are in severe financial difficulties, and two are up for sale. Spiraling inflation has resulted in the developers' running out of funds before they have adequate cash flow to begin paying back interest and principal on their bonds.

The crisis had been building for several years, but it peaked in December 1974 when Riverton came

13. U.S., Department of Housing and Urban Development, New Communities Administration, Policy Paper no. 5.

14. U.S., Department of Housing and Urban Development, New Communities Administration, Policy Paper no. 6.

15. "2 in Congress Ask Inquiry on McKissick's Soul City," *New York Times*, 9 March 1975.

16. League of New Community Developers, "Status Report."

close to financial collapse, almost saddling HUD with its $12 million obligation. HUD began negotiating refinancing deals, largely involving new guarantees for bonds to be issued by developers. Riverton has been refinanced to take care of its projected needs for the next three to five years, and several more projects are in various stages of being refinanced. Almost $2 million in interest payments has been arranged for or made by HUD itself for Jonathan, St. Charles and Riverton.

In September 1974, Park Forest South was unable to meet debt charges of more than $1 million on its $30 million of bonds. While HUD finally made the payment, as it is authorized to do, HUD did come close to foreclosing. Instead, HUD accepted a deal in which the investors bought land in the development for $5.5 million to provide the cash to keep the operations going through 1975.

Administration response

Title VII has been judged as failing because the communities have not been doing well financially. The question must be raised as to whether the projects would have been able to survive if all the authorities had been funded. Otto Stoltz, current director of NCA, claims that the HUD-guaranteed new communities are in no worse financial shape than any other real estate undertakings. This contention is supported by the former president of Jonathan Development Corporation, who feels that the current depression in the real estate industry:

. . . rapidly accelerated the present crisis. But even in a normal marketing climate, most of the federally guaranteed new towns would be having troubles.

The lack of mortgage money and the high interest rates have all but stopped construction of residential units—in new towns and everywhere else.[17]

Administration spokesmen, however, have gone beyond blaming the current economic recession for the lack of program success. They cite failure to attract large scale competent developers; lack of congressional support; failure of states and localities to become involved; and absence of developer control, that is, no discipline because HUD would be there to bail them out.

This appears to be part of the administration's tendency to downplay the program. By 1973 HUD appeared to be placing increased emphasis on the research and development aspect of the program, which was only part of the congressional intent. Speaking to the League of New Community Developers, the lobbying group for the federal program, Trevino stated that the new communities program is "neither a panacea nor the only solution to our urban sprawl and inner city troubles"; it has been an exaggerated remedy. "The Title VII program cannot substitute for other measures of shaping growth."[18] Elsewhere, Trevino had noted that part of the difficulty with the new communities program is that there is a shortage of developers with the desire and capability to build new communities.

17. Jules C. Smith, "American's New Towns . . . What Next," *Many Corners* 3, no. 3 (March 1975).

18. Remarks prepared for delivery by Alberto F. Trevino, Jr., General Manager, New Communities Administration, U.S., Department of Housing and Urban Development, at the League of New Community Developers, Dallas, Texas, 8 March 1974.

Program credibility

One justification for federal involvement was really symbolic—to establish the credibility of the new communities concept in achieving social goals. Money, totaling almost $350 million, was supposed to last through 20 years of construction. But inflation, tight money, mismanagement, and a failure of HUD to provide the communities with the assistance Congress wanted them to receive have critically damaged the credibility of the federal guarantee. NCA may have learned over the past seven years how to administer such a program, but this knowledge has come too late.

Internal and external investigation have criticized the administration of the program and have attempted to discredit federal involvement. A General Accounting Office (GAO) study accused HUD of inefficient and inaccurate financial accounting.[19] The Policy Development and Review (PD & R) Office in HUD issued a report based on other studies of new community development. It concludes that:

There is little justification for federal involvement in new community development; that the potential costs are relatively low, but still significantly higher than the benefits; and that because the costs and benefits are so low, it is difficult to assess the program's equitability.[20]

While the GAO and PD & R reports have been criticized for their inaccuracies and weak data bases, both are being widely circulated.

19. U.S., General Accounting Office, *Getting the New Communities Program Started: Progress and Problems*, B-170971, 14 November 1974.

20. Cited in *Housing and Development Reporter* 2, no. 14, December 1974.

Program prospects

Title VII is an attempt to make new communities a conscious instrument of public policy for the attainment of certain laudable, but difficult, economic and social goals. The prospects appear dim.

The federally guaranteed new communities are in a "no man's land" as far as future funding is concerned. With the termination of categorical grant programs and their replacement with community development bloc grants, the typical local government in which new communities are located has little chance of receiving the kind of assistance that might have been available through categorical grants. This is due to the fact that the Community Development Act distributes funds according to a formula which gives preference to communities in proportion to the population of the jurisdiction, the number of low and moderate income residents, and the extent of deteriorated housing.

CONCLUSIONS

There is currently no commitment to a new community program on the national level. Congressional support, while not strong, is generally favorable. However, new communities are very low on the list of present congressional priorities, and although the Republican administration claimed initially to support the New Communities Act, it has always viewed it as a Democratic program.

There has never been intra- or inter-agency coordination in the implementation of the program. Congress attempted to spread responsibility for the program throughout governmental agencies, with HUD carrying most of the burden. Unfortunately, experience has shown that it is impossible to develop any kind of coordination among agencies. The more complex the program and the longer its duration, the more difficult coordination becomes.

Another problem is that, outside of private developers, there is no real constituency for the program. Home-builders, mortgage bankers and unions were never strongly involved, because this is not a program which directly affects housing starts. The National League of Cities and other public interest groups view it as a suburban program and believe that the money should be going to central cities.

The outcome seems destined. A former NCA official says that there is:

clear danger that the new communities program will succumb, as have other HUD programs. . . . In this period of disenchantment with federal programs generally, no one can suggest that any one program is likely to be a panacea for solving the enormous problems of inner cities, urban sprawl or rural decline.[21]

Despite this dim outlook for the federal program, new communities will continue to be built in this country, perhaps not on such a grand scale and with less onerous objectives. And the odds are good that a majority of the 14 federally guaranteed communities will, with the help of federal transfusions, continue with scaled-down development.

21. Blum, "Problems and Progress," p. 47.

Suburban Foundations of the New Congress

By RICHARD LEHNE

ABSTRACT: Both Congress and the American suburbs are undergoing major reformations. The election of large and increasing numbers of suburban representatives to Congress means that, today and in the future, Congress must deal with the policy positions and reform preferences of suburbanites. This article examines the behavior of suburban legislators in the House of Representatives as a reflection of political changes taking place in the suburbs which will influence current and future congressional policy making. Competing interpretations of the political significance of the emerging American suburbs are discussed and evaluated.

Richard Lehne is an Associate Professor of Political Science at Rutgers University. He recently contributed an essay on the politics of taxation and expenditures to a collection entitled Politics in New Jersey *and is currently principal investigator on a project examining judicial strategies for school finance reform for the Ford Foundation. He has also served in the Office of the Assistant Secretary for Research, Department of Housing and Urban Development.*

HIGH on anyone's list of American institutions undergoing major reformation in this era of political turbulence stand both suburbs and the United States Congress. Ten years ago in Congress, powerful committee leaders and semiautonomous committees hammered out solutions to policy problems and then persuaded a majority of Congress to adopt these positions. Now, as a result of numerous incremental changes in committee procedures, congressional staffing patterns, and the activities of party caucuses, the men and women who chair congressional committees are no longer as powerful as they once were, and committees no longer act with the autonomy they once had. In 1965 and 1966, Congress and the country looked to an activist president to provide new initiatives in domestic policy; today, in contrast, a forthright president is resisting congressional programs to promote government housing, expand public employment, and utilize the authority of government to achieve a broad range of social goals.

The past decade has also underlined two important features of America's emerging suburbs: their dynamic growth and their enhanced diversity. The election of large and increasing numbers of suburban representatives to Congress means that, today and in the future, Congress must come to grips with the policy positions and reform preferences of suburbanites. By examining various elements of the behavior of suburban legislators in the House of Representatives, this article considers the political changes taking place in American suburbs and the implications these changes will have for congressional policy making. It appraises the size of the suburban delegation in the House of Representatives, examines the policy positions of contemporary legislators, considers the impact of party affiliation on congressional voting patterns, and concludes by scrutinizing competing interpretations of the political significance of the emergence of American suburbs.

CONGRESSIONAL REPRESENTATION PATTERNS

In *Wesberry* v. *Sanders* and *Kirkpatrick* v. *Preisler*, the United States Supreme Court ruled that population among congressional districts within a state must be "as nearly equal as practicable." These decisions put an end to the "rotten borough" system which permitted many states to heavily overrepresent sparsely populated regions and to dilute the representation of people living in the central city and suburban portions of metropolitan areas. With these decisions, the Supreme Court both established the equal population principle for the 1960s and required that it be followed when congressional district boundaries were redrawn to reflect each new decennial census.

By 1966, the districts of most members of Congress had been reshaped to adhere to the equal population standard, and by 1974 they had been reformed again to accommodate the changes contained in the 1970 census. Table 1 displays the metropolitan location of congressional districts used for the 1962 election before the Supreme Court decisions were made, in 1966 after most constituencies had been adjusted to conform to the equal population principle, and in 1974 when the congressional district boundaries were governed by the final reports of the 1970 census.

TABLE 1

LOCATION OF CONGRESSIONAL DISTRICTS

	1962	1966	1974
Metropolitan districts	254	264	305
central city	106	110	109
suburban	92	98	132
mixed metropolitan	56	56	64
Rural districts	181	171	130
Total	435	435	435

The 1970 census chronicled a decade of vibrant population mobility in the United States with a growing proportion of American citizens concentrating in the suburban portions of the country's expanding metropolitan areas. The decade's population shifts directed the redrafting of the nation's congressional district boundaries and transported 41 congressional districts—almost 10 percent of the total membership of the House of Representatives—from rural areas to metropolitan centers. This increased the number of congressional districts located in metropolitan areas from 264 to 305 and reduced the number of legislators from rural districts from 171 to 130. As expected, the suburban components of the country's metropolitan areas captured almost all of this increased metropolitan representation. The number of districts in Congress with a suburban majority increased from 98 in the years after the 1966 election to 132 after the electoral contests of 1974. The number of central city districts declined marginally during this period, while the number of mixed metropolitan constituencies divided between central cities and suburbs increased slightly. Projections for future decades indicate that suburban representation in Congress will continue to grow vigorously, while central cities and especially rural areas will be served by significantly fewer legislators in the decades ahead.[1]

POLICY IMPLICATIONS

Suburbs have undoubtedly been the prime beneficiaries of shifts in congressional representation during the past decade and will continue to benefit in the years ahead. Unfortunately, the policy implications of increased suburban representation are by no means so unequivocal. For some, the growth of suburbs constitutes a rejection of the values associated with urban life, and thus increased suburban representation will yield policies not notably different from those fashioned by legislatures dominated by rural representatives. For others, the growth of suburbs is simply the first step in an urbanization process that reflects the dissemination of urban policy perspectives to an ever larger portion of the nation's population. This section of the article examines the voting patterns of central city, suburban and rural members of Congress to establish their typical policy preferences and to appraise the impact of expanded suburban representation on congressional policy making.

Many debate whether the growth of suburbs will strengthen conservative forces in American politics or embolden liberal campaigners. The Americans for Democratic Action (ADA) and the Americans for Constitutional Action (ACA) are very much concerned with evaluating the liberalism and conservatism of in-

1. Richard Lehne, "Population Change and Congressional Representation," in U.S., Commission on Population Growth and the American Future, *Governance and Population* (Washington, D.C.: Government Printing Office, 1972), pp. 83–98.

dividual legislators. Both groups isolate a number of measures that have been voted upon in Congress to gauge the ideological positions of the men and women who serve in the House of Representatives. ADA and ACA ratings are based on the number of times each representative votes for the alternative preferred by the organization, with zero indicating complete rejection of the organization's viewpoints, and with 100 connoting full agreement with the group's perspectives. The mean values of these scores for suburban, urban and rural legislators are reported in table 2 for the Congress elected in 1966 and for the members serving in 1974, the last year for which ratings have been published.

The ACA and ADA ratings for both 1966 and 1974 consistently report that central city legislators express liberal policy positions, that rural representatives favor conservative alternatives, and that the men and women who come from suburban constituencies strike a moderate balance between the other two groups. On the ACA scale of conservatism, urban legislators averaged 26 of a possible 100 points in 1966, and 29 points of a possible 100 in 1974; members of Congress from rural districts were given an average score of 62 in 1966 and 56 in 1974; and in both years suburban delegates fit neatly between their rural and urban colleagues, with ratings of 46 in 1966 and 41 in 1974.

The ratings compiled by ADA present a mirror image of ACA offerings. Rural representatives supported the ADA-preferred side with sufficient frequency to earn scores of 22 in 1966 and 25 in 1974. At the opposite end of the spectrum were the central city representatives who voted for the alternative sanctioned by ADA more loyally than any other group, achieving ADA-approval scores of 63 in 1966 and 53 in 1974. Again, the suburban representatives appear to occupy a moderate position between the legislators from rural and urban districts, earning scores of 44 in 1966 and 41 in 1974.

The ideological implications of increased suburban representation in Congress can be established from these scores. Contrary to the belief that suburban legislators will unite with rural representatives to oppose liberal programs, the men and women who represent the nation's suburban constituencies in the halls of Congress are notably less conservative than their rural colleagues; they are also less liberal than their urban counterparts. With demo-

TABLE 2

IDEOLOGICAL RATINGS OF MEMBERS OF CONGRESS

	AVERAGE SCORE		
	CENTRAL CITY	SUBURBAN	RURAL
Americans for Constitutional Action			
1966	26	46	62
1974	29	41	56
Americans for Democratic Action			
1966	63	44	22
1974	53	41	25

graphic trends continuing to transport congressional representation from rural areas and, to a much lesser extent, from urban areas to suburban regions, the net effect on Congress will be a House of Representatives more moderate in its views, with a membership more receptive to liberal solutions to troubling policy problems.

Analysis of roll-call votes on specific issues reveals additional information about the policy preferences of suburban legislators. While the roll-call measures examined here are often procedural issues rather than votes on the final programs, these votes do reflect the pattern of legislative support for the goals of the particular pieces of legislation. Table 3 displays the percent of delegates from central city, suburban and rural districts who favored each of seven measures that came before the House of Representatives in the last year.

The first three issues are typical social service measures enlarging the role of the federal government in providing assistance to states and localities to expand their land use, education and public employment programs. The voting patterns on these social service measures reinforce the conclusions of the ACA and ADA indices. The greatest op-

position to each of these three measures comes from rural legislators, while the strongest support is voiced by representatives of central cities; the men and women who represent suburban constituencies occupy a position approximately midway between the liberally-oriented central cities and the more conservative rural areas on each of the three issues.

The next three measures offer governmental assistance to private interests to accomplish specified purposes. Suburban legislators were wholeheartedly in favor of guaranteeing funds to Penn Central and other railroads to maintain service in regions which are of direct concern to their constituents, registering a level of support equal to that of central city legislators. In contrast, suburban representatives favored repealing the subsidies that go to the oil industry through the oil depletion allowance, and they opposed increasing farm subsidies for cotton, wheat and corn more forcefully than with any other group in Congress. The final issue is one of support for military expenditures; the measure would have deleted funds for the new B-1 bomber program. Here we find that rural representatives provided the greatest support for the B-1 pro-

TABLE 3

POSITIONS ON SELECTED POLICY ISSUES

ISSUE	PERCENT OF REPRESENTATIVES IN FAVOR		
	CENTRAL CITY	SUBURBAN	RURAL
Grants for state land use programs	69	54	26
Increase education funding	76	65	52
Expanded public employment	83	60	55
Emergency railroad operations	78	79	47
Repeal of the oil depletion allowance	70	71	45
Increase cotton, wheat, corn subsidies	57	43	78
Delete funds for B-1 bomber	55	47	28

gram, while central city legislators were the group advocating deletion of the funds most unanimously. Suburban legislators again occupy a moderate position on the issue, but one that is closer to that of urban than rural members of Congress.

The growth of American suburbs has had unmistakable implications for congressional policy making. Increased suburban representation in Congress and the decline in the number of legislators from rural districts has enhanced support for typically liberal, social service measures, including railroad and mass transit measures; strengthened opposition to the oil depletion allowance and agricultural subsidies; and contributed to greater scrutiny of military expenditure requests. While the number of issues examined here (seven) is quite small, the conclusions of this presentation coincide with more extended analyses described elsewhere.[2]

PARTISAN PERSPECTIVES

Legislators from suburban districts adopt policy positions which are clearly distinct from those of the typical urban or rural representative. To the extent that the men and women elected from specific constituencies reflect the political attitudes of those districts, it is fair to conclude that public policy preferences differ from one type of district to the next. These differences are often expressed through the selection of either Republicans or Democrats to represent the constituencies in Congress. In the 1974 election, as in almost every election since World War II, a majority of congressional districts in the country selected Democratic candi-

2. *See*, for example, *Congressional Quarterly Weekly Report*, 11 April 1974.

dates to represent them—291 to 144. While electing a majority of candidates in every type of congressional district, Democratic candidates were clearly more popular in central cities, where they represented 87 percent of the districts, than in suburban or rural areas, where they served 56 percent and 60 percent of the constituencies, respectively.

Enlightening contrasts appear when we examine separately the voting patterns of the Republicans and Democrats who represent central cities, suburbs and rural areas in Congress. As Table 4 demonstrates, Democrats from every type of district support expanded social service programs more than do comparable Republicans. Democrats are more in favor of subsidizing railroads and agriculture, repealing the oil depletion allowance, and cutting funds for the B-1 bomber than are their Republican counterparts. Within both parties, rural legislators consistently adopt what are generally regarded as the most conservative policy positions.

Unmistakable patterns appear in the voting records of the men and women who represent the nation's metropolitan areas in Congress. On specific issues, legislators from the urban and suburban portions of metropolitan areas tend to vote like their party colleagues. Suburban Democrats usually vote like central city Democrats, and the voting patterns of Republicans from suburban districts resemble, although not as exactly, those of Republicans from central city districts. Thus, the characteristic differences that appear between average members of Congress from the suburbs and from central cities are a result of the different mixture of Republicans and Democrats coming from those areas.

TABLE 4

PARTISAN POSITIONS ON SELECTED POLICY ISSUES

| | PERCENT OF REPRESENTATIVES IN FAVOR | | | | | |
| | DEMOCRATIC | | | REPUBLICAN | | |
ISSUE	CENTRAL CITY	SUBURBAN	RURAL	CENTRAL CITY	SUBURBAN	RURAL
Grants for state land use programs	80	77	39	36	34	13
Increase education funding	84	92	71	29	29	26
Expanded public employment	93	99	82	25	11	15
Emergency railroad operations	86	91	55	38	62	35
Repeal of the oil depletion allowance	81	90	57	13	44	27
Increase cotton, wheat, corn subsidies	63	62	91	25	18	59
Delete funds for B-1 bomber	59	69	38	27	18	13

This does not necessarily mean, however, that partisan affiliation produces these differences. Constituencies elect different proportions of Democrats and Republicans partly because specific types of people live in individual districts. Table 5 presents a brief profile of the socio-demographic characteristics of suburban, urban and rural congressional districts. Suburban legislators in Congress represent areas that are faster growing, better educated, and financially more well-to-do than those served by other members of Congress. In urban and rural areas, the constituencies that elect candidates of one party look quite different from those who favor the other party. Republicans who come from central cities have districts whose populations are growing five times as rapidly as those in Democratic districts. In these Republican districts, the population density is only one-tenth as great; the proportion of black population is less than one-half as high; the median education level is almost one full year greater; and the average family income is approximately $1,000 more. Comparable differences appear between Democratic and Republican districts in rural areas. In both urban and rural regions, partisan differences among legislators usually amplify differences in constituency characteristics.

This is not the case with suburban districts. Surprisingly, average Republican and Democratic districts in the suburbs look quite like one another on each of the five demographic dimensions explored here: population growth rates, density, proportion black, education level and median family income. While the differences between central city Republicans and central city Democrats can easily be attributed to differences in the character of constituencies, this is not true of suburban Republicans and Democrats. While constituency characteristics provide an explanation for the voting patterns of urban and rural legislators, they are not helpful in distinguishing among suburban legislators, for whom the coincidence of ideology and partisanship is a more necessary component of an explanation of voting patterns.

TABLE 5

DEMOGRAPHIC CHARACTERISTICS OF CONGRESSIONAL DISTRICTS

	CENTRAL CITY		SUBURBAN		RURAL	
	DEMOCRATIC	REPUBLICAN	DEMOCRATIC	REPUBLICAN	DEMOCRATIC	REPUBLICAN
Population growth, 1960–1970 (percent)	6	30	23	25	9	13
Density (people per square mile)	1,237	116	191	140	10	8
Proportion of population black (percent)	22	9	7	6	13	5
School years completed	11.5	12.3	12.1	12.3	11.0	11.7
Median family income	$9,669	$10,631	$11,256	$11,522	$7,710	$8,525

An enhanced number of suburban representatives in Congress will bring more legislators with established ideological perspectives and more consistent partisan behavior into the daily workings of Congress. Since major themes in the analyses of suburban politics have been nonpartisanship in local governance and independence in popular voting, it is indeed ironic that partisan cleavages should be more basic among suburban legislators than among their rural or urban colleagues. While suburban constituencies apparently offer greater leeway for legislators' personal discretion, the contrast between a volatile electorate and representatives whose voting patterns follow partisan divisions could be a source of future tensions in American politics.

POLITICAL SIGNIFICANCE OF SUBURBIA

The policy positions of the men and women who represent the nation's suburbs in Congress have been examined and some implications of increased suburban representation have been discussed. The growth of suburbia has been such a dramatic phenomenon that it has prompted many observers to step back from the patterns of day-to-day events and appraise the basic meaning of the development of suburbia. Two analyses of the political significance of suburbia appearing in the last half-decade have been so widely received that they have shaped the rhetoric of political appeals and structured the logic of political strategists.

The first interpretation of the significance of suburbia is based on the fact that suburban areas have contained most of the nation's population growth in recent decades.[3] With this growth, an increasing proportion of the nation's voters are suburbanites, and these suburbanites have policy positions less favorable to expanded governmental services than those of urban representatives in Congress. The demography of suburban growth, according to this interpretation, is therefore very much on the conservative side, and the major thrust of the suburbanization of American politics will be a trend that is gently but profoundly conservative.

A more recent interpretation of the increasing suburban tide in Congress and in American politics generally detects not a repudiation of the role of government in society (which was advanced by the New Deal), but a continuation of that role. Community development patterns of the past decades have not suburbanized American politics, but instead have urbanized American suburbs. Suburbs are not the home of a new and powerful group in American society, but simply the new home of traditional elements of the American polity. Suburbs from this perspective are experiencing the first phase of an urbanization process, and as they age they will develop the traditional political styles and policy preferences of established urban areas.[4]

Fortunately, we can do better than blindly choose between these two interpretations of the basic significance of American suburbs. Suburban representation in Congress has undoubtedly increased in recent years, but the suburbs are not of a single type. Many people point out that Menlo Park is different from Baldwin Park, and Scottsdale does not have all the same attitudes and problems as East Detroit, yet each is a suburb. Some suburbs remain the dynamic, fast-growing home to a mobile middle class, but others have become established areas with the service demands and fiscal problems normally associated with larger urban centers.

To help evaluate the validity of the two competing interpretations of American suburban development, we have divided suburban congressional districts into two categories on the basis of their population growth rates between 1960 and 1970.[5] In this way the positions of legislators who represent older, established suburbs can be compared with those who represent the growing suburbs so frequently pictured in magazine and television advertisements. Secondly, the policy preferences of both groups of suburban representatives can be compared to those of legislators who come from central cities and rural areas. If legislators from established suburbs vote in ways quite similar to those who come from newer suburbs, we would conclude that there exists a distinct suburban perspective on policy matters which should become increasingly dominant in American politics as a growing proportion of the nation's population moves to suburban areas. If delegates from older suburbs depart significantly from representatives of new suburbs in voting patterns and adopt policy positions which closely

3. Perhaps the most popular expression of this view is found in Kevin P. Phillips, *The Emerging Republican Majority* (New Rochelle, N.Y.: Arlington House, 1969).

4. *See*, Louis H. Masotti and Jeffrey K. Hadden, eds., *The Urbanization of the Suburbs* (Beverly Hills, Calif.: Sage Publications, 1973).

5. For a further justification of this procedure, *see*, Sue Lederman, "The Impact of Suburban Residence on Political Attitudes" (Ph.D. diss., Rutgers University, 1976).

resemble those of urban members of Congress, this would lend additional support to the urbanization interpretation of suburban development.

Table 6 displays the average ACA and ADA ratings of the men and women who represent older and newer suburbs in Congress, together with their positions on the seven policy measures examined above. On almost every issue, clear differences of policy appear between the representatives of new and of established suburbs. Legislators from growing suburbs more frequently select policy alternatives favored by ACA and displeasing to ADA than do those from older suburbs. Legislators from established suburbs take more conventionally liberal positions on most issues than do delegates of new suburbs, even though the margins on some issues are not great. Only on the last issue, the proposal to delete funds for the B-1 bomber from the Pentagon budget, do representatives from older suburbs depart from the expected pattern—they provide less support to cut B-1 funding than do the legislators who represent new suburbs. These patterns do not emerge simply from the different proportions of Republican and Democratic legislators from older and newer suburbs; on the contrary, the patterns revealed in table 6—with minor exceptions—accurately reflect differences within the two major party delegations in Congress.

Not only do policy differences appear between the representatives of new and older suburbs, but the positions of suburban delegates from established areas resemble those of urban legislators quite closely. In some instances, the positions of the men and women who serve older suburbs are even more liberal or "urban" than are the positions of those from central cities. Democratic legislators from older suburbs, for example, have higher ADA ratings than do Democrats from central cities, and they voted more resoundingly to fund federal land use grants and educational aid, to expand the public employment program, to guarantee railroad subsidies, and to end the oil depletion allowance. These patterns support those who contend that the urbanization process has extended to the suburbs and who now find typically urban policy preferences among legislators from older suburban areas.

The future, however, remains un-

TABLE 6

POLICY POSITIONS OF SUBURBAN REPRESENTATIVES

	TOTAL	OLD SUBURBS	NEW SUBURBS
ACA rating	41	34	49
ADA rating	41	45	37
Federal land use grants	54%	61%	46%
Increase education funding	65	72	51
Expanded public employment	60	66	53
Emergency railroad funding	79	87	69
Repeal oil depletion allowance	71	74	68
Increase cotton, wheat, corn subsidies	43	45	41
Delete B–1 bomber funds	47	41	54

stresses the need to develop social indicators for assessing progress toward implementation of the values it espouses. In fact, with better use of available data Falk could have been more precise than he was.

The book is frustrating because certain crucial linkages are poorly drawn and because some analyses are never completely carried through. It is never very clear exactly how the institutions that are crucial elements in Falk's preferred world order would promote the four essential values. Growing public pressure for increased social and economic benefits is a fairly convincing mechanism for eventually bringing about disarmament and hence lessening the importance of the war system, and fear of nuclear and ecological disaster are potent forces leading in the direction of augmented central authority. Unfortunately, Falk is unable to suggest any equally convincing mechanism that would lead toward greater equity in the distribution of the gross global product. Falk deals with transnational corporations throughout the book, but in the end he remains ambivalent about under precisely which conditions these entities could contribute to his conception of a better world.

Falk argues that the first step toward the creation of his preferred world order must be the mobilization of segments of opinion, especially in the industrial countries and particularly the United States. His book is important because it will surely stimulate debate and consequently catalyze this mobilization. He viewed his book as a contribution to education, and he has achieved his purpose handsomely.

HAROLD K. JACOBSON
The University of Michigan
Ann Arbor

RICHARD HAMILTON. *Restraining Myths: Critical Studies of U.S. Social Structure and Politics*. Pp. 296. New York: Halsted Press, 1975. $15.00.

In this innovative work, Richard Hamilton has intelligently and persuasively challenged a number of the dominant social science theories. Much of the "conventional wisdom" in the social sciences results from three widely accepted traditions—the "centrist" position; the "mass society" theory; and the pluralist theory. Each of these theories makes a statement with respect to the capabilities of the public. Widespread acceptance of these theories results in support for restricting public participation in policy formulation. Professor Hamilton's re-evaluation of the available empirical evidence, however, raises serious doubts concerning the validity of each of these major theories. Thus, Professor Hamilton speaks of restraining myths.

The "centrist" position in the social sciences holds that the lower middle classes, due largely to extreme anxiety about maintaining their middle class position, will be a mean-spirited, reactionary force in politics. The restraining lesson here is that it would be extremely dangerous to activate this class.

The "mass society" theory emphasizes the rootlessness and isolation of the masses in contemporary urban, industrialized society. This lack of integration leaves the masses exposed and very vulnerable to the suasions of a demagogue, or to the manipulation of elites. The consequences of encouraging participation by the masses in public affairs are then very similar to the consequences of unleashing the lower middle classes in the "centrist" theory.

Pluralist theory holds that "power" has been effectively distributed within this society through the many voluntary organizations. These organizations are viewed as being responsive to the demands of the general populace and are held to be internally democratic. Through such representative, voluntary organizations every group has resources which may be used in the struggle with other groups to defend its particular interests. Hamilton sees the restraint in this theory resulting from the inhibition to promote further attempts to redistribute resources.

Hamilton offers the "group-bases" approach as a superior account of attitudes and behavior. The primary group setting is then the key in explaining differences in outlook. This is certainly a more convincing position than the "centrist" view that attitudes are essentially subject to "class" determinants. Impressive empirical evidence is marshaled against the "centrist" emphasis upon economic rewards and deprivations as the source of public attitudes and behavior. Hamilton's critiques of "mass society" and pluralist theories, while very suggestive, are somewhat less convincing since they are based upon one or two case studies which may not be typical.

This study will surely provide encouragement to those who have long believed in greater public capability. However, Professor Hamilton's alternative approach does not point to a new theory without restraints, but rather to the restraints of reality.

ALAN AICHINGER

Ohio University
Athens

ALEX INKELES and DAVID H. SMITH. *Becoming Modern.* Pp. viii, 437. Cambridge, Mass.: Harvard University Press, 1974. $15.00.

Becoming Modern, published last year, contains the authors' attempts to determine the modernity of people, in relation to what is generally considered the modern nation-state, in six countries —Argentina, Chile, India, Israel, Bangladesh, and Nigeria. The discussion of the study of the 6000 individuals who were interviewed is divided into four parts—The Fundamentals, Measuring Individual Modernity, Contexts and Causes of Modernization, and Summary and Conclusion.

In the first part Inkeles and Smith describe what they expect a modern man to embrace. They are especially interested in the characteristic mark of modern man which, according to them, has two parts: One part is external, the other internal; one deals with his environment, the other with his values, attitudes, and feelings. The change in external conditions of modern man is well known and widely documented. It can be summarized as the result of exposure to education, mass communi-

cation, urbanization, industrialization, and politicization. The citizens of a semi-modernized country live in urban surroundings which are physically modern, but not all the people in the large cities are equally affected by this modernity. We are more concerned with the internal aspects of modernization because in many urban societies the most traditional network of human relations may exist, especially in old quarters or new favelas of towns. In those areas recent immigrants or poor members of the urban community live, and their political and economic activity may not be very different from those of a hacienda or small village. But if we exclude this magnitude from the external conditions of modernization, the capitalistic or socialistic future of these societies is clearly established in the larger cities.

As for internal characteristics, consideration is given to twelve important variables which a modern individual will have: (1) readiness for new personal experiences; openness to invention and willingness to accept innovations in a variety of situations; (2) an inclination to welcome social change, such as extensive political participation and the breakdown of class and caste systems so as to permit the lifting of restrictions formerly applied to certain groups in a population; (3) a growing concern about wider issues along with the recognition and acceptance of varying opinions on them and the ability to hold opinions of a fundamental nature that may differ from the dominating opinion in the country; for example, the more educated a man is, the greater is his readiness to offer opinion and challenge accepted norms; the response is particularly advanced if he is educated in democratic principles and the society is undemocratic; (4) the desire to acquire information and facts on which to base his opinions; (5) an orientation to the present and future rather than to the past; a sense of time in general and in the organization of regular affairs; (6) faith in the ability of man to satisfactorily and successfully achieve eventual control of human life on every level and not succumb to any disastrous power exerted by nature or men; (7) an attitude favorable to long-term personal and public planning; (8) confidence that man by his actions can and will maintain an orderly and lawful world, dealing with its problems in a reasonable fashion rather than attributing them to fate or circumstances beyond those capable of explanation; (9) an appreciation of the differing value of technical skills and the ability to accept the performance of them as a valid basis for distributing rewards; (10) educational and occupational aspirations to enable him to become a member of the highly industrialized and scientific community of the world, with the prerequisite belief in the value of a scientifically and technologically oriented society; (11) an awareness and respect for the personal dignity of others; and (12) a rudimentary understanding of the logic of decision making in industry.

After having defined modernization of individuals, the authors discuss the research study, the conduct of the field work of the study, and then the OM (Overall Modernity) Scales, to measure individual modernity in general, on which the book's analyses are based. They believe that there is a syndrome of individual modernity which is reflected in responses to various aspects of daily life and in the OM Scales take into account all the components which are included in their definition.

To represent their concept of individual modern and traditional man, two Pakistani individuals are compared in Chapter V. This comparison provides readers with a clearer understanding of the depth of the study. The traditional man is Ahmadullah and the modern man Nuril, who had more or less common backgrounds in their youth and so had developed many similar attitudes which, however, in the third decade of their lives changed so that to a considerable degree one could be classified as traditional and the other as modern due to various contributing factors which are discussed in considerable detail.

The summarizing chapters raise many questions about manifestations of individual modernity and its social significance in many areas. There are several appendixes including one of the questionnaire, an excellent bibliography, and an index. The careful and thorough study and analyses which form the basis of this book are extremely interesting; some of the findings are sure to be challenged; all of it is exciting reading and I agree with Daniel Lerner who said, "*Becoming Modern* is a book for the decades."

BERT F. HOSELITZ

The University of Chicago
Illinois

PHILIP JESSUP. *The Birth of Nations*. Pp. viii, 361. New York: Columbia University Press, 1974. $14.95.

One of this country's most able and distinguished diplomats during the post World War II period has written seven case studies of the U.S. role in the culmination or, in some examples, the frustration of nation-building movements abroad. Philip Jessup's research puts many of his own experiences in the State Department and the United Nations in perspective, yet his thematic use of the metaphorical notion of the "birth" of nations hardly substitutes for an analytically useful conceptual framework.

Jessup examined diplomatic efforts which preceded the births of South Korea, Morocco and Tunisia, and Somalia, and a discussion of the legitimate but futile nationalist movement in Eritrea (about which so much more could be written since the publication of this book). The case of Manchukuo, an effort by Japan to legitimize its military aggression in Chinese Manchuria back in 1932 is also included. The latter provides a glimpse of a smaller but no less confusing State Department than today's version.

One of the most fascinating accounts of diplomatic activity describes the U.S. efforts to deal with the Palestine question in 1948. The author's disagreement with some other accounts of events during that year is clearly expressed. There was apparent vacillation of the U.S. position in the UN, supporting first partition (with economic union), then a UN trusteeship, then a UN mediation of the conflict, and finally a favorable reaction to Israel's declaration of independence on May 14, 1948. Jessup's personal account of his befuddled delegation's response to President Truman's surprise announcement of a *de facto* U.S. recognition brings to mind the embarrassment of the formal U.S. negotiating team at the conclusion of the SALT I talks in 1972. In the former case Jessup explains how the Presidential fiat threatened to undermine the diplomatic capabilities of the UN delegation.

Jessup's honest account of Bao Dai's "Abortive Empire" reveals the consensus in Washington that by the late 1940s Ho Chi Minh was a "tool of Moscow," "a Kremlin-inspired Communist" and "a Moscow stooge." Given such assumptions, the failure of Bao Dai logically led to a search for another non-communist alternative. Asian experts were well aware that Ho had the support of a majority of the Vietnamese people and they also had a sense of restraint about the limits of American power in Indochina. Nonetheless, the seeds for military intervention later were sown prior to the emergence of Ngo Dinh Diem.

One of the longer case studies—an example of difficult but ultimately fruitful U.S. and UN diplomacy—is the birth of Indonesia. A diligently constructive effort by the U.S. to cajole the Netherlands to relinquish their richest colonial possession generated much confusion and frustration in Washington, however. A 1949 telegram from Dean Rusk to Jessup asserting that the U.S. "cannot accept the role of world policeman either in a military or in a political sense if other permanent members refuse to join in action by the Security Council" is surely ironic in any other context.

As in many of the cases, the incessant flow of memoranda, conflict among bureaucratic agencies, and informal bargaining between second level officials eventually unraveled a policy shaped by forces and events over which diplomats had little control.

Impatient readers may not enjoy the highly personal and often rambling narrative. They may learn nonetheless of the ponderous machinations of the foreign policymaking bureaucracy that reacts slowly—albeit occasionally with wisdom—to the powerful forces of revolution, ideology, and nationalism in distant lands. Since Jessup has little to say about such forces, it may be difficult (for some) to distinguish the forest from the trees. Patient students of diplomatic history may find the book useful, however. The author's unique experience augmented by a judicious review of primary and secondary sources merits their attention.

PAUL CONWAY

State University College
Oneonta
New York

V. G. KIERNAN. *Marxism and Imperialism.* Pp. viii, 260. New York: St. Martin's Press, 1975. $18.95.

This is an amiably undogmatic collection of observations, by a self-styled "independent Marxist," on the history of imperialist theory. Kiernan has reworked five of his review articles and introduced them with a sort of "To the Finland Station" study of the backgrounds and main features of Lenin's concepts of imperialism. In this first essay he establishes the contributions of Angell and Brailsford to Lenin's notions, as well as the better-known work of Hobson, Bukharin, Hilferding, Kautsky, and Luxemburg; this first essay, I feel, is more useful than the now-outdated (1948) work of E. M. Winslow, *Patterns of Imperialism.*

Three of the pieces deal with imperialism in India and its crucial role in forming up Marxist and social democratic views of empire. Here Kiernan does a good job of explaining why Marx and Engels gave grudging approval to British conquest, and also how this skeleton in the closet of socialist theory has affected more recent polemics.

Another essay, "The Peasant Revolution: Some Questions," seems out of place, since its main purpose is not historiographical but rather to attack Maoist or Guevarist concepts of peasant movements in Third World countries and the impact of these concepts on the end of formal imperialism and on present thinking on neocolonialism. Unlike the other essays, this one is diffuse and superficial; it contains some absurdly romantic comments on the future of Guiné, and it is marred by today's headlines, since its predictions concerning Portuguese Africa have been shown to be embarrassingly wide of the mark.

The book's dust-jacket seems to promise that the reader will be treated to a critique of the dominant role of economics in Marxist views on imperialism and to a demonstration of the need to give "factors of political or socio-psychological order" more emphasis. But no elaborate revisionism or indeed any systematic theorizing is attempted; and this is only to be expected as soon as one realizes that the bulk of the book is composed of reworked review essays. Those who believe capitalist democracy has something positive to offer Third World countries and that capitalism can survive the end of empire without collapsing will draw only small comfort from Kiernan's critique of Leninist dogmatism, since Kiernan's discussions of non-economic causal factors are more in the nature of unsupported observations than tightly-organized theorizing. By the same token, those of the New Left who cling to neo-Leninism when considering neocolonialism will hardly feel their position is seriously threatened by Kiernan's work.

MARTIN WOLFE

University of Pennsylvania
Philadelphia

RICHARD B. MANCKE. *The Failure of U.S. Energy Policy.* Pp. vi, 189. New York: Columbia University Press, 1974. $10.00. Paperbound, $2.95.

MICHAEL TANZER. *The Energy Crisis: World Struggle for Power and Wealth.* Pp. 171. New York: Monthly Review Press, 1975. $8.95.

Two more dissimilar works covering similar ground would be hard to find. Both are useful, as they are in many respects complementary, with Tanzer valuable on the historical and power aspects of energy history and policy (for example, his survey of government policies abroad supportive of the international oil companies); Mancke useful for the analysis of the details of specific U.S. policies (pro-rationing, import policy, the Alaskan pipeline, and the effects of various kinds of taxes on supply). The differences reflect fundamental disagreement on values, methods, and thus the issues to be addressed. Mancke is firmly attached to the contemporary liberal perspectives of Heller, Okun, and in the specifically energy area, M.A. Adelman. Consistent with this outlook, Mancke is strongly wedded to free market solutions to micro-problems, and he also shares the nationalistic bent of neo-liberalism, looking at policy issues from a strictly U.S.-interest point of view. Another neo-liberal characteristic evident in Mancke is a de-emphasis on conflict and privilege as integral with and determinative of policy; for him they are abnormalities ("In the absence of clear public policy justification, governments normally [sic] do not sanction policies forcing the transfer of something valuable from one group of citizens to another"), reflecting policy errors or imperfect public understanding of the issues. These premises lead him to the absurd conclusion that our policy failures have rested on "technical" flaws—"the inability or unwillingness to coordinate existing policies" and a failure to adopt "flexible policies" adequately responsive to change.

Michael Tanzer, in contrast, an independent radical expert on the oil industry, brings to these issues an implicit Marxian-type framework in keeping with his more global, historic, and power-focused perspective. He is not fond of the free market, nor is he concerned primarily with U.S. interests. Thus, whereas Mancke disregards the historic relations between the international oil companies and Third World oil producers—Mancke's position is suggested by passing reference to the latter as "oppressed," in quotes—Tanzer deals with these relations in detail and makes no bones about his sympathy with the lesser breeds. Tanzer also sees conflict and privilege, not as abnormalities, but as built-in and *explaining* policy. Tanzer therefore devotes a great deal of his book to exploring the parties in conflict and the historic genesis of their interests, power, strategies and influence. His book is, in fact, organized on an interest group basis, with chapters on the international oil companies, the companies and their home governments, the oil exporting countries, Western Europe and Japan ("the losers"), the oil importing Third World countries, and the Communist states. This is a fruitful way of looking at energy issues, and parallels the format of Tanzer's earlier *Political Economy of International Oil and the Underdeveloped Countries* (Beacon, 1969).

Tanzer and Mancke agree that there is no energy crisis in the sense of an absolute shortage of energy resources. Both believe the crisis to be an artificial product of institutional arrangements. For Mancke it is the "immensely powerful" OPEC cartel, perhaps the most powerful cartel in history—a suggestion rather thinly based, given the fact that the cartel has been really effective for only two years, has no record of proven cohesiveness, and is subject to some potent constraints in the technological and military power of the buyer states plus the global possibilities of alternative sources of supply. (A number of experts have been forecasting an imminent collapse of this immensely powerful cartel.)

Tanzer puts a lot more weight on the historic role of the international oil companies and the supportive policies of their home governments. He stresses the post-1950 loss of energy self-sufficiency on the part of Western Europe and Japan, partly under U.S. prodding, and serving the interest of the oil companies. The lesser loss of self-sufficiency by the U.S. was also based in part on the interests of the internationals. Tanzer also discusses the evolution of the *private* oil cartel, which did the groundwork and provided the model and stimulus for producer country organization. Mancke uses "cartel" only in reference to OPEC, never as a description of the private arrangements arising out of Achnacarry in 1928 or the collective but company dominated monopoly situation before the late 1960s. Mancke suggests that the State Department played into the hands of OPEC by its interventions in 1970–1971. But Tanzer shows that the oil companies themselves dragged their feet in supporting Occidental in its dealings with Libya, and he makes a good case that the organization and firming up of OPEC was acquiesced in and partially supported by the Seven Sisters. They shared directly in the huge oil revenue increases, and the domestic impact on the value of oil company coal and uranium, and in putting constraints on the environmental movement, were favorable to the companies. In the very short-run, at least, policy was "misguided" and a "failure" only on the assumption that its ends were those postulated in a naive political model.

However, just as Mancke underrates the subordination of U.S. policy to the interests of the oil companies, Tanzer unduly plays down the conflict of interest between the Seven Sisters and OPEC. Oil company support appears to have been an opportunistic effort to maintain *some* privileged position in a situation where the Sisters saw no practicable way of avoiding their own serious loss of power. Their gains from the 1973 oil price increases were short-lived, as OPEC has quickly squeezed company per barrel returns back to pre-1973 levels or lower; and the oil companies have suffered substantial profit declines and face a highly uncertain future (inducing many of them to attempt major diversifications entirely outside the energy field).

There is some question whether before 1973 the U.S. ever had an energy "policy" in any meaningful public interest sense, as opposed to *ad hoc*, short run adjustments to immediate necessities, plus subsidies and other forms of intervention oriented primarily to enhancing the profitability of special energy interests. There was no effort made to influence the demand for energy, and supply has been left to private enterprise—aided and supported by government, but without coordination or plan. Mancke rejects any intervention on the side of demand as a paternalistic interference with free choice. And in the end there is no proposal from Mancke for any kind of plan that would amount to any radical break with the past. What he recommends is "a flexible groping strategy." On environmental matters Mancke favors "strong measures," not because of any threat of apocalypse, but because "large elements of the American citizenry now regard pollution as undesirable." This he regards as a matter of "aesthetic" taste, and if this public taste weakens, Mancke will regretfully bid environmental control farewell. This ostrich-like faith in informed choice in both markets and politics has carried Mancke successfully through both the Nixon era and his own studies of the evolution of, say, the depletion allowance.

Tanzer pulls together politics and economics in a far more sophisticated manner—his is a work in political economy. Mancke offers us competent economics in a series of useful microeconomic studies, covering matters largely disregarded by Tanzer in his more sweeping picture. In brief, both of these volumes in their own distinct ways have illuminating things to say about energy issues.

EDWARD S. HERMAN
Wharton School
University of Pennsylvania
Philadelphia

ABRAHAM YESELSON and ANTHONY GAGLIONE. *A Dangerous Place: The United Nations as a Weapon in World Politics*. Pp. 240. New York: Grossman Publishers, 1974. $8.95.

GERALD L. STEIBEL. *Detente: Promises and Pitfalls*. Pp. ix, 89. New York: Crane, Russak & Co., 1975. $4.95.

Yeselson's and Gaglione's *A Dangerous Place* and Steibel's *Detente* are concerned with international conflict and how it could be lessened. Yeselson and Gaglione contend that efforts toward world peace could be furthered if the United Nations were ignored as much as possible. Steibel analyzes the increasingly less intractable conflict between the United States and the Soviet Union. With these divergent aims, the authors also use different intellectual approaches. Yeselson and Gaglione seek to explain how states in general act in world politics; Steibel seeks to evaluate the promises and pitfalls of the United States' policy toward the Soviet Union in the 1970s.

Given Yeselson's and Gaglione's approach, the standards that they should be expected to meet would have to include essentials such as having a well-grounded conceptual framework and adequate substantiation. In their efforts to show that states act in a different way than they have been previously perceived to have acted—and, therefore, that the UN should be ignored as much as possible because it is a dangerous place, given the way states are now seen to act—they fail to meet these standards with much room to spare.

They set up a straw man (implicitly representing most political scientists interested in the United Nations) who believes that because states have ratified the UN Charter, they will always live up to it. That is, states no longer will act politically. Yeselson and Gaglione then claim to create a framework according to which states will now be seen as trying to advance their own interests. For example, they assert, as if they just recently discovered it, that states will seek to have issues brought up in the body of the UN in which they will have the greatest chance of succeeding.

Besides making very routine "discoveries" that have been written about for at least twenty-five years, their approach is terribly inadequate. Conceptually, they confuse the interests of the respective member states and the interests of the UN (p. 12) and treat the idea of a state's national interest as if it were as clear-cut as a road sign. Furthermore, they fail to substantiate many of their claims—for example, that "size, wealth, location, religion, ideology, levels of technology do not affect [the likelihood of war]" (p. 166) or that "the Soviet Union did not accept the Baruch Plan for nuclear disarmament or 'open skies' *because* [my italics] they were approved by majorities in the U.N." (p. 178).

The standards that Steibel should be expected to meet are different—to analyze perceptively recent events and to appraise objectively their significance in order to make fruitful recommendations. Steibel meets some of these standards very well. His analyses and appraisals in the first six of the seven chapters—focusing mainly on arms control (a failure), crisis management (a failure), and trade (a success)—are balanced and cogent.

In his last chapter, however, in what should have been his synthesis, Steibel is disappointing. Besides dredging up "proof," mostly from Lenin's and Stalin's writings, that Communists have fairly fixed ideological goals, he ends up recommending that the United States deal with the Soviet Union by following such maxims as "know(ing) when to be patient, when to act" and "negotiat(ing) quid pro quo." He fails to give an overall answer to the question in his title—detente: promises or pitfalls? Moreover, after evaluating the separate issues, he does not take the next step and recommend policies for making detente more productive or evaluate how productive detente ever might be.

Thus, if one wants to understand more about international conflict or a particular conflict from these books, one will only get a well-balanced analysis of recent relations between the United States and the Soviet Union. In order to find out how the tough intellectual problems are being tackled, such as explaining how states behave in international politics and the UN and using what we know about recent events in order to make better policies, one will have to read elsewhere.

ROBERT SZAKONYI

Athens
West Virginia

ASIA, AFRICA, EUROPE AND LATIN AMERICA

THOMAS J. ANTON. *Governing Greater Stockholm: A Study of Policy Development and System Change.* Pp. 259. Berkeley: University of California Press, 1975. $12.95.

Political scientist and policy analyst Thomas Anton has an important message in his excellent study of urban government and political change in the Swedish capital. In the author's own words, "mid-twentieth century cities need not be dangerous and decaying relics of a former age; efficient function need not destroy beauty and liveability; in this age, on this earth, a group of men entrusted with the future of their urban environment have behaved responsibly, and with a measure of success that the rest of the world can envy, if not emulate" (p. 208). Such conclusions are the result of Professor Anton's selective but detailed analysis of political action and institutional change in post-war Stockholm. This third volume in the Lane Studies in Regional Government also deals with a metropolitan area that experienced explosive growth since 1945; over 450,000 people were added to Stockholm's regional population by the late 1960s. This study not only treats the policies necessary to cope with these quantitative pressures, but the responses which simultaneously sought to make qualitative improvements in the nature of urban life.

The first part of this study describes the political, social, and cultural environment in which Swedish urban policies are made. Anton is quite sensi-

Nazism·Communism·Fascism

POLITICAL VIOLENCE UNDER THE SWASTIKA
581 Early Nazis
PETER H. MERKL

"Few books provide as much insight into the nature of the Nazi movement. Here we are faced with a primary source in the autobiographies, not of top leaders, but of the middle cadres of the movement, and rank-and-file followers. At the same time we are not confronted with a literary or journalistic account, but with solid empirical, quantitative, social science analysis of those data. The study is therefore a model for future research on social movements and a mine of evidence for many theoretical propositions."—*Juan J. Linz, Yale University*   Cloth, $30.00 • Limited Paperback Edition, $10.75

COMMUNISM IN ITALY AND FRANCE
Edited by DONALD L. M. BLACKMER
and SIDNEY TARROW

The contributors to this volume have addressed themselves to the growth, behavior, and prospects of the two largest Communist parties in Western Europe. The book deals in particular with the adaptation of the French and Italian Communist parties to the secular changes in their advanced societies. "This is a very significant contribution to Western European studies as well as studies of comparative communism. I expect it to be in the forefront of what is likely to be the next phase in the evolution of comparative politics."—*Samual H. Barnes, University of Michigan* $25.00

ITALIAN INTERVENTION IN THE SPANISH CIVIL WAR
JOHN F. COVERDALE

"A very important contribution based on painstaking archival research and offering new insights into a complex and highly controversial problem area. This monograph is not only important to historians of modern Spain, particularly of the Civil War and the Franco regime, but also to students of Italian Fascism and its policies. Any student of foreign interventions in internal civil conflicts would benefit from reading it."—*Juan J. Linz, Yale University* $18.50

Now in Paperback
MUSSOLINI AND FASCISM
The View from America
JOHN P. DIGGINS

"A sobering work that enhances our understanding of the appeals of Fascism and the nature of American society."—*Foreign Affairs*
Winner of the John H. Dunning Prize of the American Historical Association.
Paper, $3.95 • Cloth, $18.00

Order from your bookstore or direct from
PRINCETON UNIVERSITY PRESS
Princeton, New Jersey 08540

tive to the different normative aspects of local government, and, as in previous works, he is able to capture concisely important elements of Swedish political culture. He raises the hypothesis to which he frequently returns that in the trade-off between citizen participation in local government and the competence and service of local political institutions, Swedes overwhelmingly have placed greater value on the latter. Local government and community are means to an end. To be certain, opportunities for participation do exist, but except for the most recent developments, Anton's discussion of Stockholm's government focuses on the policy-making elites. Among the many interesting facts brought to light in this part is the administrative and legal flexibility of Swedish local government. Particularly interesting is the ability of urban polities to create nominally "private" companies to carry out policy ends. Although not uniquely Swedish, such entities have easier access to capital and are freed of many political constraints.

The second section of the book provides solid case studies in three major policy areas: planning, housing, and transportation. Although discussions of Swedish efforts in these critical areas have been available in English before, Anton's study is surely among the first to integrate them so well and provide a critical perspective. Housing particularly has been a controversial domain, because Swedes want urban housing to be easily available (which it was not until the early 1970s), inexpensive (which it is not, although various subsidies help large segments of the population), and physically attractive (which it is, comparatively, but not without justified criticism).

The final section discusses "patterns of participation" as can be deduced from the case studies. Two images emerge forcefully. The first is the powerful and aloof position of urban political leaders (City Commissioners). Anton introduces a cast of determined and resourceful men, for whom Stockholm's prosperity and growth repre-

sented a vital political goal. The personality and career of long-term Social Democratic commissioner Hjalmar Mehr is extensively depicted. A second image is that of general deference by the population to the urban administrative and political elites. Given proportional representation of city and county councils, there is a remarkable continuity of policy-makers even though elections may occasionally change portfolios. Anton suggests that the major confrontations of the post-war expansion of Stockholm were between urban and suburban politicians and, less frequently, between those demanding greater resources for the cities and national political leaders. Citizens often voiced their frustrations, but rarely did they trouble the narrow circle of policy elites. The press as well gave minimal coverage to urban policy controversies. Anton suggests as have other observers of Swedish politics that Swedes treat political competition as a variable sum game, in which a successful compromise and outcome will benefit all and a failure will hurt all (albeit not equally). Contemporary politics in American urban centers has more closely resembled a negative or at best zero game.

Professor Anton's well-written and thoughtful study is thus an invaluable addition to the policy literature. Students of urban regional government and comparative public policy, as well as those seeking hope that urban problems can be treated at times with considerable success, will find this a work into which they may profitably sink their teeth.

ERIC S. EINHORN
University of Massachusetts
Amherst

RAMÓN L. BONACHEA and MARTA SAN MARTÍN. *The Cuban Insurrection, 1952–1959.* Pp. 451. New Brunswick, N.J.: Transaction Books, 1974. $12.95. Paperbound, $4.95.

Fidel Castro's ascent to power in 1959 has stimulated an extensive body of historical and political literature, much of which is either superficial, biased, or both. The recent study by Bonachea and San Martín, however, is a scholarly, well-documented, and exceptionally well-written account of the attempt to overthrow dictator Fulgencio Batista during the period from 1952 to 1959.

This book is not exclusively or even primarily an examination of the revolutionary activities of Fidel Castro. Rather it describes the loosely-coordinated and heterogeneous efforts of a number of anti-Batista groups. The authors examine the Moncada attack of 1953, the early student movement, the Granma expedition of 1956, the palace attack and Cienfuegos uprising of 1957, the abortive urban strike of spring 1958, the government's equally ill-fated summer offensive and the victorious westward march of the rural guerrillas.

Writing from the "point of view of the Cuban insurrectionists," the authors hold certain frankly-stated opinions. For one, they express contempt for the role played by the established Communist party. "Like their comrades in Latin America, Cuban Communists were as comfortably bourgeois as the members of the oligarchy with whom they were always on the best of terms" (p. 25). "Far more to the right than Batista . . ." (p. 221), they actively collaborated with the dictatorship throughout most of the period, reversing that policy only in mid-1958 when it became apparent to practically everyone that Batista's days in office were numbered.

Similarly, Bonachea and San Martín hold strong opinions about Fidel Castro. Although they describe him as a consummate politician and a valiant and dedicated revolutionary, they also depict him as an opportunist capable of intrigue and double-dealing. Fidel, they note, was not above privately soliciting financial support from the same traditional politicians he often denounced in public. Also, in April of 1958, Castro instigated but subsequently failed to support an urban uprising in Havana which resulted in the liquidation by the police of many of Fidel's potential rivals within the guerrilla movement. Finally, in May of the same year, he formed a pact with the Communist Party whose members had, scant weeks before, served as government informers during the bloodily-suppressed strike.

Another interesting aspect of this book is its treatment of the important role played in the insurrection by concepts such as honor, personal dignity, and the mystique of manliness— "machismo," if you will. The information which the authors provided clearly indicates that the Cuban revolution might never have taken place had not thousands of Cuban youths made virtually-suicidal individual commitments to rid their country of a dictator whom each viewed as an affront to his or her personal dignity. Their frequent and usually ill-fated acts of violence slowly demoralized the dictatorship, drained its *jefe* of his mystique and ultimately gave an almost supernatural aura to Fidel Castro, the symbol and most important survivor of the insurrectionary process.

In sum, this book is a scholarly and unusually engrossing treatment of a very important subject. Though certain opinions are expressed, the authors are thorough and effective in their documentation of those positions. *The Cuban Insurrection* is highly recommended not only for classroom and professional use but also as enjoyable reading for the interested public.

THOMAS W. WALKER
Ohio University
Athens

LOWELL DITTMER. *Lin Shao-ch'i and the Chinese Cultural Revolution: The Politics of Mass Criticism*. Pp. 404. Berkeley: University of California Press, 1974. $12.95.

The Chinese biographical tradition was a straightforward one—biographies, praised or blamed, were exercises in hagiography or demonology. That tradition still lives, certainly in the case of Liu Shao-ch'i, who holds an all-time record for villification. Mr. Dittmer's study of the demon and poisonous weed, now exterminated, is also an examination of the process and the means of his transformation from Mao Tse-tung's successor into the enemy of the people. Mr. Dittmer uses two biographical techniques. First, he gives a straightforward chronological account of Liu's rise and fall. The result of Mr. Dittmer's voluminous research is tantalizing: he gives a gripping account of Liu's *via dolorosa* during the Great Proletarian Cultural Revolution, but much of Liu's earlier career remains shrouded in mystery. There is very little on a critical formative experience, as director of underground work in Kuomintang-ruled north China. Mr. Dittmer's second technique is biographical comparison, between the victim and his vanquisher. He sets up a dichotomy between the revolutionary romantic and the organization man, a dichotomy which gradually moves into polarization and hostility. The attractions of this approach are obvious; it corresponds to the Chinese version, and it permits a systematic, formal analysis using models, statistics and charts. But it also distorts. It sets up two individuals in exaggerated, stereotypic roles. Seeing Liu as an organization man downplays the fact that he achieved his greatest praise (and his greatest blame) in a different role, as a moral philosopher, as the author of *How to be a Good Communist*. It is easy to equate organization with bureaucracy, with formality, with pettiness, and to juxtapose it with the excitement, and panache of revolutionary romanticism, but it does not necessarily enlighten us about Liu. Mr. Dittmer makes many perceptive comments on Liu and on Mao, but his basic dichotomy forces him to simplify and pigeonhole two highly complex people: sober, upright, cautious, boring, plodding Liu; fiery, dynamic, unpredictable, brilliant Mao. Mr. Dittmer's attempt to objectify, to give a rational interpretation places his subjects in a framework which constricts and distorts them. Nor does it solve the problem of objectivity. Fitting what is often highly subjective material into an objective framework gives no guarantee of transforming subjective into objective.

Mr. Dittmer seems to realize this, to feel that formal analysis, frequency counts, charts, models and the like may not produce a deep understanding of complex individuals. But he assumes that concepts evolved in western political science (in this case communications theory) must have direct relevance to China. This is a dangerous assumption, one that Ezra Vogel has called "Right Adventurism." All the detail and the careful tabulation of the charges launched against Liu seem secondary to the fundamental questions about Liu's downfall. Mr. Dittmer implies, almost by the way, the workings of an agent which is not quantifiable— accident. He shows disparate pressures converging on Liu, turning him into a symbol of evil, or a scapegoat for others, a man then who is not an obvious candidate for destruction, but whom the historical process has grabbed by the throat.

DIANA LARY

York University
Ontario
Canada

JOHN K. FAIRBANK. *China Perceived: Images and Policies in Chinese-American Relations*. Pp. xx, 245. New York: Alfred A. Knopf, 1974. $7.95.

C. L. SULZBERGER. *Postscript with a Chinese Accent: Memoirs and Diaries, 1972–1973*. Pp. 401. New York: Macmillan, 1974. $10.00.

For the most part this is an edited, slightly revised and abridged collection of articles written since 1946 by the dean of American historians of modern China. Not only has Professor Fairbank lived parallel with many of the trends interpreted; he also puts China's cultural and political relations with the West in still longer historical perspective. Whether lecturing or writing, he is a master at summation, analytical observation, and the art of the historical essay. His brush is, therefore, often broad. These pieces reveal again his long interest in American and Chinese perspectives and images of each other as sojourners, transactors and civilizations. He calls China "the most distinctive and separate of the great historical cultures," and tends to minimize the degree to which China, in some periods, has borrowed from abroad.

With respect to China and its foreign relations, and to U.S. policies in East Asia, this volume can be considered part of the re-evaluation process that has been underway since the tide turned against the American intervention in Vietnam. But the author has all along been a reputable critic of what he again calls two decades of "mindless American activism" toward China. As a leading educator he is doubtless correct in stressing the need for more knowledge about East Asian countries, especially China, and for the utilization of such insights in the making of national policies. Yet the records show that American official policy-makers have not so much lacked information, even analyses, as they have been narrowed by preconceptions, entrenched interests, and power political considerations in reaching decisive judgments. One cannot be sure that a larger reservoir of well trained linguists and historians of China would have avoided the pitfalls. In these essays one finds an admirable, illuminating grasp of Chinese history and the modern Chinese revolution, but not much linkage of world politics to foreign policy-making.

Dilemmas have existed in Sino-American relations; some of them are mentioned as such in this volume. The author asserts (and makes a partial case for) but would not satisfy some observers that Taiwan has become the "last of the treaty ports." He advocates its reintegration with the mainland despite the significant differences in living levels; that nearly 15 million Chinese would be forced to live under one of the most powerful—certainly the most minutely manipulative—of dictatorships seems not to trouble him. On pages 168–69 one finds his apologia for the guided tour. There is no mention of the closed society and only oblique reference to the problems of the free exchange of ideas. Ideological problems, and particularly those that reached a crescendo during the Cultural Revolution, are detoured.

One of the most interesting essays (in Part Three) is an illustrated study of Chinese perceptions of the West and of Westerners in the 1880s. The next part contains accounts of five Americans who were able to travel in and write about China in critical periods of change. In certain passages (for example, on pages 4, 9, 10, 14, 18, 19, 57, 60, 197–198) Professor Fairbank waxes prophetic in ways that are stimulating to thought and expectation.

In a journalistic sense, Mr. Sulzberger prepared for the visit he and his wife made to parts of People's China (for one month: September to late October 1973) by interviews with chiefs of state and officials—especially in Asian affairs sections—of foreign ministries in Paris, Washington and in several capitals from Israel to Japan. During his talk with Secretary Kissinger he was told part of the rationale for the U.S. tilt toward Pakistan during the struggle in which East Pakistan became Bangladesh. Kissinger commented that "we know perfectly well that Peking will continue to be our opponent." Still, as the world is aware, he regards the PRC as such an important counterpoise to the Soviet Union that American-Chinese détente is regarded as essential.

Most of what appears here concerning China was currently reported in the author's well known column in *The New York Times*. Sulzberger is an intelligent, articulate, energetic journalist in the field. His visit to the Inner Mongolian capital of Huhehot was a rare opportunity. His report from Sian is especially interesting. In addition he spent a few days each in and around Tatung in northern Shansi, Yenan, Nanking, Shanghai, and Hangchow. Just before departing from Peking, he was given a two-and-a-quarter hour interview with Premier Chou. The most interesting part of that exchange was Chou's rather comprehensive statement regarding Sino-Soviet boundary problems. Sulzberger agrees with others that, on the Chinese side, too, there are no illusions about détente. He adds his impression that the Chinese are basically anti-foreign, though polite.

One who is not an Asian expert should have had his manuscript checked so as to avoid such a resented term as "Chinaman" and a number of misspelled historical and geographical references. On page 341 it is apparent that he did not know that K'ung was the surname of Confucius.

ALLAN B. COLE

The Fletcher School of Law and
   Diplomacy
Tufts University
Medford
Massachusetts

HARRY N. HOWARD. *Turkey, the Straits and U.S. Policy.* Pp. xii, 330. Baltimore, Md.: The Johns Hopkins University Press, 1974. $14.50.

The author, for over twenty years a State Department official involved with Middle Eastern affairs, has produced his fourth addition to the history of American foreign relations in the region. The present work analyzes U.S. reponses to the centuries-old Straits Question. Chapters I through V summarize the very minor role played by the U.S. up to the Second World War; the remaining three chapters describe American policy from 1941 to approximately 1960, as the U.S. took over Britain's position in defending the western democracies against Russian expansion into the Mediterranean.

The U.S., though involved commercially in the Middle East since the nineteenth century, consistently refused to become involved politically in the Straits Question until the 1940s. The first direct association came in 1941 with the Lend-Lease Agreement. Following the war, American policymakers deemed Turkey and the Straits vital to the accessibility of the Suez Canal and Middle Eastern oil—ultimately to the safety of western Europe. In 1947, when the Soviets appeared determined to absorb Turkey, President Truman offered American assistance. Turkey's usefulness to American global strategy in the Cold War was reciprocated by U.S. financial and military aid; her membership in NATO (1952) crowned the relationship.

Contrary to what the book jacket implies, the author unfortunately devotes only ten pages to the period after the mid-1960s. Though he speaks of "anti-American and neutralist sentiments" in Turkey by 1964, he does not mention the cause: President Johnson's overbearing demand that Turkey cease its invasion of Cyprus—an undertaking the Turks felt vital to their national security. He also fails to explain the genesis of those American policies which, since 1967, have virtually assured Soviet access to ports in several Mediterranean Arab states, and which caused the Turks to fear that such bases make them as vulnerable to the Russians as ever in the nineteenth century.

Despite these flaws, the author explains clearly America's historic interest in the Straits: their strategic importance in regard to Russian expansion, and their commercial importance in regard to Mediterranean trade. He notes recent Soviet moves to neutralize Turkish ties with the West, and strongly implies that continuing cordial relations with the Turks will best serve the interests of the U.S.

WILLIAM J. GRISWOLD

Colorado State University
Fort Collins

HUBERT C. JOHNSON. *Frederick the Great and His Officials.* Pp. vi, 318. New Haven, Conn.: Yale University Press, 1975. $17.50.

Most famous of Prussia's rulers, Frederick the Great achieved reputation primarily for his conduct of war and diplomacy. His role within his realm, however, has always been difficult to understand. While admirers have pictured him as autocratic and omniscient, critics claim that he was little more than the servant of his own vassals and officials. Johnson's opinion is that the truth lies between these extremes and that Frederick governed in close partnership with those officials fortunate enough to enjoy his almost unlimited trust.

Frederick's conquest of Silesia made Prussia a first-rank power in Europe, but one very much hampered by a third-rate civil service and conservative ministers unwilling to adapt to the challenges of Prussia's new position. The Seven Year's War gave Frederick the chance to overhaul the machinery of his administration. He gave immense authority over the entire excise system to a consortium of French entrepreneurs and to the remarkable minister Hagen. Although his dream of a modern state and his loose direction of this amalgam of forces were ultimately defeated by the conservatism of a serf-ridden, noble-dominated society, they hold important lessons for administrative history, political sociology, and political science.

Johnson has produced a book of real distinction, the fruit of thirteen years of research in both published and unpublished material; the archives of the old Prussian state, now in Merseburg and Potsdam, provided both new material and new insights. Probably no reader will go through the detailed work from cover to cover, well-documented throughout, but those who will will be also generously rewarded.

JOSEPH S. ROUCEK

Bridgeport
Connecticut

VICTOR D. LIPPIT. *Land Reform and Economic Development in China: A Study of Institutional Change and Development Finance.* Pp. xi, 183. White Plains, N.Y.: International Arts and Sciences Press, 1974. $15.00.

DWIGHT H. PERKINS, ed. *China's Modern Economy in Historical Perspective.* Pp. viii, 344. Stanford, Calif.: Stanford University Press, 1975. $13.85.

Victor Lippit's fine little book analyzing and taking the measure of the role that land reform played in providing an important portion of the wherewithal to finance the economic development of the People's Republic of China (PRC) is a modest yet quite praiseworthy contribution to the political economy of the PRC. The author felicitously combines analytic tools and quantitative measures within a framework of institutional change to help explain how the Chinese successfully generated a high level of national savings and investment (over 20 percent) where before the revolution that level was quite low (about 2 percent).

The author makes a strong case that China's land reform led to a contradiction in the consumption of owners of land and other property in agriculture and in consumption made possible by their loans thus enabling an increase in national savings available for development investment—an outcome at variance with the conventional wisdom that China was too poor to develop by herself except at the expense of the peasants. The author concludes that the land reform changed "the institutional structure in China's countryside, . . . solidified support for the new regime, increased the income of those who needed it most, laid the basis for egalitarian, socialist economic development, and channeled a portion of the agricultural surplus into increased national savings and investment."

The surplus from the countryside making higher levels of investment possible came from luxury consumption and dissaving in agriculture that the land reform eliminated. Since the property owners whose consumption was reduced did not contribute much labor input to production, incentives were not unfavorably affected. The redirected income flows made potentially available almost 19 percent of net domestic product for investment finance at very little cost in foregone investment. Part of this newly released surplus was siphoned off through taxes and part through terms of trade unfavorable to agriculture (though this latter situation was reversed in later years).

Professor Lippit not only has clarified for students of the Chinese revolution the role land reform has played in facilitating the PRC's development, but he has also drawn some useful inferences from China's experiences to apply to other developing economies. In the Chinese case the impact of land reform on income distribution rather than on productivity has been stressed. Some of the experiences of the Chinese are relevant in the cases of other countries though political possibilities are often constraining factors. This book, thus, not only sharpens one's view of the Chinese development process but suggests re-thinking of the different positive roles land reform can play in struggling to overcome poverty.

Dwight H. Perkins' collection of ten papers from a Bermuda conference in 1973 deals mainly with the extent to which China's post-revolution economy was shaped by continuities of the past. In doing this the nine authors, scholars from Canadian, British, and U.S. universities, have performed an important service since the historical underpinnings of the Chinese economy have been much neglected in the rush to throw light on the economic development process of the People's Republic of China (PRC).

Most of the papers focus on China's twentieth century economy and those conditions which determined the structure and technology of its industrial sectors and their social relationships. Several deal with traditional and pre-Republican China: its skills and resources (Elvin), the "standard market" which patterned economic and social institutions (Fei), cooperative institutions in agriculture (Myers), and the role of the foreigner in economic development (Dernberger). Once again the balance in coverage is heavily skewed toward the contemporary period, a function both of differential scholarly interest and availability of data.

The papers on twentieth century China provide a quite useful perspective and significant data on a slowly emerging modern economy. Professor Perkins, editor and contributor, emphasizes the power of continuity in his assertion that "traditional Chinese society appears to have nurtured within itself certain values and traits more compatible with modern economic growth than those of many other less-developed states." These included a high degree of commercialization, a bimetallic monetary system, numerous heavily populated cities, private land ownership, high man-land ratio, literary requirements for government officials, and high value accorded to education and literacy.

And yet one still wonders why China did not develop rapidly, as Japan did, for so long. The papers by Dernberger, Riskin (on surplus and stagnation), and Schran (Yenan origins of current economic policies), supplemented by data and generalizations from the other contributors (Chao and Rawski), help to throw some light on the question. Dernberger sees both positive and negative impacts from foreign trade and investment. Among the negative were impacts on the structure of trade and investment which impeded the development of a modern sector. Riskin demonstrates that despite China's poverty she did have the potential surplus that "dwarfed the highest investment rates . . . of now-industrialized countries"; and Schran shows strong continuity from the Yenan period (1937–45) when the Chinese Communist Party (CCP) developed economic policies and mechanisms that were key to the PRC's later rapid development. There seemed to be an important element after 1949 that reaped from the continuities of the past but also changed them—the policies and programs of the CCP. This is not boldly stated in the book but it is a reasonable inference that one can draw.

Collections of papers often suffer the deficiency of unevenness and lack of focus. This work avoids these pitfalls: it is of good quality throughout and all papers relate effectively to the main concern—the continuities of the past.

The data and the analysis provide a helpful historical introduction to the contemporary Chinese economy and revolution.

CHARLES HOFFMANN
State University of New York
Stony Brook

JAMES W. MORLEY, ed. *Prologue to the future: The United States and Japan in the Postindustrial Age.* Pp. v, 232. Lexington, Mass.: Lexington Books, 1974. $15.00.

This is an interesting compendium of essays by American and Japanese scholars in diverse fields. The disparate chapters, each by a different scholar, are seemingly held together by a thin strand of expectational experiences in the postindustrial period. In fact, only Morley's introductory essay attempts to hold to the stated theme—the others each take off in their respective fields of interest with meandering relevance to the main motif. There is little agreement among the scholars as to what is meant by "postindustrial" society.

Morley, Heilbroner and Huntington examine the term in some depth but emerge with little common ground in conceptualization. Huntington is perhaps the most definitive. Leaning heavily on Daniel Bell, Huntington maintains that individual postindustrial society theorists, while stressing different aspects of the concept, would generally agree on the following as central elements distinguishing postindustrial from industrial and agrarian society: (1) "The economic predominance of the service sector in contrast to that of the industrial and agricultural sectors"; (2) "The predominance in the labor force of white-collar in contrast to blue-collar workers and, particularly, the large size and critical role in the economy of professional, technical and managerial workers"; (3) "A central role in the economy and society of theoretical knowledge, technology, research and development in contrast to physical capital and consequently the central role of institutions such as universities, think tanks, and media, which—in contrast to factories—are devoted to the creation and transmission of information"; (4) "High and widespread levels of economic well-being and affluence, leading to increased leisure of the bulk of the population, with a few isolated 'pockets' of poverty, in contrast to a small well-off elite and widespread poverty"; (5) "Higher levels of education for the bulk of the population with a college education becoming the norm, in contrast to a norm of primary education"; and (6) "A new 'post-bourgeois' value structure concerned with the quality of life and humanistic values, in contrast to a 'protestant' inner-directed work ethic."

Heilbroner enters a number of demurrers. For example, noting that the industrial core has remained constant, and that the percentage of blue-collar workers constituted 25.5 percent of the labor force in 1900 and 34.9 percent in 1968, he declares: "Thus, if postindustrial society in fact represents a new stage of socioeconomic relationships, the cause must be sought elsewhere than in any disappearance of the industrial sector as a milieu for work." And, as he moves on to critique another of the alleged attributes of postindustrial society, he notes: "As in the case of the definition of postindustrialism that emphasizes the shift in the locus of employment, I do not want to denigrate the importance that has been attached to human capital. Nonetheless it is important, as before, that we scrutinize this characterization of postindustrialism with a certain reserve. For when we do so, we encounter some disconcerting considerations." He says, for example, that we cannot assume that a postindustrial society is one in which the general level of "know-how" is raised along with the general level of formal education.

Heilbroner's view of the evasive definitional term is that "If there is one ultimate definition for postindustrial society, then I would suggest it is that stage of socioeconomic organization in which men gradually escape from the thralldom of blind mechanisms to enter the perilous, but potentially liberating, terrain in which human beings finally assert themselves, for better or worse, as the makers of their fate." Whether the United States or Japan has reached, or is likely to reach, this terrain, Heilbroner does not say.

Morley, too, takes issue with some of the definitional concepts of postindustrialism. "Lebanon, for example," he states, "has probably the highest percentage of its labor force (two-thirds) in the service sector of any country in the world, but it is not usually considered to be the most 'advanced' society in the world." He would not attempt to press Japan and the United States into the same postindustrial definitional mold because of the very considerable divergence in their problems, preferences and philosophies.

A word about the contents of the book. The first essay by James Morley of Columbia University is entitled "The Futurists' Vision." There follow two essays on "The Economy." Robert Heilbroner writes on "Economic Problems of a Postindustrial Society," while Hirofumi Uzawa, of the University of Tokyo paints a broad canvas entitled, "The Transition to a Welfare Economy in Japan." There are two essays on "The Polity." Joji Watanuki of Sophia University describes "Japanese Politics in Flux," while Samuel P. Huntington of Harvard University dilates on "Postindustrial Politics: How Different Will It Be?" Next are two essays on "The City." The first, by Nathan Glazer, of Harvard University, is entitled "Information, the Postindustrial Society, and the American City." There follows "An Approach to the Measurement of the Levels of Welfare in Tokyo" by Kenichi Tominaga of the University of Tokyo. The two final essays on "Information" were written by Yoshimi Uchikawa of the University of Tokyo, on "New Trends in the Media of Japan," and by Charles Frankel of Columbia University, on "Information and Communication in the Not-So-New Society."

The only thing that these essays have in common is that they are wholly unrelated to each other. Each scholar has written, provocatively and stimulat-

ingly, about his own theme and subject, and if treated as a series of readings, rather than as a cohesive whole, there is much concentrated wisdom in this "prologue to the future."

JEROME B. COHEN

Senior Editor, *Bankers Magazine*
New York

DAVID E. POWELL. *Antireligious Propaganda in the Soviet Union.* Pp. 206. Cambridge, Mass.: MIT Press, 1975. $25.00.

The Supreme Court of the United States long acted on the first dictionary definition of "religion" as attitudes toward a Supreme Being with consequent duties of behavior. Lately the Court has acted on a second definition of "religion" as any system of beliefs which control conduct. By this definition, the doctrines of the Communist Party are recognized as a "religion" in these United States; our legal definition would say Communism is the established "religion" in China and the U.S.S.R. A writer or a reader who wishes to consider "antireligious propaganda" finds himself in some difficulties.

Many Americans hold to the creed, "My country—right or wrong!" By this creed it is "sin" to criticize any act of our government or its officers. Such citizens should feel at home in the U.S.S.R., where criticism of the Communist Party has many punishments.

The Russian Orthodox Church was part of the power structure of the tsarist government overturned by revolution. Coming to power, the Communist Party fought the Church with all the weapons at its command. It had good political reasons for doing so. It had also docrinal reasons inherited from Marx and Lenin. Since the late 1950s, the Party has sustained a massive propaganda effort against religion, dropping terror as a policy. After a brief review of the record, Dr. Powell in this book seeks to describe and assess the efforts of the past two decades. He gives the new regime credit for having brought a backward state into one of the world's great powers, with industrialization, urbanization, and improved standards of living and education for masses of people.

The Communist Party invests real money and effort in the antireligious program. Would you believe 679,000 lectures on atheistic themes in a single year? But lectures are only one part of the program; add closing about nine out of ten churches and church institutions of all sects, and prohibition of any proselyting efforts. Add pamphlets, books, exhibits, posters, slogans, clubs, libraries, drama, films and slides, museums, newspapers and magazines, radio, television. Add programs involving most subjects in public schools and training of teachers to teach atheism. Assign teachers and workers for face-to-face confrontations with believers. Substitute secular holidays and ceremonies for religious observances for birth, coming of age, marriage, death, substitute "Red Corners" for religious shrines in schools, homes, factories. Venerate the bodily remains of Lenin rather than religious relics. Make sacred texts of the writings of Marx, Engels, Lenin. The Party and/or the Supreme Leader serve as functional equivalents of God's will on earth, with doctrine made dogma, with priesthood and hierarchy and missionary spirit!

Dr. Powell judges that the Soviet regime has been successful in destroying the political and economic strength of the church, limiting access of the church to children and other citizens, inducing people not to attend church, reducing observance of religious rituals and holy days. He counts it less successful in convincing religious believers that their views are "wrong," less successful still in molding citizens into militant atheists and "New Soviet Men."

Such achievements may have cost more than it has been worth, he suggests, for some religious motivations might be brought to the support of the party and the country. Almost all denominations now actively support Soviet domestic and foreign policy, and leading church figures lavish praise on the political system, echoing the Party line on questions such as arms control, peaceful coexistence, elimination of colonialism. But he thinks "scientific atheist propaganda" will continue, as functional to the atheist and to the Party.

I enjoyed the half-dozen full-page cartoons from *Krokodil*, and was interested in the maps and appendices—but the $25.00 price will limit the book's market.

As I write, the Apollo-Soyuz mission is launching. Perhaps man can learn in outer space to work together on Spaceship Earth. For such unity, one finds imperatives both in Secular Humanism and the theology of One God.

ROLFE L. HUNT

New Rochelle
New York

THOMAS P. ROHLEN. *For Harmony and Strength: Japanese White-Collar Organization in Anthropological Perspective.* Pp 285. Berkeley: University of California Press, 1974. $12.50.

ROBERT J. SMITH. *Ancestor Worship in Contemporary Japan.* Pp. viii, 266. Stanford, Calif.: Stanford University Press, 1974. $12.50.

Both Professors Smith and Rohlen have written well researched and carefully thought out descriptive studies which fill in major gaps in the Western language literature on modern Japanese society. Professor Smith's work is a study of how the Japanese treat their dead and is particularly significant because of his unique census of memorial tablets in households in various cities and villages. Professor Rohlen's book is an ethnographic account of white collar workers in a major regional bank and is of special interest because the author himself participated in the bank's introductory spiritual training program. Since the two books deal with divergent themes, before adding a few comparative comments, I would like to introduce the contents and conclusions of each separately.

Professor Smith begins his study with a detailed treatment of the history of ancestor worship in Japan. Among other things, he discusses prehistoric burial practices, the subsequent Buddhist influence (particularly important since in modern times funerals and anniversary services for the dead are largely Buddhist rites), the nineteenth century government's attempt to create an "emperor system" and to establish the emperor as national father descended from the national ancestors, and the 1898 civil code which made the eldest son of each family heir and keeper of the family tombs and genealogical records. Next he presents a fascinating discussion of the types of ancestral spirits, ghosts and gods in Japanese religion and folklore, and then describes the nature of the rites and ceremonies for both the newly dead and the more distant collective ancestors. In the fourth chapter he treats those occasions such as the mid-summer Festival of the Dead on which Japanese approach the dead either for their help or to help them or both. These first four chapters are based on an impressive command of the English and Japanese language literature touching on burial and memorial practices.

In the last two chapters, Professor Smith makes an even greater contribution to our knowledge of how the Japanese treat their dead. In Chapter Five, he presents a discussion of who the ancestors are based on the census of memorial tablets in almost 600 household Buddhist altar shelves, and on interviews and questionnaires with household members about the altar contents in five urban and three rural communities. He finds, not surprisingly, that most tablets are for ancestors—that is, people in the line of succession or unmarried siblings and children of the present household head —but he also reveals that almost 10 percent of the tablets are for non-lineal and occasionally even non-kin dead. In the last chapter, therefore, he introduces evidence from interviews about these exceptions as well as about duplicate tablets, tablets found both in the altar they should be in and others, to show that the "realm of personal attachments" as well as the lineage system is important. Professor Smith closes his book with the rather limited conclusion that ancestor worship in Japan in the future is more and more likely to be focused on the one or two generations of parents and grandparents, people whom the living genera-

tion remembers. As the conjugal family replaces the stem family, so too worship of the immediate kin who have died will replace an emphasis on the collective dead, lineage and family continuity. One only wishes that a scholar with Professor Smith's deep knowledge of and feel for Japan had ventured a more daring conclusion and shown a bit more problem consciousness (*mondai ishiki*).

Professor Rohlen opens his study of white collar workers in Uedagin, the fictitious name of a large regional bank, with a short discussion of the problems of the study of modern industrial organization in Japan. After this, he turns to Uedagin and introduces the company, its history, workers, their sex, age, rank and concludes the first chapter with a discussion of the importance of group unity, and vertical, hierarchical relationships in the bank as well as in Japanese society as a whole. It is here, on page 33, that the major theme of the book, that Uedagin fits the "vertical society" model, is introduced. This theme along with that of "lifelong employment" occurs throughout the book. Professor Rohlen then deals successively with the company ideology and its concomitant songs and oaths, how people are recruited and leave the bank, a typical work day, senior-junior (sempai-kohai) relations, the qualities, seriousness, perseverance and harmoniousness necessary for advancement, the company's salary policy, union, introductory training course, dormitory and apartments, and its employees' marriages and family life. I found five of the eleven chapters particularly important and provocative. Chapters One and Two, which deal with the bank's ideology and recruitment policies, raise a number of unanswered questions about the company's alleged concern for public service. How does the bank's public commitment to protecting the local environment and its private goal of maximizing profits, for example, affect its loan policy to local industry if that company is a known polluter? Or when the personnel section conducts thorough background investigations of candidates for employment (pp. 71–73), are Koreans and outcastes (*burakumin*) excluded? Perhaps Professor Rohlen's admitted lack of skepticism and inclination "to credit all people with good intentions" prevented him from asking such "hard" questions. Chapter Five contains a discussion, unique in English language literature on Japan, of the dependency of younger people on older ones who are still usually members of the same generation, the *sempai-kohai* relationship. This type of dependency is more an elder-younger brother (or sister) one than the better known vassalage type relationships of the fictive father-son ties of the *oyabun-kobun* system, and is also probably more prevalent in contemporary Japan. In Chapter Eight, the author describes the bank's submissive company union, and in Chapter Nine he develops some very plausible ideas about the impact of "spiritual training" in the company's introductory course for recruits. The author closes his book by stating that the Uedagin system in fact works, and should be judged in its own terms, not by a Western model—a conclusion which does not seem particularly earth-shaking to a specialist in Japanese society and history. In fact, the descriptive part of Professor Rohlen's book is so thorough and readable that it too deserves a forceful and broad conclusion.

The two authors' books contrast sharply in two areas: the authors' sense of history and their style of writing and presentation of their evidence. Professor Smith has a rare quality among contemporary social scientists—a deep feeling for history. He not only devotes one of six chapters to the historical perspective, but the influence of history permeates much of the rest of the book. Professor Rohlen's book, on the other hand, lacks an historical context. Altogether he devotes only two pages of the book to the bank's past, and he describes many of the bank's activities as if they are unique to contemporary Japan. This is surprising since much in the bank's ideology, organization and training program sounds similar to practices of such prewar organizations as the military reserve and youth associations. He would have benefited from historical knowledge. For example, in his discussion of staff planning (pp. 153–154), Professor Rohlen indicates some surprise that the bank's top officials delegate important staff planning functions to young, talented subordinates. Through a knowledge of prewar bureaucratic organization, the author would know that this tradition has hoary antecedents, and that in the past (and still today?) the plans were drawn up without specific delegation from above. Only after the subordinates completed their study, as in the case of the plan which led to the 1931 Manchurian incident, did they inform their superiors of what they had planned by submitting it to them for approval. And again, in his conclusion, Professor Rohlen describes the bank's lifetime employment practice as non-economic, used by the company out of a feeling that commitment to its employees is more important than profit (pp. 259–261). A look at its origins would reveal that the lifelong employment system did not develop naturally out of Japan's premodern past, but was adopted by Japanese companies in the early twentieth century to help them obtain a stable work force, avoid labor problems and keep wages and salaries low. In other words, in its origins (and in Japan's pre-1970 expanding economy), lifelong employment was extremely economical.

The two authors' methods of presenting their material are also very different. Professor Smith meticulously discusses his methodology, presents tables with his data, and makes conclusions only after carefully introducing the supporting evidence. Because of this, the book is at times difficult to read, but one comes away with confidence that the author has proven his limited conclusions. Professor Rohlen, on the other hand, although he does discuss his methodology in his conclusion, rarely documents his points with specific attributions. In his several discussions of how women bank employees docilely accept their subordinate position to men, for example, he gives us no idea of how many women he interviewed or what questions he asked them. Thus, not overburdened with data, Professor Rohlen's book is the more readable of the two; but one would like to have more specific knowledge about his sources.

RICHARD J. SMETHURST

Kyoto
Japan

RICHARD SANDBROOK. *Proletarians and African Capitalism: The Kenyan Case, 1960–72.* Pp. v, 222. New York: Cambridge University Press, 1975. $23.50.

In this highly successful book, the author undertakes an analysis of the political, social, and economic forces composing the labor union movement in Kenya and its relationships with the government. The author examined a sample of unions carefully. He attended meetings, interviewed a great number of people, and carefully researched materials available in Kenya. He concludes that neither the Kenya national party (KANU), which *is* the government, nor the union movement, can be referred to either as independent or as entities. Rather, they both are conglomerations of patron-clientele relationships, always in states of factionalism. Nevertheless, the governing elite is sufficiently cohesive, in the main, to work its will upon the unions and to prevent them from disrupting its objectives of economic development to the gain of a specific elite. Much substantive evidence is introduced for this thesis, including not only a scholarly presentation, but also several anecdotes that illustrate the major points.

The book suffers from starting and ending in a marxist framework, using the terminology of believers, thus giving a first impression that Kenyan unionism is to be made to fit the marxist mold. Why else would the book be named as it is, and why else would the author stress that the prevailing form of economy in Kenya is *capitalist*, despite its early protestations in favor of African *socialism*? But the author drops the mold very quickly, and proceeds to an objective and highly informative presentation of the inner workings of unionism and its relationships with the government.

He is aware of, and deftly describes, the principal pressures upon union leaders from all sides. On one, the government is imposing restraints, not only in wages but also in the ability to strike, in order not to disrupt the national development process (and presumably its own gain), while on the other, leaders must respond to pressure from the rank and file for wage increases (and occasionally for strikes), or support will be lost. The strength of the book lies in the author's ability to describe the balancing of political forces and their net impact.

On the economic side, the book is somewhat weaker. The author recognizes that unions are working within a difficult framework of widespread unemployment and rural-urban migration, whose pressures constantly limit their ability to increase wages. Furthermore, urban workers are often accused of being an "elite" because they earn twice as much in real terms, and ten times as much in money terms, as their rural counterparts. Increased wages would not only aggravate unemployment (by causing employers to use machines instead of people) but would also increase the discrepancy in living standards between city and country. These problems are mentioned, but not answered. Rather, the author reflects his sympathy for the unions by making the obviously striking comparisons between the mode of living of the rich (and their houses in Westlands and Karen) and the poor (in Pumwani).

Had he carried his argument further, however, he might have discovered a host of reasons *why* the rich are rich, in terms of the tax, tariffs, subsidy, interest-rate, and other incentives that the government has bestowed upon them. Indeed, the unions recognize that these economic policies in favor of the rich create a pool of profits that labor would like to tap. Thus the "elite" unions become "co-conspirators" with the rich, against the rural poor. This does not mean that urban laborers share the wealth to a great extent, but it does explain why the labor movement and the government are often able to conform to each other.

Let us desist here. It is not fitting for an economist reviewer to criticize a primarily political book for not containing more economics. It is a good book, insightful and well written. I wish I had read it before I went to Kenya.

JOHN P. POWELSON
University of Colorado
Boulder

JAMES D. THEBERGE. *The Soviet Presence in Latin America*. Pp. vii, 107. New York: Crane, Russak & Co., 1974. $4.95.

This study traces the recent Soviet influence in Latin America. It is an interpretative overview with Cold War undertones, and it is speculative with many unsupported observations.

The ten brief chapters include a summary of Soviet interest in Latin America as well as discussion of topics such as Soviet diplomacy, trade and aid, espionage and subversion, and naval presence in the Caribbean. There is concern with Moscow's support for revolutionary violence, relations between the Soviet and Latin American communist parties, and Soviet interest in Cuba, Chile, and Peru.

This book contains a multitude of perspectives, many in need of further analysis and evidence. According to the author, the Soviet Union views Latin America as an area of "relatively mature capitalism," yet he ignores the implications of feudalism, a theme stressed in the documents of the Latin American communist parties. The author argues that Soviet perceptions are "ideologically weighted down by Marxist class analysis" without acknowledging the obfuscation which results in contemporary social science emphasis on institutional forces in Latin America.

Dubious is his assumption that the disadvantages of Soviet aid are greater than those of U.S. aid. The discussion of Soviet espionage and subversion could be related to U.S. activities in these areas so as to obtain an objective perspective of external influences into Latin American affairs. The attention to Cuba's dependence on the Soviet Union is distortive in that there is no recognition of the significant socio-economic developments that have occurred there. The focus on violence as strategy does not coincide with the prevailing practice of the Latin American communist parties. The reference to Fidel Castro's August 1968 speech supporting the Soviet invasion of Czechoslovakia does not acknowledge Fidel's criticism of the undemocratic nature of Soviet socialism. The fall of Allende in Chile is seen as a Soviet defeat without offering analysis of domestic contradictions, the "invisible blockade" which stifled relations in the world economy, and CIA manipulations. All these concerns are deserving of elaboration and supporting detail.

Thus, this book stands as a general synthesis of traditional North American perspectives of the Soviet role in Latin America. It is a strong affirmation of official views that perceive political changes in Latin America as being persistently threatened by outside communism. As such, there is little attention to U.S. imperialism, and there is no attempt to delve into internal conditions that have brought about many changes in Latin America.

RONALD H. CHILCOTE
University of California
Riverside

LAWRENCE L. WHETTEN. *The Canal War: Conflict in the Middle East*. Pp. xii, 520. Cambridge, Mass.: MIT Press, 1974. No price.

The reader will look forward to a sequel to this book. It brings him up to the end of 1973, when the Arabs had just realized what a trump card they held in their control of so much of the world's oil. It is not easy to read. It is crammed with detailed material, and it assumes a familiarity with the area and a good atlas handy for consultation. In a way it recalls Arnold Toynbee's *Survey of the Islamic World since the Peace Settlement*, published in 1927, but it is much more detailed and it caters to the soldier as well as the historian and diplomat.

The Canal War is a study of the reluctant involvement of two great powers, both operating in an unfamiliar environment, both anxious to achieve a lasting settlement based on a local balance of power, and both frustrated by the intransigence of their respective protegés. Lessons emerge for the practitioner as well as the student, of power politics in peripheral areas, of strategy and tactics of the deployment of weapons and the uses and shortcomings of air power, and of the interdependence of all these activities. The predominant local factors are the confidence of Israel and the evasive skills of Egypt. The former led Israel to reject various opportunities of achieving a favorable settlement. The latter enabled Egypt to avoid the consequences of disaster. She was fortunate in finding two successive leaders capable of playing a poorish hand with consummate skill, equipping herself with a Russian defense system without sinking to the status of a satellite, and dealing drastically with internal Communist conspiracy while retaining the advantages of external alliance with the leading Communist power. Nasser may remain the national hero, but history will probably reckon Sadat the greater man.

Professor Whetten enjoys the advantage of having participated in the events which he describes, as a special assistant in the office of the Secretary of Defense. The most painstaking of chroniclers and ablest of historians are bound to make mistakes unless they have first hand experience of their subject matter. So far as one can see there is only one trivial slip in the book, the spelling of the name Nimeri as Numerei.

This book should find a place on the shelves of every department of modern history and every military academy.

K. D. D. HENDERSON

Salisbury
Wiltshire
England

WINTHROP R. WRIGHT. *British-Owned Railways in Argentina: Their Effect on the Growth of Economic Nationalism, 1854–1948*. Pp. xii, 305. Austin: University of Texas Press, 1974. $10.00.

This careful monograph is traditional in content and method; it is a descriptive, chronological presentation of the political-economic history of its subject. It is also the valuable kind of building-block monograph still much needed in the field of Latin American history and the other social sciences.

In execution, the study is much wider than the apparently narrow scope given it in the main title. The key to that breadth lies in the subtitle, for the book's true and most interesting focus is on the stages of evolution of Argentine economic nationalism from the days just after the fall of the dictator Rosas and the coming of the first railroad in 1857 to the politically successful but economically debilitating purchase and nationalization of the railroads by the authoritarian, populist-nationalist government of Juan Perón in 1948.

Needless to say, the author is here grappling with a major topic in the history of dependency, which is not the same as polemicizing about the evils revealed by that mode of analysis. Those evils exist in plenty in the Argentine story, and the author treats the grasping deeds of the national dependent oligarchy, the spoils of internal colonialism, and the intricate ways of informal empire with nicely factual objectivity.

The author has made use of all available source materials; sadly, the Argentine records of the Anglo-Argentine railway corporations were destroyed by Peronist mobs in 1948.

Professor Wright has written a well-balanced, significant book.

THOMAS F. McGANN
The University of Texas
Austin

UNITED STATES

JUDITH BEST. *The Case against Direct Election of the President: A Defense of the Electoral College.* Pp. 235. Ithaca, N.Y.: Cornell University Press, 1975. $9.95.

Political engineering is among the more enduring and perhaps endearing qualities of American culture. Throughout the nation's history, there have been recurring efforts to modify those institutions intended to give operative meaning to the ambitious but still ambiguous and elusive ideals of democracy. Not the least of these are the institutions that govern the electoral process. Over the years, these essential institutions of democratic society have provided reformers of varying political hues endless opportunities to demonstrate their ingenuity and their resourcefulness. The results are evident in the variety of election practices employed locally, and in such historical, if not historic, innovations as: the popular election of judges and United States Senators; proportional representation; off-year elections; permanent registration; and the secret ballot.

That political engineering of this sort remains a viable cultural trait is clear from the main concern of this book—the complex and consequential way in which a president is chosen. The present system, as more than one critic has argued, is something of an anomaly in a society that professes, however vaguely at times, its commitment to majority rule. In theory, the Electoral College violates this ideal—a distinction it shares with a number of other prominent national institutions, most notably the Supreme Court and the United States Senate—and this has

given rise to a number of proposals designed to remedy the disjuncture between the ideal and the real.

Of the proposals advanced, the most serious contender today, according to Professor Judith Best, is the direct election of the president. Under this plan, presidential elections would be decided by a national plurality of at least forty percent of those voting, or, failing this, by a run-off election between the two highest vote-getters. There have been other alternatives, each of which modifies but maintains the Electoral vote, but these alternatives—the automatic plan, the proportional plan, the district plan—no longer enjoy the support they once did. Direct election, on the other hand, has powerful backers, among them the American Bar Association, the House of Representatives of the 91st Congress, and an estimated eighty percent of those polled in a national survey.

As Professor Best acknowledges, the case for the direct election of the president is persuasive. Its appeal rests in part, as noted above, on the ideal of majoritarianism. Granted, achieving this goal completely would require that the voting population and the total population be identical, a condition seldom, if ever, realized in any society. But a plan that promises a closer approximation of this ideal has a strong presumption in its favor.

This presumption would be even stronger if, as its critics insist, there are serious perils in the workings of the Electoral College. For those addicted to election night television, these perils are no doubt sufficiently familiar, in as much as the potential discrepancies between the popular and the Electoral College vote have provided useful filler-material for television's political commentators. Most are familiar, that is to say, with the possibility a popular majority may not be an Electoral majority, or the possibility an election may be "thrown into" the House where, regardless of size, each state is entitled constitutionally to only one vote.

Unquestionably, these and other dangers are inherent in the Electoral College, but the probability of their occurring is quite another matter. It is Professor Best's contention that the perils have been exaggerated, and, along with them, the potentials for constitutional crisis. True, one election (1824) was resolved in the House, and another (1888) witnessed the defeat of the candidate (Cleveland) with the largest share of the popular vote. In addition, in at least twenty elections, "a shift of less than one percent of the popular vote would have produced a runner-up President." The author presents a critical appraisal of these historical precedents and concludes that much of the concern with the Electoral College is prompted by ahistorical speculation. In most, though not all, the instances cited by critics—the major exception is the election of 1888—the outcomes, or near-misses, resulted mostly from factors other than the Electoral College. Moreover, much of this speculation is highly misleading. As Professor Best points out: "By proposing minor and imaginary shifts in the popular vote, critics suggest the electoral-count system can easily and frequently produce a runner-up President . . . [However] it is a simple matter to move an exact and limited number of votes from one paper column to another in a political vacuum; it is more difficult to move an exact *and limited* number of voters from one candidate to another in the political world" (p. 206, emphasis in the original). In other words, in the real world there is no guarantee that a hypothetical shift would be unidirectional, and whatever moves a candidate might have made to gain additional votes might well have cost him some of the votes he actually received.

If the perils of the Electoral College are not as serious as its critics claim, its advantages, according to Professor Best, are considerable, particularly when compared to the potential risks of direct election. Among other things, the Electoral College has produced "definite and accepted winners,"—the sole contingency election (1824) pre-dates the universal adoption of the unit rule by the states—and in so doing has minimized the uncertainty and turmoil that could so easily accompany the transfer of presidential power. By contrast, "the 40-percent runoff rule could make frequent resort to a contingency election necessary. Once the unit rule, with its bias in favor of the two major-party candidates is abolished, the 40-percent runoff rule could serve as an open invitation to multiple candidacies and thereby facilitate a contingency election strategy" (p. 210).

Such a strategy, of course, would offer numerous opportunities for political mischief—and more. In fact, the author contends, "the direct election would constitute a fundamental change in our established institutions," (p. 44) not only in the College itself, but in the presidency, the parties and the federal system. Whether this would occur is unclear, for despite our heritage of political engineering we know all too little about the intricate and subtle ways in which political systems function. Still, the book is well worth reading, and pondering. The author presents a thoughtful and balanced appraisal of both the Electoral College and the proposed direct election plan, and her analysis should give considerable pause to those who would replace the seemingly archaic and "undemocratic" Electoral College with the more modern and "democratic" direct election of the president.

RUSSELL D. MURPHY

Wesleyan University
Middletown
Connecticut

SURENDRA BHANA. *The United States and the Development of the Puerto Rican Status Question, 1936–1968.* Pp. viii, 293. Lawrence: The University Press of Kansas, 1975. $11.00.

The publication of this volume on the development of commonwealth status for Puerto Rico is timely, for it coincides with the disclosure that the United States may soon gain another "Puerto Rico" in the Pacific, when the Marianas are transformed into a new American commonwealth. And like Puerto Rico, the inhabitants of these islands will enjoy the advantages of becoming American citizens, paying relatively few Federal taxes, and securing liberal infusions of Federal funds. The United States will also have an opportunity to benefit from its Puerto Rican experience in developing a system of bilingual and bicultural education, offering the Islands' schools a blend of their native (Chamorro) language and culture and instruction in the English language, using American curricula.

As its title indicates, this book is concerned principally with the evolution of Puerto Rico's political status, that is, its relationship with the United States. At its outermost limits, the book's time frame extends from 1915 to 1972, but it focuses chiefly on the period from 1936, when the movement to free Puerto Rico from its colonial status emerged as a lively issue, until 1952, when the Commonwealth came into existence. Puerto Rico had previously gone through several stages under American rule: administration by a military regime, governance as an "unincorporated territory," and special status, such as United States citizenship for its inhabitants, in the Jones Act of 1917. In the 1930s, the island's two great unresolved questions were its economic and political status. The former related to its condition of grinding poverty, aggravated by the Great Depression; the latter to its structure of government, complicated by its cultural divergence from the United States and its search for *dignidad*.

Several of the book's features are particularly noteworthy. The first is Bhana's analysis of the balance the island's leaders struck between its economic needs, which required a continuing association with the United States, while cultural differences and the passionate demands of the *independistas* impelled it in the opposite direction. The final solution, of course, was neither statehood, nor independence, but the "Middle Way" —the fashioning of a new and unique political form, an "Associated Free State." Secondly, the author has made a systematic and thoroughgoing canvass of relevant government publications and personal papers of American officials, supplementing these sources with his own correspondence with surviving participants in the events he describes. This extensive documentation has enabled him to develop his theme in great detail, with special emphasis on the personalities and programs of political leaders and the shifting names, compositions, and creeds of their respective political parties. As the foregoing statements suggest, he has unearthed many little known details, which will provide rich supplements to our present state of knowledge. Undoubtedly they will interest specialists in this area, but the inexorable massing of facts occasionally impedes readability.

As previously suggested, the lessons learned from Puerto Rico's experience with Commonwealth status may be relevant to the projected new American government in the Pacific, especially if the five remaining Micronesian districts in the Trust Territory of the Pacific outside the Marianas also decide to join the United States under comparable terms. In addition, this volume may prove valuable as a basic resource for curriculum experts and textbook writers dealing with Puerto Rican affairs. The recent proliferation of Spanish bilingual-bicultural programs in the United States has revealed a shortage of texts relevant to that island, particularly since most materials prepared for Hispanic students are appropriate for the Chicanos of our Southwest. This book may help fill the gap.

FREDERICK SHAW

Office of Bilingual Education
Board of Education
City of New York

JAMES O. BREEDEN. *Joseph Jones, M.D.: Scientist of the Old South.* Pp. xiii, 275. Lexington: The University Press of Kentucky, 1975. $13.25.

Relatively few books can bring across to the reader the horrors of war or the sad fact that the "good old days" weren't the days of milk and honey and simplicity and happiness for all that we like to recall.

The life of Joseph Jones, at least that portion of it described in this book (from birth until shortly after the end of the

Civil War) is one that takes us from the cradle of a wealthy plantation owner, through the good life of the antebellum South and the horrors of the Civil War.

Son of a wealthy clergyman, living always within a religious framework and the recipient of an excellent classical education (at South Carolina College and Princeton), Jones graduated in 1856 from the University of Pennsylvania medical department, which was the finest medical institution in the United States at that time.

Most of the biography is devoted to Jones' involvement in the Civil War. From October, 1861 until March, 1862 he served as a private in a local Georgia militia unit, then in the middle of 1863 he joined the staff of the only Confederate hospital in Augusta, Georgia, as a civilian contract surgeon. Here he became increasingly interested in the etiology, prevalence and effect of camp diseases. Late in 1862 he passed a medical exam at Charleston and was appointed a surgeon in the Confederate army. From this time until the end of the war, he was an inveterate collector and preserver of Confederate medical records. Indeed, his study of prison life at Andersonville was used by the Union prosecution to convict and hang the former commandant Henry Wirz. I agree with the author's statement that "No one, with the exception of (Confederate) Surgeon General Samuel P. Moore, was as well informed on the medical history of the Confederacy." His study of hospital gangrene and the conditions at Andersonville certainly bear this out. There probably are no better records of the horrors of war.

There are only minor points I would quibble about. Breeden, an associate professor of history at Southern Methodist University, somewhat favors his central figure, as many biographers tend to do. Yet, he does make such comments as that Jones "still had not learned to accept criticism" by 1858 and that he showed "a characteristic self-assurance which often bordered on brashness." Breeden also states in his Prologue that only three short studies of Jones have previously been published, but he omits the article on Jones written by James Phalin in the DAB.

I highly recommend this biography to those interested in late antebellum Southern history, the Civil War buff as well as the student, and to the medical historian. I also hope that Breeden will chronicle the later career of Jones, who became a noted physician and sanitation expert in New Orleans.

HENRY S. MARKS
Northeast Alabama State Junior
  College
Rainsville

WILLIAM A. BULLOUGH. *Cities and Schools in the Gilded Age: The Evolution of an Urban Institution.* Pp. 183. Port Washington, N.Y.: Kennikat Press, 1974. $12.50.

William Bullough examines how urban schools in the late 19th century—the Gilded Age—met massive socio-economic dislocations in "ambivalent, peripheral and incomplete ways." He also suggests that many problems facing today's urban and suburban schools are legacies of the Gilded Age.

According to the author, educators in the 1880s attributed pupil absenteeism to greed rather than economic need among poor immigrant families. Moreover, schools met the exploding population of the cities with inadequate facilities and irrelevant curricula. Urbanization gave impetus to professionalism but not to great accomplishment among educators. Teachers' organizations proliferated, but teachers were still underpaid and poorly trained even after the emergence of the normal school. National efforts concentrated on retirement and insurance plans, while policy was left to local school boards which were subject to political manipulation in the absence of clear standards for certification. As school administrators became more highly professionalized, they increasingly emphasized the need for an efficient, centralized bureaucracy. Schools became part of a system administered by men who saw themselves more as executives than as educators. Bullough portrays them and reformers as victims of an era, not as "ignorant, blind or purposively self-seeking men."

Reformers shared an ideology antipathetic to politics and committed to Spencerian evolution, a business mentality, and the Protestant Ethic. They blamed the schools' failings on characteristics of the pupils, totally ignoring the socio-economic dislocations endemic to urban areas. They sought to inculcate in the students the values of self-sacrifice, patriotism, industry, and morality; they strove for child labor laws and compulsory attendance laws in order to maintain harmonious relations among the social classes and to Americanize the immigrants. Educators and reformers alike were ambivalent if not hostile to the city. They yearned for the rugged individualism, simplicity and security of the rural-agrarian community. They sought a panacea for school problems in nature study and manual training in traditional crafts irrelevant in an urban setting.

Although benevolent in intention, compensatory education was a "reform" geared to bringing about conformity among the "deprived and defective" who deviated from existing socio-political norms. What little real social change occurred in the schools was the result of efforts by isolated individuals who frequently were lower echelon educators or non-professionals.

By the end of the 19th century, urban schools were inadequate. The prevailing ideology peculiarly combined intellectual traditionalism (a rural mentality with emphasis on morality) with intellectual modernism (an undying faith in progress and the ability of urban problems to solve themselves). The prevailing structure was a rigid bureaucracy geared to internal efficiency and devoid of meaningful contacts with other institutions or the communities supposedly served. Bullough concludes that this ideology and structure, coupled with the ways they led people to perceive and solve problems, comprise the destructive legacy of the Gilded Age for today's school system.

If this book has a major shortcoming, it is the constant emphasis on negative aspects of the early school system. The book is also somewhat repetitious, but quite readable. The researcher focuses on primary materials, especially National Education Association and Bureau of Education documents. Throughout the analysis, if the reader substitutes the word "ghetto" for "slum," and "Black, Puerto Ricans or Indians" for "immigrants," he is persuaded by Bullough's basic argument. Perhaps nowhere is this more clear than in the discussion of compensatory education which was in the Gilded Age and is now more an attempt at social control and assimilation than one of reform. This short book is an excellent example of the relevance of historical analysis for insight into the evolution and current plight of a social institution. It is recommended to urban historians, sociologists, and educators.

MADELINE H. ENGEL
Herbert H. Lehman College
City University of New York

DAVID BRION DAVIS. *The Problem of Slavery in the Age of Revolution, 1770–1823.* Pp. 576. Ithaca, N.Y.: Cornell University Press, 1975. $17.50.

In this book Professor Davis has maintained the meticulous research, the careful selectivity of materials, the objectivity of treatment and the superb stylistic approach to his subject that he did in his earlier volume, *The Problem of Slavery in Western Culture.* Indeed, both of these splendid treatises represent scholarship and narration at its best.

The author is not concerned with slavery in Asia or in Africa, except incidentally, African slave trade, not even in eastern Europe, but confines his treatment of the problem almost wholly to England, France, the United States and Latin America. In this expansive area Professor Davis found materials that kept him busy for fifteen years doing the research which went into the writing of this book.

The author says that slavery corrupted

the well springs of true religion and also that the abolishment of slavery was basically a question of power. Over sixty percent of the Africans crossing the Atlantic were dumped on Europe's western islands. In fact, free Negroes in the United States increased more than slaves from 1790–1810, but slaves increased more rapidly thereafter; an increase due largely to Whitney's cotton gin and the development of the sugar industry.

Although some attempts were made toward general emancipation, success was attained only in Northern states and that by gradual emancipation. In England complete emancipation was linked to national interests, while in the American Southern states the issue was intimately connected with localized land ownership and the necessity of labor sources. Whether in England or in France or in the United States slavery was always a divisive issue in legislative assemblies, correctly concludes Professor Davis.

A widely known fact, not familiar to many students of United States history, is that America had many anti-slavery organizations but that they were concentrated in the Southern slave states by a 4 to 1 ratio. Unfortunately there were not many ties of endeavor between the anti-slavery organizations in the South and elsewhere in the United States. England and France likewise had groups interested in the abolition of slavery. Quakers wherever found were usually in the forefront of the abolition movement. They created anti-slavery societies and initiated reforms throughout the culture generally in the United States and abroad.

By pamphlets, letters and books some Americans before and during the Revolutionary War urged the emancipation of slaves. During the war itself British generals offered freedom to slaves who joined the British in the war against their masters. A great American paradox was the rise of liberty and equality contemporaneously with the expansion of slavery. Yet another inconsistency, of which the author reminds us, was the Americans holding slaves and at the same time resisting England's efforts to enslave them. The Great Awakening witnessed whites converting slaves to Christianity to encourage meekness, docility and obedience.

Although some thought slavery an efficient and beneficial institution, others contended the issue was the Negro's capacity for self-determination. All, however, made race the chief issue of the slave problem. Wherever found slavery epitomized the market wrought by multiple conflicts of interest. In England especially there were parallels between the rise of anti-slavery sentiment and the changed attitudes toward the English poor.

England, France and America found in slavery conflicting jurisdictional problems. In all areas some began to appeal to the "higher law" in an effort to solve the slavery issue. The author discusses a number of cases which arose in American and European courts to show the complex problem of legal acceptance of the numerous phases of the slavery issue. Moreover, those for and against slavery tried to best the other in their appeals to the Bible for support of their cause.

This book surpasses anything published on this problem and will serve those interested in the problem of slavery for years to come.

GEORGE OSBORN
University of Florida
Gainesville

EMORY G. EVANS. *Thomas Nelson of Yorktown: Revolutionary Virginian.* Pp. x, 204. Charlottesville: University Press of Virginia, 1975. $8.95.

Although it is possible to quibble with caveats of interpretation, Emory G. Evans has written a solid, engaging biography about Thomas Nelson, an eighteenth-century Virginian whose good works during the American Revolution generally have been neglected by scholars. Evans has rescued Nelson from undeserved obscurity; and in a text that must be noted for its unburdensome length places him squarely in the center of Virginia's revolutionary politics. As an assembly leader, member of the Continental Congress (he signed the Declaration of Independence), militia general, and war governor during the crucial battlefield year of 1781, Nelson demonstrated real talent for disinterested and enlightened public service, certainly producing a record comparable with Patrick Henry, Thomas Jefferson, and other illustrious Virginians of more enduring fame. Despite almost chronic bouts with illnesses, especially intestinal disorders and what must have been asthma, Nelson persisted with the cause; it wore him out physically, and as Evans hints, led to his premature death in 1789 at fifty years of age. Perhaps it was this lack of good health, along with personal financial problems, that cut short the life of a man who would have been of substantial service to the struggling new nation.

Given Professor Evans's earlier scholarship on the role of debts in Virginia as they related to the American Revolution, readers will not be surprised to find that this biography belongs to the "neo-whig" genre. Evans implies throughout that eighteenth-century Virginia society was open, fluid, and tending toward the democratic. It was not a world, according to Evans, that was filled with class antagonisms which affected the course of revolution. Thus Evans tells us, for example, that pre-revolutionary planter and merchant elite leaders were consistently "responsive to the electorate . . . since the franchise was broad and the voter independent" (p. 19). But we also learn (p. 20) that Nelson's father in 1761 arranged for his son's election to the House of Burgesses, apparently just before the youthful Thomas returned to Yorktown after several years of education in England. Somehow such facts might lead some readers to question how open and "democratic" politics really were in Virginia. Professor Evans would have served readers more exactly had he admitted that Nelson was the product of a well-educated, socially- and politically-dominant elite,

and that it probably was that exceptional, favored, enlightenment training that undergirded Nelson's noteworthy career in revolutionary politics.

As Volume X in the "Williamsburg in America Series," this volume putatively has been prepared for the dust jacket creation known as the "general reader." But the book should not be slighted by scholars. Despite its awkward neo-whiggism, it has been well-researched and carefully documented; it represents a definite contribution to knowledge, not only about Thomas Nelson but also about Virginia in the American Revolution. Evans has written a worthwhile biography.

JAMES KIRBY MARTIN

Rutgers University
New Brunswick, N.J.

RICHARD G. HEWLETT and FRANCIS DUNCAN. *Nuclear Navy, 1946–1962.* Pp. v, 477. Chicago, Ill.: The University of Chicago Press, 1974. $12.50.

In 1946 a relatively obscure Navy captain named Hyman Rickover arrived at Oak Ridge, Tennessee, to head a small-scale, experimental nuclear reactor project. By 1962, the U.S. Navy had 27 nuclear powered submarines and 3 nuclear powered surface ships, including the aircraft carrier, *Enterprise*—and Admiral Rickover was a national figure.

In this, the first account to be authorized by Rickover, authors Hewlett and Duncan meticulously narrate one of the great engineering achievements of the century: the development of America's nuclear navy. Working against time, and often in the face of bureaucratic opposition, Rickover and his associates convinced the Navy of the imminent possibilities of nuclear power for naval propulsion. Within four years they completed a prototype plant and, in 1955, the *Nautilus*, the first nuclear submarine, went to sea. During these same years, Rickover's group built the first full scale commercial nuclear power plant in Shippingport, Pennsylvania; a model for subsequent water-reactor design and development. Thus did Rickover's work not only revolutionize naval warfare; it also accelerated and influenced nuclear technology development for decades to come.

How did it happen so quickly and so successfully? A definitive analysis of the Rickover method eludes the authors. Yet, the parts of the book that describe Rickover's highly personalized and interactive network of relationships with engineering associates, Navy bureaucrats, Congress, and private corporate contractors should be highly interesting to political scientists. If politics is the purposive struggle for, and exercise of, power, then Rickover's mode of operation is quintessentially political.

Hewlett and Duncan, chief historian and assistant historian of the Atomic Energy Commission (AEC), have given us a definitive history of the nuclear Navy from 1946–1962. Comprehensive, scholarly, interesting, enhanced by good illustrations and three helpful appendices, this book is a worthy companion to the two other volumes in the AEC's historical series: *The New World, 1936–1946* and *Atomic Shield, 1947–1952.*

There are shortcomings. The authors promise us a mix of historical narrative and analysis. We get much more of the former than the latter. And the narrative itself has a run-on effect, a problem that could be reduced by better chapter overview and summaries and by a less crowded publisher's format.

The most striking shortcoming for this reader, however, is the uncritical quality at the level of the most basic questions about nuclear technology. Neither the authors, nor the AEC, nor Rickover nor any of the actors in this story address themselves to these questions: How much nuclear power is enough? How long are we going to follow the siren lure of nuclear military technology from reactors to submarines to MIRVs? When are AEC historians going to be able to write a book about how the U.S. learned to say, selectively, "No" to nuclear technology?

JOY MILLER HUNTLEY
Ohio University
Athens

D. CLAYTON JAMES. *The Years of MacArthur, 1941–1945.* Volume II. Pp. xix, 939. Boston, Mass.: Houghton Mifflin, 1975. $15.00.

Hardly any of his contemporaries and none of his chroniclers have been objective in their appraisal of Douglas MacArthur. However, D. Clayton James's three-volume biography is as close to an impartial appraisal as MacArthur is likely to get. This is not to say that James writes without passion; as he puts it in the preface, he found himself "alternately admiring and despising MacArthur" (p. viii.) Like most biographers who compare their subjects to human rather than ideal standards, James probably admires more often than he despises, but he is invariably balanced and just in his judgments.

This volume is as much a history of World War II in the Southwest Pacific as it is a biography of MacArthur. James carefully delineates the tactical and strategic considerations of each major operation and assesses MacArthur's role therein, from the loss of Bataan and Corregidor in 1942 to the triumphant reconquest of the Philippines in 1945. James blames MacArthur for the poor provisioning of troops on Bataan, which was in large part responsible for "the worst disaster ever suffered by an American army" (p. 65). On the other hand, he says that MacArthur learned from his mistakes and seldom repeated them. Furthermore, his leadership was frequently brilliant and bold. Nor was MacArthur a coward, as the "Dugout Doug" slur common among some soldiers implied. In fact, James finds that MacArthur braved enemy fire many times; unfortunately, he offers no explanation as to why MacArthur exposed himself to dangerous situations for no apparent reason.

Throughout the war MacArthur displayed an inability or unwillingness to understand the political necessity of the "Europe first" policy; this was exacerbated by his petty rivalry with European army commanders and quarrels with Navy leaders in the Pacific. Other damaging character traits included his blindness toward the Rasputin-like qualities of his Chief of Staff General Richard Sutherland and his "desperate need to save face, even if it involved lying" (p. 765). Yet MacArthur was a welter of contradictions; for every such damaging instance there was some redeeming quality: his concern for his men, his spiritual and moral values, his complete lack of racial prejudice.

James seems at times to have difficulty in subordinating less significant events to the more important ones. His tendency to tell us more than we want or need to know may account for the book's great length. Nevertheless, even given an unexceptional prose style, James's prodigious research and penetrating analysis more than offset any flaws in the book. Volume two concludes with the Japanese surrender in Tokyo Bay and sets the stage for volume three, dealing with MacArthur's "most significant contributions . . . when he served as an administrator during the Japanese occupation" (p. x). This biography will not lay to rest the controversies which still swirl about the MacArthur name and legend, but it will certainly make the debate better-informed.

FREDERICK J. DOBNEY

Saint Louis University
Missouri

ARTHUR S. LINK et al., eds. *The Papers of Woodrow Wilson: 1908–1909*. Vol. 18. Pp. xii, 672. Princeton, N.J.: Princeton University Press, 1975. $22.50.

ARTHUR S. LINK et al., eds. *The Papers of Woodrow Wilson: 1909–1910*. Vol. 19. Pp. viii, 785. Princeton, N.J.: Princeton University Press, 1975. $22.50.

Wilson, in this continuing series, at least from hindsight, moves almost visibly toward the Presidency. Yet the details of his forward movement reveal enigmas. His personal milieu is amazingly narrow, emphasizing parochial details of Princeton life, with its courses, student clubs, and the like, the personalities and wants of benefactors, and, in the long view, second-rate litterateurs like Robert Bridges: "Bobby" to Wilson. Wilson exposes his deepest feelings to a Mary Allen Hulbert Peck. He lets down his guard in private talk while visiting Great Britain (18:386) to voice views of "darkies" extremely derogatory to their hopes and future.

Yet there is power and enormous control in his numerous public statements and speeches which say much for him and his ability to sway a Progressive generation. He avers his conservatism, and offers indirect, and sometimes direct contrasts with Theodore Roosevelt and Bryan. He accuses the former of overdoing executive power (18:264), though he himself has praised leaders as self-appointed and emphasized the unique prerogatives of the Presidency, which public opinion alone limits. He urges law rather than regulation, fears it can lead to socialism, later softens this by accepting the "principle" of regulation. He praises business, but also warns that businessmen are too "selfish." He lectures often on the need for rigid standards of study, but draws laughter and applause by criticizing his own establishment: "To be studious in the ordinary conventional sense, if I may judge by my observation at a university, is to do the things you have to do and not understand them particularly" (19:39). Wilson sweeps aside sectional differences. Abraham Lincoln is "our" Lincoln. It is a "delightful" thing that Robert E. Lee is now, he believes, a national hero. He is for incorruptibility in public affairs, but: "The peculiarity of a politician is that he is a fellow very much like what you would be in the same circumstances" (18:601).

Wilson is a master of popularization. As the *Nation* nicely puts it, his lectures published in *Constitutional Government in the United States* (1908) are "suggestive, but not very profound." Indeed, it employs the most obvious details in hailing John Marshall, commenting on the Tariff of 1828, and the Presidential crisis of 1876. Wilson's method permits him to say anything at all which serves his argument: "Frederick did for Prussia more than Elizabeth did for England. He made it a compact and potentially powerful kingdom, and then himself called it into consciousness" (18:90). Whatever this meant, his rhetoric impressed readers and auditors on all elite and semi-elite levels, and thrilled them, as when he honored Robert E. Lee for having avoided the "weak course of expediency" and having preferred the "spending [of] his people's blood and his own." This once-famous speech was delivered at the University of North Carolina, but admired elsewhere by readers who saw him as the orator they sought: one who would "go about and make men drunk with [the] spirit of self-sacrifice" (18:641, 645).

Speaking to municipal clubs, chambers of commerce, college assemblies, at commencements, annual meetings, and special occasions everywhere across the country, Wilson mixes wholly serious and even exalted charges with anecdotes and jokes, all thoroughly dated but all heartily received. Volume 19 of this series gives in definitive detail yet to be completed the struggle over the site of the graduate school. On the surface it amounts to little: whether the school should be set among undergraduate buildings, or set aside from them as a sanctuary for scholars. But if Wilson staked his academic prestige on the "democratic" alternative, it needs to be noted how determined were his foes to win victory for their version of elitism.

LOUIS FILLER

Antioch College
Yellow Springs
Ohio

DAVE RICHARD PALMER. *The Way of the Fox: American Strategy in the War for America, 1775–1783.* Pp. xx, 229. Westport, Conn.: Greenwood Press, 1975. $12.50.

The author of this volume is a 1956 graduate of West Point and a former member of its faculty. Currently a Lieutenant Colonel assigned to the Office of the Army Chief of Staff, he is now writing a book on the recent campaigns in Vietnam. The first half of the present book is devoted to the principles of military strategy already apparent in the 18th century and the yet-to-be-formulated strategic ideas of the 19th century. Colonel Palmer maintains that the strategic capabilities of Washington compare favorably with those of other military leaders of the period. He concludes that Washington, although lacking formal military education, was happily endowed with hard common sense and successfully applied principles that had not yet been formally introduced. Palmer deals with the Revolutionary War in New England, New York, Pennsylvania, and Virginia, but devotes little time to the war in the South, presumably because Washington was not involved in these campaigns. He does not treat in detail the battles and incidents of the war, but takes care to show how Washington adapted his strategy to fit each phase of the conflict. Palmer recounts his successes and explains away his failures, emphasizing the non-military problems which confronted him. The last half of the book is in deep praise of Washington, the "Fox" of the title, and Palmer borrows the words of Lighthorse Harry Lee in describing him as "first in war." The book is easy to read and is not burdened with details that do not fit into the story.

CECIL JOHNSON

University of North Carolina
Chapel Hill

CABELL PHILLIPS. *The 1940s: Decade of Triumph and Trouble.* Pp. xi, 414. New York: Macmillan, 1975. $12.95.

This volume in the *New York Times' Chronicle of American Life* series is well suited to adorn the coffee tables and mantles of college-educated businessmen in their fifties or older. Its bulk will restrict its appeal to insatiable readers or those who wish to appear as such. Its substance will appeal primarily to those who were active participants in the United States of the 1940s.

Its conclusions that the 1940s democratized American society and that today's middle class dominates American government and society will appeal to successful middle-class businessmen.

Phillips advances no startling interpretations. The journalist-author's thesis is that the 1940s served as a decade of transition from depression to affluence and from isolationism to internationalism. His method is to recapture the events and moods of the decade as experienced and expressed by literate Americans, continuing the genre of *Only Yesterday*. Those who remember their own role during the 1940s will enjoy the review of the decade. The sections devoted to wartime subversion as viewed from Phillips' position as Press Information Officer for the Department of Justice, the postwar "Red Menace," and presidential campaigns are particularly interesting.

It is difficult to distinguish this volume from many written in the 1950s, and understandably so since few of the secondary sources cited by the author were published after 1960. Domestically, Phillips concludes by quoting from John Kenneth Galbraith's *The Affluent Society* and citing the problems of an increasingly wealthy middle class. Internationally, he demonstrates a belief in a continuing Cold War, states that Germany is the greatest postwar issue, practically ignores Southeast Asia, and totally neglects the collective Third World.

Phillips relied heavily on the *New York Times* and other contemporary newspapers and magazines as sources. His own journalistic experiences and interviews with colleagues at the *Times* provide the most interesting commentary in the book. He also utilized the memoirs of participants without noting the hazards of such sources. Although he consulted several published government documents of the period, the author has done little archival research. Lack of such research is not surprising or distressing in a book of this type, but the author's failure to profit from the

scholarship of the last fifteen years dictated the 1950s' tone of his writing.

MARTIN I. ELZY

Lyndon B. Johnson Library
Austin
Texas

RICHARD J. STILLMAN, II. *The Rise of the City Manager: A Public Professional in Local Government.* Pp. 170. Albuquerque: University of New Mexico Press, 1974. $8.95.

This study deals with over half a century of experience with a unique American contribution to politics—the council-manager plan. We follow the plan from its early days as a movement to achieve the twin objectives of popular control of local government and efficient management through its emphasis on scientific management to today when the plan seeks to meet the complex needs of suburbia. The position of manager as community leader is traced from the early days when the supposed separation of policy making and administration led proponents of the manager plan and the code of the profession to maintain that the manager was not a political leader, to today when it is widely recognized that the manager must exercise leadership functions in the policy-making area. Efforts of the managers to establish their status as a professional are dealt with sympathetically and the professionalism of the manager is compared with that of the career diplomat and the school superintendent with the conclusion that managers are the least protected by their professionalism from external pressures. This study concludes with the plea that the manager profession develop "a more coherent image of its functions and purposes on the modern urban scene"—one with more emphasis on process and political leadership, more understanding of the broad developments of our civilization, and greater skill in dealing with group relationship. The manager must become an engineer of group behavior rather than a bureaucratic manager. There are some

nated classes. Rather, in plural societies, ideologies are varied, sometimes flexible, sometimes polarizing, sometimes unitary and almost always determined by racial rather than class differences. They are also at times independent, rather dependent variables in social change.

The theme of the social change essays and the book review is that neither Marx nor Durkheim adequately explains change in plural societies. Again with some oversimplification: according to Durkheim, internal differentiation in time breaks down the isolation of the segments of a mechanically solidary society leading to the rise of a functionally differentiated organically solidary society—and change is evolutionary; according to Marx, class differentiation oriented to the means of production grows increasingly polarized as the productive potential of a given technology is exhausted, turning society into a structure of coercive domination that can only be overthrown by violence —and change is revolutionary. Primarily following M. G. Smith, Professor Kuper argues that in plural societies neither Durkheim's concept of the role of continuities nor the Marxian concept of the role of discontinuities is appropriate, for both are subordinated to forces resting on differences of race. While race-based differences almost always tend to polarize in a head-long rush to violent revolution, this is not an inevitable outcome. The proper cultivation of trans-racial continuities could make possible the liberal dream of peaceable change in plural societies.

This schematic outline hardly does justice to Professor Kuper's subtlety and insight; his essays must be read to be appreciated. Unfortunately they are repetitious with the same argument recurring in sometimes similar, sometimes different language and with minor unresolved differences. Throughout the volume one feels stuck at the same point. Also the essays employ two rather disconcerting stylistic devices; the author periodically fires off volleys of rhetorical questions only some of which are answered in the ensuing analysis; and many of his arguments are of a conclusory nature—that is, appearing to be deductions from theories or empirical matter not in evidence. One can only regret that the author did not scrap his essays and write a new monograph which could well have been half as long and twice as good.

As things stand, *Race, Class and Power* seems to have a hidden biographical theme that may be phrased as "one man's Odyssey from Marxism to liberal functionalism." While this is of intrinsic interest it detracts from the analytical task of developing the full conceptual resources for the analysis of plural societies. Gumplowicz, a contemporary of Marx, had always placed racial and ethnic differences, war, conquest and politics at the core of the problems of stratification and socio-political change. Max Weber, a contemporary of Durkheim, developed a flexible typology of stratification concepts which assigned significance to party and status group as well as class for the analysis of the dynamics of internal societal differentiation and change. Yet though both Gumplowicz and Weber appear in Kuper's bibliography, he does not exploit them in his analyses.

Appendix II in which Professor Kuper accuses the Clarendon Press of "surrogate censorship" for omitting his chapter on African nationalism (while leaving it in the international edition) from Volume II of the South African edition of the *Oxford History of South Africa*, strikes me as a bit over zealous. If the Clarendon editors were correct: by omitting Kuper's chapter they were protecting their South African editor; they would have been unfair to other authors had they proceeded on a course that would have led to the banning of the book altogether; by binding blank pages in the South African edition where Kuper's chapter would have been, they were voicing a quiet but insistent protest against the South African Suppression of Communism Act. Incidentally, the Clarendon Press's manner of handling the problem not only gave Professor Kuper world wide publicity, but may well have caused the South African authorities to reconsider whether it was not really better to have the chapter published than to remain as a reproach of bigotry. Perhaps Professor Kuper, who opts for nonviolent social change, should consider the possibility that in the world of publishing, too, there may be procedures short of the "violence" of abrupt confrontation and censorship to bring about change.

DON MARTINDALE
University of Minnesota
St. Paul

LOUIS SCHNEIDER. *The Sociological Way of Looking at the World.* Pp. ix, 343. New York: McGraw-Hill, 1975. $12.50.

There is a brilliant insight behind this book. The way to produce a manageable introduction to sociology, one that does not miss the forest among the trees, is to focus on what it means to think sociologically. Professor Schneider expounds four "pathways" involved in "the sociological way of looking at the world": (1) irony, (2) culture, social structure, and personality, (3) cultural and social change, and (4) what might be labeled the values of sociology.

So far so good. Unfortunately, Professor Schneider fails to heed sufficiently his own warning: "If one tries a bland reconciliation of 'everything' there is a danger of coming out with pap." Though he tries mightily, Professor Schneider never succeeds in reconciling the split between so-called "conflict" and "consensus" sociology.

The most blatant manifestation of this failure is Professor Schneider's unwillingness (and/or inability) to integrate his fascinating treatment of irony (Part I) with the rest of the book. He declares several times that sociology must refrain from "irony-mongering." Irony, Professor Schneider believes, "does not set down the very foundations of the field."

If irony "does not set down the very foundations," we never discover what does. Even if irony is not the basis, Professor Schneider's treatment is just sufficient to suggest that the ironic theme might have served as a focus for the whole book and provided the missing link between "conflict" and "consensus" sociology. Irony comes very close to the "debunking" activities of the conflict sociologists but with more of the "objectivity" demanded by the consensus sociologists.

As it turns out, there are really two books here, one on irony, and one on the usual sociological concepts of culture, social structure and personality. The more challenging book (both to write and to read) would have been to use the theme of irony as the rubric within which to develop the sociological way of looking at the world. This might not have been so difficult as it might at first seem. Though Professor Schneider tries to quarantine irony in Part I, the theme reappears softly throughout the rest of the book. (Even the index fails to note the consistent references to irony beyond Part I.)

If ultimately Professor Schneider's intention is to justify the sociological way, to convince us that sociology goes beyond the "obvious," the "trivial," the "irrelevant," the "jargonistic," and the "pseudomathematical," then, ironically enough, he should have rested his case at the end of Part I.

RANDY HUNTSBERRY
Wesleyan University
Middletown
Connecticut

JAMES L. SUNDQUIST. *Dispersing Population: What America Can Learn from Europe.* Pp. xi, 290. Washington, D.C.: The Brookings Institution, 1975. $9.95.

This is another well-written, competently researched economic study from Brookings. While population deconcentration has been given much political attention in the U.S., as well as in Western Europe, here we have done relatively little to bring it about compared with the programs in Great Britain, France, Italy, Netherlands, and Sweden which Sundquist analyzes.

The actions taken by the Europeans are two-fold and essentially economic in character: slowing manufacturing and service industry growth in the heavily populated areas while stimulating such growth in the areas of declining population. The intended results are to arrest growth or even decrease population in the metro areas while causing people to stay in the declining areas. Job creation is the key. The many incentives and disincentives offered by governments to plan for and regulate where new jobs are offered workers are examined and evaluated. Tax incentives, direct grants, infrastructure creation, improved government services, low-interest loans are only some of the devices employed since World War II by the Europeans. One gains the impression, substantiated in part by limited data, that on balance these programs have been successful. On the other hand there are uncertainties as to the future. Dispersion plans are not backed by long range planning, assured political determination, and skilled administration. Sundquist presents the future prospects for each country studied.

The first and last chapters are devoted to an analysis of the American experience with population dispersal. Very little has been accomplished. On the other hand, Sundquist points out why the European policies are not necessarily suitable in every instance to our country. We are much larger, more diverse, have more complex urban areas and have different migration flows, to say nothing of the sharp philosophical differences existing among Americans as to the desirability of government action in this area. To Sundquist, whether or not we should have a dispersal policy is a separate question. He does assert that the Europeans have shown that dispersal policy and execution can be fairly simple, not too costly and it works. Interested readers should know beforehand, however, that the social, psycho-

logical, and cultural consequences of these policies are not dealt with in this book.

JAMES R. BELL
California State University
Sacramento

ANTHONY SUTCLIFFE and ROGER SMITH. *Birmingham, 1939–1970*. Pp. vii, 514. New York: Oxford University Press, 1974. $38.50.

In 1938 the City Council of Birmingham and, recently, the Birmingham Corporation commissioned a history of the city of which this is the third volume. Anthony Sutcliffe and Roger Smith are lecturers at the University of Sheffield and at the University of Glasgow, respectively. Sutcliffe and Smith did not strive for continuity from the two earlier volumes authored by others but set out to write an independent social history of Birmingham focusing on its modernization in the last 30 years and its recent extensive urban renewal.

This book will interest social scientists and urbanists other than urban historians and persons interested in Birmingham *per se*. As an urban sociologist, I found hospitable the authors' treatment of the recent history of the second largest metropolitan center in Great Britain. Stressing themes that are "essentially urban," their description of the public life of the community resembles a social survey and is reminiscent of the American community-studies tradition in sociology, though the authors stress they have approached their task as historians.

Beginning with a chapter on the impact of the War, there follow discussions on the role of mass media in the life of the city, issues in public education, an assessment of the extent to which the black West Indian and Asian minorities are absorbed by the city's economy, and other aspects of the city's public life. The authors, moreover, sought to make a case study that is generalizable to the process of metropolitanization of all the great urban regions in Great

Britain. Finally, they draw certain parallels with the rebuilt cities on the Continent and the American industrial city.

The authors insightfully treat Birmingham as an integral part of a metropolitan complex and of a national system of cities. In noting "the city's declining power to shape its own destiny," they are, in effect, describing a process well known to urban community sociologists. They also give attention to the impact of the suburbanization after the War on the life of the city, though I think more analytic attention to this process would have better elucidated the sources of the urban problems that Birmingham has faced and dealt with so admirably.

There is a lesson in Sutcliffe and Smith's book for students of the American city. In coming to be what the authors call "Britain's most transatlantic city," Birmingham has also come to share many of the social and urban problems of the American city. The authors, however, could have omitted the naive cliché, "a certain materialism and acquisitiveness among [Birmingham's] people," from their otherwise instructive comparison. This book serves not only as a thorough and scholarly description of the recent development of Birmingham, but it also can be taken as a cross-national comparison showing the similarity of basic urban processes and attendant problems in post-industrial cities and societies.

IRVING LEWIS ALLEN
University of Connecticut
Storrs

HANS TOCH, J. DOUGLAS GRANT and RAYMOND T. GALVIN. *Agents of Change: A Study in Police Reform*. Pp. 437. New York: Halsted Press, 1975. $16.50. Paperbound, $5.95.

One may wonder why on the dust jacket of this book the policeman, with a contented faint smile, peers between two Greek Ionic columns. Perhaps he caught someone who made an illegal left turn at the Erechteum (a lucrative business of police officers who are supposed to be busy with keeping another kind of law and order in the society), or, maybe, he is one of those whom the authors propose to transform to be a pious law enforcement agent who can shoot his way from earthly violence to the peaceful heaven.

The book is conspicuously a flat research report that responds to an NIMH grant; this might be suspected also from finding in the 437 pages only 37 footnotes (not too much even in a research report), 28 of them placed at the end of the 14 page-short introduction, another 2 in a later chapter printed at the foot of the page, and 7 more in one of the appendices. Since the 50s and 60s when violence has developed to be a stylish mode of demanding a variety of rights and privileges, primarily the police (and not the demanding masses) started to be charged with violent behavior, and this prompted publication of a number of studies on the violence of the law enforcement agents. This book is one of them, in quality not much different from the others. It is sailing with the winds of fashion.

As a police reform venture, this project suggests "to build a violence-oriented problem-solving component" into police departments. The authors want the policeman "to address" the problem of violence in an objective way. Through induction process, review of aims, suspended motivation, sugar-coated deterrence, catalytic discussions, defining the mission, faith and exploration, peer influence, systematizing knowledge and experience, solution of social problems (*sic!*), and other psychological kinds of strategies, the authors propose a program to proceed in cumulative, gradually re-cycling, stages. They would start working with a small group of men who would inform themselves about "the problem" and would prepare the men to take on roles as leaders for a larger problem-solving group. They would, then, extend the effort further, and ultimately, so the authors think, an institutional arrangement would develop in the form of a permanent problem-solving body within the police department. Their exploration has been demonstrated by several quantifying tables and charts.

When the authors are asking the questions, "Are people capable of change?" and "Specifically, can policemen change when they have a history of involvement in violent incidents?", as this reviewer can read them, they are asking two unrelated questions. The problem of the authors, as stated, appears to be simple enough; however, on detailed analysis it turns out to be highly complex, much more than the authors are presenting it, and it reaches spheres far beyond the scope of the investigators' design. The authors' technique in changing men is much too well known, but when it comes to the police (and here is the point where so many other "police books" hit a dead end) they display a curious naivety in failing to distinguish between individual attitudes and an irresistible social environment, also in missing the evaluation of reactions to stress, mainly if it arouses emotion, that depends on a host of factors with which the authors simply do not cope.

There is, of course, nothing harmful or wrong with what the authors want to do with policemen, but doctoring the mind of individual police officers is simply hopeless in a given social situation. It may seem to succeed until the law enforcement agent stays within the bricks of his total institution, or better "total organization," but once he steps out to the real world, a most significant difference between intended direction and the actual activation of human behavior will become obvious and almost always unavoidable. As opposed to a system-analysis or a structural-functional investigation, the authors' basis is chosen in preference to the examination of individuals (moreover, not even all who participate in violent incidents) that diverts attention from the societal environment which so strongly affects the behavior of the actors within the system.

The authors do not present causes, consequences, and cure in a unit, but as if they were independent elements. Moreover, by presenting only consequences and proposing cure, they neglect elaborating on causes. One of the most difficult subjects that man ponders is the relation between how man acts and how he believes he should act. Are the policemen's actions determined wholly by the values they hold, or are they dictated by stronger social forces which their ethical beliefs merely neutralize. The history of the American police would be a fertile field for this inquiry—but the authors missed it.

The book does not appear substantial enough to succeed; the real issue far exceeds the scope of this project. The inadequacies of the book stem from the faulty starting point and the designed arena which permit the real topic floating in a vacuum, and from the fault of the method which did not perceive the real perspective. It is just helping to perpetuate the often federally supported "let's change the police" type projects which re-emerge again and again with an all-absorbing passion of proposing cure without analyzing causes.

STEPHEN SCHAFER

Northeastern University
Boston
Massachusetts

ECONOMICS

MICHAEL F. COLLINS and TIMOTHY M. PHAROAH. *Transport Organization in a Great City: The Case of London.* Pp. 648. Beverly Hills, Calif.: Sage, 1974. $37.50.

If one is interested in the institutional origins of London's transportation problems, then this is the volume designed to satisfy that want. Such a specialized want, however, may not apply to a very large audience. And herein lies the problem of the book.

The book focuses on the nature and operation of the complex structure of institutions which was responsible for planning and operating transport in London. This focus is effected through 15 major case studies which comprise approximately 60 percent of the book. In these case studies attempts are made to show how the major insti-

tutions entered into the particular transportation matter at hand, what problems and delays arose, what arguments were used, and how powers were used to arrive at decisions relating to the matter-at-hand. The studies thoroughly trace the matter-at-hand from its inception through the latest decision.

While these cases make fascinating reading (having been chosen to represent a diverse series of events) and even though problems of a similar nature exist or will exist elsewhere, the lessons to be learned from such studies are likely to be so idiosyncratic to the situation and personalities involved as to be of only limited use for others. Nevertheless, the descriptions of how the institutional process constrains and influences decisions is indicative of problems faced world wide.

Several not too startling conclusions emerge from the book. Since this is a book dealing with institutions, it is not surprising that the conclusions are institutional and organizational in nature, for example, planning should take a systems approach with the transport, land use and environmental planners working together. This is a well known result from other research. It is, however, easy to discuss but very difficult to implement since total control is not possible and the causal relationships are not well understood.

A systems approach for transport planning is also advocated, that is, planners should study auto, bus, mass transit, and others as a system and not one mode at a time. Operating and investment policies should be coordinated so that cross purposes are not served. These ideas are also well known.

Finally, some other conclusions such as exclusive bus lanes (already implemented in the U.S.) and better pedestrian facilities are given.

In the English tradition, the case studies are qualitative in nature rather than quantitative. This is to be somewhat expected given the objectives of the study. However, since recommendations are a part of the study, a quantitative, generalizable methodology for assessing the likely impact of implementing those recommendations as well as assessing the impact of the current situation seems logical. It is not, however, presented.

In toto the book is well written and interesting. I would imagine, however, that it will find a very limited audience (especially at the price of $37.50).

W. BRUCE ALLEN
University of Pennsylvania
Philadelphia

STEPHEN J. DECANIO. *Agriculture in the Postbellum South: The Economics of Production and Supply.* Pp. xii, 335. Cambridge, Mass.: MIT Press, 1974. No price.

The author's zeal to define aspects of postbellum agriculture in the South deserves a more satisfactory outcome. His effort is to quantify what can only be approximately described. The project does not lend itself to key punching and computing. If the comparative advantage of cotton cultivation and comparative competence of black and white agricultural labor could be precisely calculated, the light shed on the postbellum economy of the South would be limited. With further enquiry, which it is hoped Professor DeCanio will pursue, he will deepen and broaden his understanding of the place, the period, and the people. The attempt at statistical statement is vitiated by the multiplicity and variety of influences at play, and even so more were present than are here comprehended. Cotton was not only a crop, it was a constitution of society. Soil exhaustion, migration to new lands, military government, political hostility, ignorance, routine, poverty, race prejudice, unabashed exploitation of the weaker members of the community, emergence of industry as against staple agriculture, legal restraints, and a confining credit system were some of the forces present.

What the author calls "the impressionistic evidence," the testimony of participants in and observers of the scene, is the genuine evidence, needing fullest possible collection and checking. Statistical array and mathematical calculation can do no more than confirm the results of careful inspection. The hope that manipulation of quantitative data according to a model can reveal secrets otherwise obscured is alchemy. The more the field is narrowed, the less meaningful the answers obtained. In addition to other complications not sufficiently included in this study, are changes over time. The development of cotton manufactures in the Southern Piedmont, commencing in a determined way a dozen years after the Civil War, fetched increasing numbers of tenant farmers into the mill villages, as the author recites. Indeed, the motive of the factory enterprisers was in instances semi-philanthropic, to relieve distressed whites on the land, and enliven the economy, as well as to turn a neat profit for promoters and investors. The slogan "bring the cotton mills to the cotton fields" was both a supplement to cotton growing and a protest against sub-marginal production of cotton. The advocacy of alternative crops ere long received impetus from ravages of the boll weevil, as witness the erection of a monument to the pest in a delta county which was forced to venture on dairying and vegetable canning.

The capture of private profits from cotton growing, whatever its extent, reflected little benefit to public welfare. The gains to the individual planter or merchant-creditor were speculative, and class cleavages in the society inhibited public spirit and generosity. Hence the scrutiny of market manifestations, which latterly has attracted practitioners of the "new economy history," is not informing, where the South is concerned, about social progress and prosperity.

Professor DeCanio, this reviewer feels, has painted himself into a corner. His talents will be better appreciated when he remains more in the open of Southern postbellum experience.

BROADUS MITCHELL
Rutgers University
New Brunswick, N.J.

YOEL HAITOVSKY, GEORGE TREYZ, and VINCENT SU. *Forecasts with Quarterly Macro-Econometric Models.* Pp. xix, 363. New York: National Bureau of Economic Research, 1974. $15.00.

This book is written for the specialist in econometric forecasting, that statistical art which seeks to provide ways of forecasting GNP and its components, as well as other "endogenous" variables, by setting up a mathematical model of the economy, determining statistically the parameters that relate changes in one variable to changes in others, and then inserting various "exogenous" variables—Government spending, perhaps categories of investment spending, exports, and the like—on the basis of informed judgment of the forecasters, and thus predicting what is going to happen. Econometric models in a full *ex post* sense are frequently used also to explain in systematic fashion past events—they may, if not too elaborate and complicated, provide a framework for economic historians to work in.

The authors of the volume, all research associates with the National Bureau of Economic Research as well as teachers, concentrate on two key models for forecasting quarterly events in the U.S. economy: that developed by the Office of Business Economics (OBE) of the Department of Commerce, and that developed under one of the greats in the field, Laurence Klein, at the Wharton School of the University of Pennsylvania. After a brief introduction on econometric models, although even this is not for the layman, the authors describe (but never fully lay out, even in an appendix) the OBE and Wharton School models. Their main efforts, then, involve ways to get at errors in the models, with the objective presumably to improve their accuracy. Again, most readers would have appreciated first some general picture of the errors (for example, the GNP forecast was generally off by two–six percent over the period of the late 1960s which the authors consider) before getting into details on pinpointing why the errors occurred, that is, whether because the model was faulty in some respect (not true), estimates of the exogenous variables proved wrong, or the parameter values involving the behavior of endogenous variables were at fault. The authors do eventually do this, in Chapter 7 (the last chapter), but even there no general summary picture is given.

In attempting to assign responsibility as between the latter two factors the authors use the parameters the model-builders use, but draw on *ex post* knowledge of the exogenous variables—they make exogenous values accord with actual facts. They find, surprising to this reviewer, that to do so frequently *worsens* the accuracy of the forecasts, implying that in some way the forecasters' judgments, perhaps linked to their knowledge about parameter values, proved to be better than the facts.

Part Two of the work involves an intricate "decomposition" of the forecasting errors in the two models—trying to pinpoint the sources of error. This is the most valuable part of the book, for the specialist. The results are impossible to summarize, for the sources of errors prove to be varied indeed.

The book seems to this reviewer to be of high quality and of considerable use for the specialist, but not something that the layman can really use to gain insights into this steadily improving, yet still-deficient art.

Philip W. Bell

University of California
Santa Cruz

Mary A. Holman. *The Political Economy of the Space Program*. Pp. vi, 398. Palo Alto, Calif.: Pacific Books, 1974. $24.95.

After 15 years of spectacular accomplishments and debates, the space program—the spender of one–two percent of all governmental outlays—has become the subject of comprehensive economic analysis. Professor Holman deserves compliments for writing a book which can be simultaneously valued by space scientists, political scientists, historians, the intelligent layperson, without sacrificing economic theory. The scope of the study ranges from a general survey of the program to its effect on employment and business organization.

The book does not skirt the fact that economic policy is frequently the servant of political and social policies, so that military, political, employment, cultural considerations all tend to influence the decision making process. An example is the measurement in dollar terms and the priority ranking of such elements as national prestige and good will (pp. 102–3). Notwithstanding such fictive quantities, most of the analysis is applied to more tractable cases: the cost comparison for possible launch sites to support the manned lunar landing program, the cost evaluation of possible sites for a NASA electronic research center, appraisal of business contracts, and so on.

It is the adaptation of cost-benefit analysis to her novel topic wherein the author's grasp of economic theory as well as political reality sheds new light on the space program. In due awareness of the many criticisms against the method, she leads the reader to perceive that after the objectives of a governmental program have been defined, they should be achieved at the lowest possible cost. This is, of course, the raison d'être of cost-benefit analysis. Namely: for optimum efficiency within the space sector, or any branch of it, it is necessary to measure the rate at which costs and benefits change when resources are alternatively allocated.

But this is a significant step forward from the rather intuitive approach widely used. For example, NASA has not applied specific discount rates, "although those economic factors are implicit in our consideration of alternative programs and assessment of priorities" (p. 98). Professor Holman, on the other hand, firmly adheres to the principle that "the proper discount rate for cost-benefit studies should reflect the opportunity cost of the use of resources on the proposed project. Opportunity cost, as used here, is the cost of not being able to put the resource to work on alternative projects" (p. 92).

This reviewer encountered one rather inconvenient error in the book where a table attempts to appraise satellite-obtained information systems: the ratios do not jibe with the costs and benefits (p. 107). Finally, it occurred to me how well this topic would lend itself to a "grants economy" analysis, that is, tracing the grant elements versus exchange elements and then identifying the beneficiaries of the program within the public sector (various agencies) and the private sector (Telestar, atomic energy industry) of the national economy.

JANOS HORVATH

Butler University
Indianapolis
Indiana

THEODORE H. MORAN. *Multinational Corporations and the Politics of Dependence: Copper in Chile.* Pp. vii, 286. Princeton, N.J.: Princeton University Press, 1974. $12.50.

Theodore H. Moran has written a thoroughly researched and judicious analytical history of Chile's Gran Mineria, the premier export industry formerly dominated by U.S. mining interests. In the second, third and seventh chapters, Moran's work demonstrates a skillful blending of political and economic concepts as he analyzes the structure and strategy of the international copper industry (past and future) and the growth of economic nationalism in Chile from 1945 to 1954.

In contrast to my own view, the author appears to minimize the positive results of the "New Deal" copper legislation of 1955 (see Chapter 4). As I have shown elsewhere (*National Tax Journal*, Vol. 14, No. 1, March, 1961), Chile benefited considerably from this legislation. It set in motion intensive prospecting operations and these led to the discovery of two major ore bodies by Anaconda (El Salvador and Exotica) and a third deposit (Rio Blanco) by the Cerro Corporation. Production was increased from available capacity and an expansion program totaling $200 million was initiated. Consequently, output of the Gran Mineria increased 50 percent between 1953–54, the two years preceding the "New Deal" Law, and 1959–60, on completion of the investment program. Further, Chile increased its total copper income by about one-half despite a one-cent drop in the average price of copper between the two periods. Finally, had the Chilean government extended its 1955 agreement regarding stable tax rates, the U.S. copper companies would have launched a second major expansion program during the early sixties. By failing to reach an accommodation with Anaconda and Kennecott at that time, Chile lost, according to my estimates, roughly $1.5 billion of net foreign exchange income.

In Chapter 5, Moran shows the diverging strategies of Kennecott and Anaconda in trying to cope with political pressures for greater national ownership and control over the Gran Mineria. Clearly, of the two enterprises, Kennecott had a much better perception of Chilean political realities and behaved accordingly. Unfortunately, the author does not distinguish sufficiently between President Frei's "Chileanization" and "pacted nationalization" agreements (that involved in every instance effective compensation to the U.S. copper companies) and the Allende regime's *de facto* confiscation of their remaining assets.

In Chapter 6, the analytical core of the volume, Moran develops a "dynamic balance of power model" that illuminates the changing relationship between the foreign mineral investor and the "host country." The relative weight of bargaining strength tilts in favor of the "host government" after the foreign company's lump-sum investment in new production capacity in mines and smelters has been completed. The government is then in a position, particularly if its nationals have developed the technical and managerial capacity to operate the mineral complex, to force a "renegotiation" of the agreement (p. 161). The author argues convincingly that U.S. pressure for Chilean land reform through the Alliance for Progress in the 1960s ultimately undermined the political support that Chilean conservative groups had given Anaconda and Kennecott in the 1950s.

In the concluding chapter, "Economic Nationalism and the Future," Moran recommends a new resource company-host country relationship that minimizes equity ownership or includes the option of systematic divestment, and provides regular procedures for renegotiation of terms.

ERIC N. BAKLANOFF

The University of Alabama
University

ARTHUR M. OKUN. *Equality and Efficiency.* Pp. vii, 124. Washington, D.C.: The Brookings Institution, 1975. $6.95.

This timely book is the expanded version of the Godkin lectures presented by the author at the John F. Kennedy School at Harvard University in April, 1974.

The objective is to explain the conflicts in our society between equality among citizens and economic efficiency. The author explains how, in America, by the process of gradual adjustment and counterbalance, there is a constant tradeoff. He describes how economic efficiency gives a few people a great amount of power, privilege, and the possibility of influencing others.

The following phenomenon is not described by the author: Some economic activities under the name of economic efficiency may be in the long run inconsistent with this efficiency. Individual economic efficiency may have high social overhead—such as the production of alcohol, uncontrolled publication of questionable books, and other activities.

Measures which help individual equality and are considered irrelevant to economic efficiency sometimes have a positive tradeoff in the long run in favor of economic efficiency. If, for example, citizens are unable to exercise their free choice of work due to ill health or other uncontrollable factors, and they are helped, economic efficiency is also helped in the long run. There are no pure tradeoffs, but an acceptable investment and an act of pure economic efficiency.

The author entertainingly describes various attempts in our society to create more equality of opportunity and to help individuals exercise their rights. The following fundamental concept is not mentioned: If citizens are to exercise their basic rights, they must have the minimum tools and means to live. A person who loses health or job due to uncontrollable events cannot be considered as having the necessary freedom to exercise certain basic rights. His life is reduced to a degrading slavery. His basic rights and freedom become non-operational.

Those who lose their subsistence means should be given an opportunity to work in subsidized enterprises along with free minimum health care for all. Such enterprises need careful planning and organization to be realized well. If realized well, they will be cheaper and less degrading than welfare and unemployment subsidies. These socially organized enterprises could increase and decrease in size and activity in the areas of predetermined economic activities, depending on the size of the existing unemployment. No doubt, in government subsidized enterprises, there will be some undesirable results, as there certainly are in our present welfare and unemployment policies.

The author does not explain carefully that we have in many fields, powerful quasi-monopolistic industries which hinder the working of the competitive system. A better tradeoff between this unbalanced power and principle of equality among citizens is needed. The fact that punishment of the violation of private property by individuals is far greater than punishment of its violation by big corporations (by fixing prices and other monopolistic or illegal procedures) distresses all who see the injustice, and particularly our youth. Recent disclosures regarding the illegal use of contributions and trading of an undesirable nature, make the concept of economic efficiency in its puritan form seem highly debatable as a workable concept.

The author does not give due emphasis to the ethical and moral aspects of economic efficiency and equality among citizens. He mentions that defense of economic efficiency and free enterprise on moral principles is not a "persuasive factor." This attitude is a common one in universities, special business schools, chambers of commerce, and many other institutions. This is unfortunate. A competitive economic system is more ethical than a socialist or Communist system. A revival of ethics and morality could bring about more balance between individual rights and economic efficiency than the most intricate legal and legislative acts.

I recommend this excellent scholar's book for its intelligent and meaningful presentation of important topics. Such books create an interest in economic issues. It has been fashionable to devote time and energy to the discussion of overly abstract and irrelevant economic topics. This book, or books like it, may create a new trend that will give economics its proper place of leadership in our society.

ALLEN O. BAYLOR
University of Texas
El Paso

ARTHUR B. SHOSTAK, JON VAN TIL and SALLY BOULD VAN TIL. *Privilege in America: An End to Inequality?* Pp. v, 150. Englewood Cliffs, N.J.: Prentice-Hall, 1973. $6.95.

BARRY R. CHISWICK. *Income Inequality.* Pp. x, 212. New York: National Bureau of Economic Research, 1974. No price.

The two books under review could not be more different, and in the face of obvious space limitations a unitary review is virtually impossible. Shostak and the Van Tils have set out to challenge the prevailing structure of inequality in American society. Their book is divided into three parts. The first part explores the origins and major dimensions of inequality and presents a brief but adequate overview of the degree and stability of inequality in America. Part Two considers intellectual-*cum*-political responses to inequality, including a spirited and intelligent discussion of populism, democratic socialism, and ethnic group politics. Part Three consists of a discussion of meliorative programs, especially cash transfer programs.

It would be easy to fault this slender volume for missing this or that (for example, it is not noted that much of the terribly small reduction in family income inequality over the past thirty years may in fact be the result of the increasing number of households with more than one wage earner) or for failing to explore the full range of political responses to inequality; this would be unfair. The book is clearly not intended to be anything but an opening, or better, a re-opening of serious deliberation. As a vehicle for introducing students and general readers to a discussion of inequality it serves very well but it is not a substitute for more detailed and exhaustive analysis. The great virtue of this volume, in this reader's mind, is that it does not attempt to preclude or close off argument. Rather, it pointedly demonstrates that inequality is not a given; inequality results from particular social arrangements and the political struggles, large and small, that create, sustain, and, let it be said, change those arrangements. As the conservative response to the re-opened debate over our society's harsh inequalities swells, books such as *Privilege in America* are all the more needed. As importantly, as this book makes clear again and again, more than books are needed: the call to action, and the analysis of alternative courses of action, pose a challenge to all of us.

That simply more books are not the answer is ably demonstrated by the Chiswick monograph. I should say at the outset that I am utterly unable to render a judgment on what I take to be the central point of *Income Inequality*; namely, the elaboration of an econometric model embodying the major factors of a human capital analysis. In this, Chiswick may be a virtuoso. But the reader who hopes to learn something substantive about inequalities of income had best look elsewhere. The income inequality Chiswick is concerned with is the inequality between income distributions among the 50 states (plus the District of Columbia). This, I hasten to add, is not irrelevant for some important purposes (state and regional planning, for example), but it is a focus that tells us little or nothing about why some few are very rich and most barely manage to get by. We learn that a state's income distribution is affected by the investment in education and the character (type and amount) of employment sustained by a state's policy. In other words, if all states had identical economic structures and made available identical opportunities for schooling, the income distributions for all states would be quite similar—providing, of course, the residents of all states had similar age distributions, work experiences, racial backgrounds and sex ratios. As I said, the major contribution of Chiswick must be in the econometric models he derives. I hope that my review does not preclude his book's being reviewed by someone competent to judge its merits in that regard.

JAN DIZARD

Amherst College
Massachusetts

OTHER BOOKS

The ABS Guide, 1975 Supplement: Recent Publications in the Social and Behavioral Sciences. Pp. 210. Beverly Hills, Calif.: Sage, 1975. $15.00.

AIZCORBE, ROBERTO. *Argentina: The Peronist Myth*. Pp. v, 313. Hicksville, N.Y.: Exposition Press, 1975. $10.00.

AKHTAR, SHADID. *Health Care in The People's Republic of China. A Bibliography with Abstracts*. Pp. 182. Ottawa, Ca.: International Development Research Center, 1975. $1.00. Paperbound.

ALLAND, ALEXANDER, JR. *When the Spider Danced: Notes from an African Village*. Pp. 240. New York: Doubleday, 1975. $8.95.

ANDRESKI, STANISLAV, ed. *Reflections on Inequality*. Pp. 159. New York: Barnes & Noble, 1975. $14.75.

ATKINSON, A. B. *The Economics of Inequality*. Pp. 295. New York: Oxford University Press, 1975. $17.75. Paperbound, $6.25.

AVAKUMOVIC, IVAN. *The Communist Party in Canada: A History*. Pp. v, 309. Toronto, Ca.: McClelland and Stewart Limited, 1975. $5.95. Paperbound.

AVRUTIS, RAYMOND. *How to Collect Unemployment Benefits*. Pp. 128. New York: Schocken Books, 1975. $1.25. Paperbound.

BAIROCH, PAUL. *The Economic Development of the Third World since 1900*. Pp. 274. Berkeley: University of California Press, 1975. $12.00.

BALL, GEORGE W., ed. *Global Companies: The Political Economy of World Business*. Pp. 179. Englewood Cliffs, N.J.: Prentice-Hall, 1975. $7.95. Paperbound, $2.95.

BARNARD, JOHN and DAVID BURNER, eds. *The American Experience in Education*. Pp. v, 268. New York: New Viewpoints, 1975. No price.

BECKER, ABRAHAM S., BENT HANSEN and MALCOLM H. KERR. *The Economics and Politics of the Middle East*. Pp. v, 131. New York: American Elsevier, 1975. $7.95.

BECKER, CHARLOTTE. *Four Years to Go*. Pp. 111. Hicksville, N.Y.: Exposition Press, 1975. $6.00.

BECKER, GARY S. and WILLIAM M. LANDES, eds. *Essays in the Economics of Crime and Punishment*. Pp. 268. New York: National Bureau of Economic Research, 1974. $12.50. Paperbound, $5.00.

BELLRINGER, ALAN W. and C. B. JONES. *The Victorian Sages: An Anthology of Prose*. Pp. v, 241. Totowa, N.J.: Rowman and Littlefield, 1975. $10.00. Paperbound, $5.00.

BENDER, LYNN DARRELL. *The Politics of Hostility*. Pp. ix, 156. San Juan, P.R.: Inter American University Press, 1975. $7.95. Paperbound, $2.95.

BENJAMIN, JACQUES. *Planification et Politique au Quebec*. Pp. 142. Portland, Ore.: ISBS, 1975. $7.25. Paperbound.

BENNETT, W. LANCE. *The Political Mind and the Political Environment*. Pp. vii, 207. Lexington, Mass.: Lexington Books, 1975. $16.00.

BENSMAN, JOSEPH and ARTHUR J. VIDICH, eds. *Metropolitan Communities*. Pp. vi, 296. New York: New Viewpoints, 1975. $5.95. Paperbound.

BERG, ALAN, NEVIN S. SCRIMSHAW and DAVID L. CALL, eds. *Nutrition, National*

Development, and Planning. Pp. vi, 401. Cambridge, Mass.: MIT Press, 1975. No price.

BERNARD, H. RUSSELL. *The Human Way.* Pp. v, 391. New York: Macmillan, 1975. $5.95. Paperbound.

BERNARD, JESSIE. *Women, Wives, Mothers: Values and Options.* Pp. v, 286. Chicago, Ill.: Aldine-Atherton, 1975. $15.00. Paperbound, $5.95.

BINKIN, MARTIN. *The Military Pay Muddle.* Pp. vii, 66. Washington, D.C.: Brookings Institution, 1975. $2.50. Paperbound.

BIRD, RICHARD M. and OLIVER OLDMAN. *Readings on Taxation in Developing Countries.* 3rd ed. Pp. viii, 555. Baltimore, Md.: Johns Hopkins University Press, 1975. $16.50.

BLACK, EDWIN R. *Divided Loyalties: Canadian Concepts of Federalism.* Pp. xii, 272. Quebec, Ca.: McGill-Queen's University Press, 1975. $13.00. Paperbound, $6.00.

BLACKMER, DONALD L. M. and ANNIE KRIEGEL. *The International Role of the Communist Parties of Italy and France.* Pp. x, 67. Cambridge, Mass.: Harvard University Press, 1975. $2.75. Paperbound.

BLACKWOOD, R. T. and A. L. HERMAN, eds. *Problems in Philosophy, West and East.* Pp. vii, 474. Englewood Cliffs, N.J.: Prentice-Hall, 1975. $11.95.

BLINDER, ALAN S. *Toward an Economic Theory of Income Distribution.* Pp. viii, 176. Cambridge, Mass.: MIT Press, 1974. No price.

BLOOMER, D. C. *Life and Writings of Amelia Bloomer.* Pp. 410. New York: Schocken Books, 1975. $7.50. Paperbound, $3.95.

BOSWORTH, BARRY, JAMES S. DUESENBERRY and ANDREW S. CARRON. *Capital Needs in the Seventies.* Pp. vii, 85. Washington, D.C.: Brookings Institution, 1975. $2.50. Paperbound.

BRUCE, NEIL. *Portugal: The Last Empire.* Pp. 160. New York: Halsted, 1975. No price.

BUCHAN, ALASTAIR. *Change without War: The Shifting Structure of World Power.* The BBC Reith Lectures, 1973. Pp. 112. New York: St. Martin's Press, 1975. $8.95.

BURNS, HENRY, JR. *Corrections: Organization and Administration.* Criminal Justice Series. Pp. 578. St. Paul, Minn.: West Publishing Company, 1975. No price.

BURNS, JAMES MACGREGOR and J. W. PELTASON. *Government by the People.* 9th ed. Pp. 876. Englewood Cliffs, N.J.: Prentice-Hall, 1975. $12.95. Paperbound, $9.95.

BUTLER, DAVID and DONALD STOKES. *Political Change in Britain: The Evolution of Electoral Choice.* 2nd ed. Pp. 500. New York: St. Martin's Press, 1975. $19.95.

CAMPBELL, THOMAS M. and GEORGE C. HERRING, eds. *The Diaries of Edward R. Stettinius, Jr., 1943–1946.* Pp. xii, 544. New York: New Viewpoints, 1975. $6.95. Paperbound.

CAPLOW, THEODORE. *Sociology.* 2nd ed. Pp. vi, 420. Englewood Cliffs, N.J.: Prentice-Hall, 1975. $11.95.

CAPOUYA, EMILE and KEITHA TOMPKINS, eds. *The Essential Kropotkin.* Pp. vii, 294. New York: W. W. Norton, 1975. $12.50. Paperbound, $3.95.

CARLTON, DAVID and CARLO SCHAERF, eds. *The Dynamics of the Arms Race.* Pp. 244. New York: Halsted Press, 1975. $17.95.

CARTER, ROBERT M., RICHARD A. MCGEE and E. KIM NELSON. *Corrections in America.* Pp. v, 497. Philadelphia, Pa.: J. B. Lippincott, 1975. $10.95. Paperbound, $7.95.

CARVER, TERRELL. *Karl Marx: Texts on Method.* Pp. vii, 230. New York: Barnes & Noble, 1975. $17.50.

CAYER, N. JOSEPH. *Public Personnel Administration in the United States.* Pp. 178. New York: St. Martin's Press, 1975. $10.95. Paperbound, $4.50.

CHATOV, ROBERT. *Corporate Financial Reporting: Public or Private Control?* Pp. vii, 363. New York: Free Press, 1975. $15.00.

CHEIT, EARL F. *The Useful Arts and the Liberal Tradition.* Pp. xiii, 166. New York: McGraw-Hill, 1975. $10.00.

Chemical Disarmament: New Weapons for Old. A SIPRI Monograph. Pp. v, 151. New York: Humanities, 1975. No price.

CHENERY, HOLLIS and MOISES SYRQUIN. *Patterns of Development, 1950–1970.* A World Bank Research Publication. Pp. v, 234. New York: Oxford University Press, 1975. $14.50. Paperbound, $5.00.

CHESTER, EDWARD W. *Sectionalism, Politics, and American Diplomacy.* Pp. iii, 348. Metuchen, N.J.: Scarecrow Press, 1975. $12.50.

CHOUE, YOUNG SEEK. *Toward the Brighter Future.* Pp. 259. Seoul, Korea: Moon Wha Printing Company, 1974. No price.

CHUDACOFF, HOWARD P. *The Evolution of American Urban Society.* Pp. iii, 280. Englewood Cliffs, N.J.: Prentice-Hall, 1975. $12.50.

CHURCHWARD, L. G. *Contemporary Soviet*

Government. 2nd ed. Pp. v, 368. New York: American Elsevier, 1975. $19.00.

CIECHANOWSKI, JAN M. *The Warsaw Rising of 1944*. Pp. v, 332. New York: Cambridge University Press, 1974. $19.50.

CLARK, BURTON R., ed. *The Problems of American Education*. Pp. 342. New York: New Viewpoints, 1975. $5.95. Paperbound.

CLARKE, ANN M. and A. D. B. CLARKE, eds. *Mental Deficiency: The Changing Outlook*. 3rd ed. Pp. vi, 886. New York: The Free Press, 1975. $25.00.

CLARKSON, KENNETH W. *Food Stamps and Nutrition*. Pp. 85. Washington, D.C.: American Enterprise Institute for Public Policy Research, 1975. $3.00. Paperbound.

Congressional Roll Call 1974: A Chronology and Analysis of Votes in the House and Senate 93rd Congress, Second Session. Pp. 170. Washington, D.C.: Congressional Quarterly, 1975. $8.50. Paperbound.

COOK, ADRIAN. *The Alabama Claims: American Politics and Anglo-American Relations, 1865–1872*. Pp. 261. Ithaca, N.Y.: Cornell University Press, 1975. $13.50.

COOK, CHRIS and JOHN PAXTON. *European Political Facts, 1918–1973*. Pp. 363. New York: St. Martin's Press, 1975. $14.95.

COOK, CHRIS. *Sources in British Political History, 1900–1951. A Guide to the Archives of Selected Organizations and Societies*. Vol. I. Pp. v, 330. New York: St. Martin's Press, 1975. $16.95.

COOPER, CLARE C. *Easter Hill Village: Some Social Implication of Design*. Pp. vii, 337. New York: The Free Press, 1975. $15.95.

COSTELLO, FRANK BARTHOLOMEW. *The Political Philosophy of Luis De Molina, S.J. (1535–1600)*. Pp. xiv, 242. Spokane, Wash.: Gonzaga University Press, 1974. No price.

COXE, JACK WOODLEY. *The Science of Influence*. Pp. v, 174. New York: Vantage Press, 1975. $6.95.

CREWE, IVOR, ed. *British Political Sociology Yearbook: The Politics of Race*. Vol. II. Pp. 298. New York: Halsted, 1975. $23.50.

CRUICKSHANK, CHARLES. *The German Occupation of the Channel Islands*. Pp. xii, 370. New York: Oxford University Press, 1975. $21.00.

CULL, JOHN G. and RICHARD E. HARDY, eds. *Career Guidance for Black Adolescents: A Guide to Selected Professional Occupations*. Pp. v, 148. Springfield, Ill.: Charles C. Thomas, 1975. $13.75.

DAVID, ARIE E. *The Strategy of Treaty Termination: Lawful Breaches and Retaliations*. Pp. vii, 324. New Haven, Conn.: Yale University Press, 1975. $20.00.

DAVIDSON, J. W. *Peter Dillon of Vanikoro*. Edited by O. H. K. Spate. Pp. vii, 351. New York: Oxford University Press, 1975. No price.

DEAKIN, F. W., H. SHUKMAN and H. I. WILLETTS. *A History of World Communism*. Pp. 177. New York: Barnes & Noble, 1975. $13.50.

DECKARD, BARBARA. *The Woman's Movement: Political, Socioeconomic, and Psychological Issues*. Pp. v, 450. New York: Harper & Row, 1975. $6.95. Paperbound.

DE FRANCESCO, HENRY F. *Quantitative Analysis Methods for Substantive Analysis*. Pp. vii, 431. Los Angeles, Calif.: Melville, 1975. No price.

DENTON, DAVID E., ed. *Existentialism and Phenomenology in Education: Collected Essays*. Pp. 223. New York: Columbia University, 1974. $9.95.

DERTHICK, MARTHA. *Uncontrollable Spending for Social Services Grants*. Pp. 139. Washington, D.C.: Brookings Institution, 1975. $2.50. Paperbound.

Development and Participation: Proceedings of the XVIIth International Conference on Social Welfare. Pp. 388. New York: Columbia University Press, 1975. $20.00.

DEVOS, TON. *Introduction to Politics*. Pp. iii, 278. Englewood Cliffs, N.J.: Prentice-Hall, 1975. $6.95. Paperbound.

DICARA, LEO V. et al., eds. *Biofeedback & Self-Control, 1974*. Pp. xi, 534. Chicago, Ill.: Aldine-Atherton, 1975. $27.50.

DOBSON, CHRISTOPHER. *Black September*. Pp. ix, 179. New York: Macmillan, 1974. $8.95.

DREW, DAVID E. *Science Development: An Evaluation Study*. Pp. iii, 182. Washington, D.C.: National Academy of Science, 1975. No price.

Education on the Move: A Companion Volume to Learning to Be. Pp. iv, 307. New York: UNIPUB, 1975. $12.50. Paperbound.

EVANS, MICHAEL. *Karl Marx*. Pp. 215. Bloomington: Indiana University Press, 1975. $10.00.

EVANS, ROBERT R., ed. *Readings in Collective Behavior*. 2nd ed. Pp. vi, 430. Chicago, Ill.: Rand McNally, 1975. $6.95. Paperbound.

FAN, K. H. and K. T. FAN. *From the Other Side of the River: A Self Portrait of China Today*. Pp. 429. New York: Doubleday, 1975. $3.95. Paperbound.

FLINK, JAMES J. *The Car Culture*. Pp. x, 260. Cambridge, Mass.: MIT Press, 1975. No price.

Foreign Relations of the United States, 1948. Vol. I. Pp., iii, 505. Washington, D.C.: United States Government Printing Office, 1975. $8.10.

FOSTER, JOHN L., THOMAS A. HENDERSON and DANIEL G. BARBEE. *National Policy Game: A Simulation of the American Political Process*. Pp. 108. New York: John Wiley & Sons, 1975. $4.95. Paperbound.

FRANK, ISAIAH, ed. *The Japanese Economy in International Perspective*. Pp. 306. Baltimore, Md.: Johns Hopkins University Press, 1975. $16.00. Paperbound, $3.95.

FRIEDMANN, JOHN and WILLIAM ALONSO, eds. *Regional Policy Readings in Theory and Applications*. Pp. viii, 808. Cambridge, Mass.: MIT Press, 1975. No price.

FULLERTON, HERBERT H. and JAMES R. PRESCOTT. *An Economic Simulation Model for Regional Development Planning*. Pp. v, 133. Ann Arbor, Mich.: Ann Arbor Science Publishers, 1975. $12.50.

FURNIVALL, J. S. *Experiment in Independence: The Philippines*. Pp. 103. Detroit, Mich.: Cellar Book Shop, 1974. $4.00. Paperbound.

GALLIMORE, RONALD, JOAN WHITEHORN BOGGS and CATHIE JORDAN. *Culture, Behavior and Education: A Study of Hawaiian-Americans*. Pp. 256. Beverly Hills, Calif.: Sage, 1974. $11.00. Paperbound, $7.00.

GAMBS, JOHN S. *John Kenneth Galbraith*. Twayne's World Leaders Series. Pp. 131. Boston, Mass.: Twayne Publishers, 1975. $6.95.

GAMMAGE, ALLEN Z. *Basic Police Report Writing*. 2nd ed. Pp. 273. Springfield, Ill.: Charles C. Thomas, 1975. $17.50. Paperbound.

GAPPERT, GARY and HAROLD M. ROSE, eds. *The Social Economy of Cities*. Pp. 640. Beverly Hills, Calif.: Sage, 1975. $25.00.

GELLATELY, ROBERT. *The Politics of Economic Despair: Shopkeepers and German Politics, 1890–1914*. Pp. 318. Beverly Hills, Calif.: Sage, 1974. $15.00.

GELLES, RICHARD J. *The Violent Home: A Study of Physical Aggression Between Husbands and Wives*. Pp. 232. Beverly Hills, Calif.: Sage, 1974. $10.00. Paperbound, $6.00.

GIL, RICHARD and ERNEST SHERMAN, eds. *The Fabric of Existentialism: Philosophical and Literary Sources*. Pp. v, 640. Englewood Cliffs, N.J.: Prentice-Hall, 1975. $14.95.

GILISON, JEROME M. *The Soviet Image of Utopia*. Pp. 192. Baltimore, Md.: Johns Hopkins University, 1975. $9.00.

GILLESPIE, GILBERT. *Public Access Cable Television in the United States and Canada: With an Annotated Bibliography*. Pp. v, 157. New York: Praeger, 1975. $14.00.

GOLEMBIEWSKI, ROBERT T. and JACK RABIN, eds. *Public Budgeting and Finance: Readings in Theory and Practice*. 2nd ed. Pp. v, 513. Itasca, Ill.: F. E. Peacock, 1975. $11.95.

GOODMAN, JAY S. *The Dynamics of Urban Government and Politics*. Pp. vii, 413. New York: Macmillan, 1975. $6.95. Paperbound.

GOODWIN, GEOFFREY L. and ANDREW LINKLATER, eds. *New Dimensions of World Politics*. Pp. 127. New York: Halsted Press, 1975. $11.00.

GORDEN, RAYMOND L. *Interviewing: Strategy, Techniques, and Tactics*. Revised Edition. Pp. ix, 587. Homewood, Ill.: Dorsey Press, 1975. $12.95.

GOUGH, BARRY. *Canada*. Pp. viii, 182. Englewood Cliffs, N.J.: Prentice-Hall, 1975. $7.95.

GRACE, JOHN. *Domestic Slavery in West Africa*. Pp. 294. New York: Barnes & Noble, 1975. $23.50.

GROOM, A. J. R. and PAUL TAYLOR, eds. *Functionalism: Theory and Practice in International Relations*. Pp. v, 354. New York: Crane, Russak, 1975. $23.50.

GROSMAN, BRIAN A. *Police Command: Decisions and Discretion*. Pp. 154. Toronto, Ca.: Macmillan, 1975. $13.95. Paperbound, $6.50.

GROW, LUCILLE J. and DEBORAH SHAPIRO. *Black Children-White Parents: A Study of Transracial Adoption*. Pp. 239. New York: Child Welfare League of America, 1975. $5.95. Paperbound.

GUTTERIDGE, W. F. *Military Regimes in Africa*. Pp. 195. New York: Barnes & Noble, 1975. $12.75. Paperbound, $7.00.

HAFFENDEN, PHILIP S. *New England in the English Nation, 1689–1713*. Pp. vi, 326. New York: Oxford University Press, 1974. $17.50.

HALLECK, SEYMOUR et al., eds. *The Aldine Crime & Justice Annual, 1974*. Pp. v, 541. Chicago, Ill.: Aldine-Atherton, 1975. $27.50.

HAMERMESH, DANIEL S., ed. *Labor in the Public and Nonprofit Sectors*. Pp. v, 272. Princeton, N.J.: Princeton University Press, 1975. $11.50.

HAMMOND, THOMAS T., ed. *The Anatomy of Communist Takeovers*. Pp. xi, 664.

New Haven, Conn.: Yale University Press, 1975. $25.00. Paperbound, $5.95.

HARRISON, LOWELL H. *The Civil War in Kentucky*. Pp. ix, 115. Lexington: University Press of Kentucky, 1975. $3.95.

HARRISS, C. LOWELL, ed. *Inflation: Long-Term Problems*. Pp. 214. New York: Praeger, 1975. $15.00.

HAYWARD, JAND and MICHAEL WATSON, eds. *Planning, Politics and Public Policy: The British, French and Italian Experience*. Pp. vii, 496. New York: Cambridge University Press, 1975. $37.50.

HAZARD, LELAND. *Attorney for the Situation*. Pp. xvii, 314. New York: Columbia University Press, 1975. $9.95.

HEIKOFF, JOSEPH M. *Management of Industrial Particulates: Corporate, Government, Citizen Action*. Pp. v, 260. Ann Arbor, Mich.: Ann Arbor Science Publishers, 1975. $14.50.

HENSHEL, RICHARD L. and ROBERT A. SILVERMAN. *Perception in Criminology*. Pp. x, 471. New York: Columbia University Press, 1975. No price.

HERTZ, FREDERICK. *The German Public Mind in the Nineteenth Century*. Edited by Frank Eyck. Pp. 422. Totowa, N.J.: Rowman and Littlefield, 1975. $18.75.

Hierarchies of the People's Republic of China. Pp. ii, 262. Kowloon, Hong Kong: Union Research Institute, 1975. $7.00.

HOOVER, KENNETH R. *A Politics of Identity: Liberation and the Natural Community*. Pp. 171. Urbana: University of Illinois, 1975. $7.95.

HOROWITZ, IRVING LOUIS and JAMES EVERETT KATZ. *Social Science and Public Policy in the United States*. Pp. vi, 187. New York: Praeger, 1975. $16.50. Paperbound, $5.95.

HUREWITZ, J. C., ed. *The Middle East and North Africa in World Politics: A Documentary Record*. Vol. I. Pp. vii, 616. New Haven, Conn.: Yale University Press, 1975. $30.00.

HUSEN, TORSTEN. *The Learning Society*. Pp. viii, 268. New York: Barnes & Noble, 1974. $13.75.

HUTT, W. H. *A Rehabilitation of Say's Law*. Pp. v, 150. Athens: Ohio University Press, 1975. $8.00.

ICHIMURA, SHINICHI, ed. *The Economic Development of East and Southeast Asia*. Pp. 393. Honolulu: University of Hawaii, 1975. $15.00. Paperbound, $10.00.

IMMIRZI, ELIZABETH and TREVOR BLACKWELL. *Paper Voices*. Pp. 262. Totowa, N.J.: Rowman and Littlefield, 1975. $12.50.

INGHAM, KENNETH. *The Kindgom of Toro in Uganda*. Pp. v, 186. New York: Barnes & Noble, 1975. $14.50.

IQHAL AFZAL. *The Prophet's Diplomacy: The Art of Negotiation as Conceived and Developed by the Prophet of Islam*. Pp. xii, 142. Cape Cod, Mass.: Claude Stark & Co., 1975. $8.00.

ISAAK, ALAN C. *Scope and Methods of Political Science*. Revised edition. Pp. ix, 253. Homewood, Ill.: Dorsey Press, 1975. $9.95.

JOHNSON, D. GALE. *World Food Problems and Prospects*. Foreign Affairs Studies. Pp. 83. Washington, D.C.: American Enterprise Institute for Public Policy Research, 1975. $3.00. Paperbound.

JOHNSON, RAY and MONA MCCORMICK. *Too Dangerous to be at Large*. Pp. x, 174. New York: Quadrangle, 1975. $6.95.

JOHNSTONE, RONALD L. *Religion and Society in Interaction: The Sociology of Religion*. Pp. 345. Englewood Cliffs, N.J.: Prentice-Hall, 1975. $9.95.

JOST, FRANCOIS. *Introduction to Comparative Literature*. Pp. v, 349. New York: Bobbs-Merrill, 1974. No price.

KANTHWICZ, EDWARD R. *Polish-American Politics in Chicago*. Pp. v, 260. Chicago, Ill.: University of Chicago Press, 1975. $12.95.

KAPP, ROBERT A. *Szechwan and the Chinese Republic: Provincial Militarism and Central Power, 1911–1938*. Pp. viii, 198. New Haven, Conn.: Yale University Press, 1973. $10.00.

KARON, BERTRAM P. *Black Scars*. Pp. vii, 204. New York: Springer, 1975. $8.95. Paperbound, $5.95.

KATZ, ZEV, ROSEMARIE ROGERS and FREDERIC HARNED. *Handbook of Major Soviet Nationalities*. Pp. v, 481. New York: Free Press, 1975. No price.

KEARNEY, ROBERT N., ed. *Politics and Modernization in South and Southeast Asia*. Pp. iv, 277. New York: Halsted Press, 1975. $15.00. Paperbound, $6.50.

KENKEL, WILLIAM F. and ELLEN VOLAND. *Society in Action*. Pp. v, 534. San Francisco, Calif.: Canfield Press, 1975. No price.

KIM, ILPYONG J. *Communist Politics in North Korea*. Pp. vi, 121. New York: Praeger, 1975. $13.50.

KINDLEBERGER, CHARLES P. *The World in Depression, 1929–1939*. Pp. 336. Berkeley: University of California, 1975. $11.25.

KING, EDMUND J., CHRISTINE H. MOOR and JENNIFER A. MUNDY. *Post-Compulsory Education: A New Analysis in Western Europe*. Pp. 486. Beverly Hills, Calif.: Sage, 1975. $17.50.

KLINEBERG, OTTO and COLETTE GUIL-LAUMIN. *Race as News*. Pp. 173. New York: Unipub, 1975. No price.

KOHLER, FOY D. and MOSE L. HARVEY, eds. *The Soviet Union: Yesterday, Today, and Tomorrow. A Colloquy of American Long Timers in Moscow*. Pp. iii, 220. Coral Gables, Fla.: University of Miami, 1975. No price.

KOLINSKY, MARTIN. *Continuity and Change in European Society: France, Germany and Italy since 1870*. Pp. 234. New York: St. Martin's Press, 1974. $16.95.

KORIN, BASIL P. *Statistical Concepts for the Social Sciences*. Pp. v, 407. Cambridge, Mass.: Winthrop, 1975. $11.95.

KRAMER, RALPH M. and HARRY SPECHT, eds. *Readings in Community Organization Practice*. 2nd ed. Pp. viii, 386. Englewood Cliffs, N.J.: Prentice-Hall, 1975. $8.50. Paperbound.

KRISTOL, IRVING et al. *America's Continuing Revolution: An Act of Conservation*. Pp. vii, 398. Washington, D.C.: American Enterprise Institute for Public Policy Research, 1975. $12.00.

KURLAND, PHILIP B., ed. *The Supreme Court Review 1974*. Pp. vii, 360. Chicago, Ill.: University of Chicago Press, 1975. $25.00.

KUTCHER, ARTHUR. *The New Jerusalem: Planning and Politics*. Pp. 183. Cambridge, Mass.: MIT Press, 1975. $6.95. Paperbound.

LANDIS, PAUL H. *Making the Most of Marriage*. 5th ed. Pp. v, 533. Englewood Cliffs, N.J.: Prentice-Hall, 1975. $11.95.

LAVE, CHARLES A. and JAMES G. MARCH. *An Introduction to Models in the Social Sciences*. Pp. iv, 421. New York: Harper & Row, 1975. $6.95. Paperbound.

LAWRENCE, ALAN. *China's Foreign Relations since 1949*. World Studies Series. Pp. v, 261. Boston, Mass.: Routledge & Kegan Paul, 1975. $18.50.

LEBRA, JOYCE C. *Japan's Greater East Asia Co-Prosperity Sphere in World War II*. Pp. vi, 212. New York: Oxford University Press, 1975. $21.75.

LEIFER, MICHAEL. *The Foreign Relations of the New States*. Studies in Contemporary Southeast Asia. Pp. vii, 114. New York: Longman, 1974. $8.50. Paperbound, $3.50.

LEIK, ROBERT K. and BARBARA F. MEEKER. *Mathematical Sociology*. Pp. v, 242. Englewood Cliffs, N.J.: Prentice-Hall, 1975. $12.95.

LEVINE, ARTHUR L. *The Future of the U.S. Space Program*. Pp. v, 198. New York: Praeger, 1975. $16.50.

LEVY, EUGENE and JOHN RENALDO. *America's People*. Pp. 191. Glenview, Ill.: Scott, Foresman, 1975. No price.

LEVY, REYNOLD. *Nearing the Crossroads: Contending Approaches to American Foreign Policy*. Pp. ix, 180. New York: Free Press, 1975. $9.95.

LEWANSKI, RICHARD. *Guide to Polish Libraries*. Pp. iii, 209. New York: Columbia University, 1975. $11.00.

LeWARNE, CHARLES PIERCE. *Utopias on Puget Sound, 1885–1915*. Pp. vii, 325. Seattle: University of Washington, 1975. $12.50.

LIEBERMAN, PHILIP. *On the Origins of Language: An Introduction to the Evolution of Human Speech*. Pp. v, 196. New York: Macmillan, 1975. $.95. Paperbound.

LINDZEY, GARDNER, CALVIN HALL and RICHARD F. THOMPSON. *Psychology*. Pp. 802. New York: Worth, 1975. $13.95.

LIPSET, SEYMOUR MARTIN and DAVID RIESMAN. *Education and Politics at Harvard*. Pp. ix, 440. New York: McGraw-Hill, 1975. $15.95.

LISKE, CRAIG, WILLIAM LOEHR and JOHN McCAMANT, eds. *Comparative Public Policy Issues: Theories and Methods*. Pp. 300. New York: Halsted Press, 1975. $20.00.

LOWENTHAL, MARJORIE FISKE, MAJDA THURNHER and DAVID CHIRIBOGA. *Four Stages of Life*. Pp. ix, 292. San Francisco, Calif.: Jossey-Bass, 1975. $13.95.

MADAY, BELA C., ed. *Anthropology and Society*. Pp. v, 116. Washington, D.C.: Anthropological Society of Washington, 1975. $5.00. Paperbound, $2.50.

MALE, GEORGE A. *The Struggle for Power: Who Controls the Schools in England and the U.S.* Pp. 200. Beverly Hills, Calif.: Sage, 1974. $10.00. Paperbound, $6.00.

MARIN, PETER, VINCENT STANLEY and KATHRYN MARIN. *The Limits of Schooling*. Pp. vii, 150. Englewood Cliffs, N.J.: Prentice-Hall, 1975. $7.95. Paperbound, $2.45.

MARKS, CLAUDE. *Pilgrims, Heretics, and Lovers: A Medieval Journey*. Pp. 338. New York: Macmillan, 1975. $14.95.

MARSDEN, RALPH W., ed. *Politics, Minerals, and Survival*. Pp. v, 86. Madison: University of Wisconsin Press, 1975. $10.00. Paperbound, $2.45.

McGRATH, WILLIAM J. *Dionysian Art and Populist Politics in Austria*. Pp. ix, 269. New Haven, Conn.: Yale University Press, 1974. $12.50.

McINNES, NEIL. *The Communist Parties of Western Europe*. Pp. x, 209. New York: Oxford University Press, 1975. $16.00.

MCKEE, JOHN D. *William Allen White: Maverick on Main Street.* Pp. x, 264. Westport, Conn.: Greenwood Press, 1975. $12.95.

MCLAURIN, R. D. *The Middle East in Soviet Policy.* Pp. vii, 206. Lexington, Mass.: Lexington Books, 1975. $13.50.

MCWILLIAMS, WILSON CAREY. *The Idea of Fraternity in America.* Pp. 695. Berkeley: University of California, 1975. $4.95. Paperbound.

MEEROPOL, ROBERT and MICHAEL MEEROPOL. *We Are Your Sons: The Legacy of Ethel and Julius Rosenberg.* Pp. vii, 419. Boston, Mass.: Houghton Mifflin, 1975. $10.00.

MEIER, GERALD M. *Problems of Cooperation for Development.* Pp. viii, 249. New York: Oxford University Press, 1974. $4.95. Paperbound.

MEISELMAN, DAVID I. and ARTHUR B. LAFFER, eds. *The Phenomenon of Worldwide Inflation.* Pp. 215. Washington, D.C.: American Enterprise Institute for Public Policy Research, 1975. $8.50. Paperbound, $4.00.

MELTSNER, ARNOLD J. *The Politics of City Revenue.* Pp. 319. Berkeley, Calif.: 1975. $4.25. Paperbound.

MERKLIN, LEWIS, JR. *They Chose Honor: The Problem of Conscience in Custody.* Pp. xiv, 325. New York: Harper & Row, 1974. $8.95.

MOLLO, JOHN and MALCOLM MCGREGOR. *Uniforms of the American Revolution.* Pp. 228. New York: Macmillan, 1975. $5.95.

MONAGHAN, JAY. *Chile, Peru, and the California Gold Rush of 1849.* Pp. 320. Berkeley: University of California, 1973. $11.95.

MONROE, ALAN D. *Public Opinion in America.* Pp. v, 296. New York: Dodd, Mead & Co., 1975. $6.95. Paperbound.

MOODIE, T. DUNBAR. *The Rise of Afrikanerdom: Power, Apartheid, and the Afrikaner Civil Religion.* Pp. 344. Berkeley: University of California, 1975. $12.50.

MORRIS, MILTON D. *The Politics of Black America.* Pp. xi, 319. New York: Harper & Row, 1975. $6.50. Paperbound.

MOSSE, GEORGE L., ed. *Police Forces in History.* Pp. 334. Beverly Hills, Calif.: Sage, 1975. $13.50. Paperbound, $6.00.

NA'AMAN, S. *Die Konstituierung Der Deutschen Arbeiterbewegung, 1862/63.* Pp. v, 967. Assen, The Netherlands: Royal Vangorcum Ltd., 1975. $70.00.

NAIDU, M. V. *Alliances and Balance of Power.* Pp. viii, 306. New York: St. Martin's Press, 1975. $12.95.

NICHOLAS, H. G. *The United States and Britain.* Pp. v, 195. Chicago, Ill.: University of Chicago, 1975. $10.00.

NICHOLLS, DAVID. *The Pluralist State.* Pp. 179. New York: St. Martin's Press, 1975. $18.95.

NICHOLLS, DAVID. *Three Varieties of Pluralism.* Pp. 69. New York: St. Martin's Press, 1975. $8.95.

NICOLAEVSKY, BORIS I. *Power and the Soviet Elite.* Edited by George I. Kennan. Pp. v, 275. Ann Arbor: University of Michigan, 1975. $8.95. Paperbound, $4.95.

NOSSITER, T. J. *Influence, Opinion and Political Idioms in Reformed England.* Pp. viii, 255. New York: Barnes & Noble, 1975. $22.50.

NYE, ROBERT A. *The Origins of Crowd Psychology: Gustave LeBon and the Crisis of Mass Democracy in the Third Republic.* Pp. 226. Beverly Hills, Calif.: Sage, 1975. $13.50.

OAKESHOTT, MICHAEL. *Hobbes on Civil Association.* Pp. 162. Berkeley: University of California, 1975. $10.00.

ODELL, PETER R. *Oil and World Power: Background to the Oil Crisis.* Pp. 245. New York: Taplinger, 1975. $9.95.

O'NEILL, JOHN. *Making Sense Together: An Introduction to Wild Sociology.* Pp. ix, 83. New York: Barnes & Noble, 1975. $7.00.

OTT, DAVID J. et al. *State-Local Finances in the Last Half of the 1970s.* Domestic Affairs Studies. Pp. 105. Washington, D.C.: American Enterprise Institute for Public Policy Research, 1975. $3.00. Paperbound.

OWEN, JOHN. *L. T. Hobhouse: Sociologist.* Pp. vii, 225. Columbus: Ohio State University Press, 1975. $11.00.

OWEN, JOHN B. *The Eighteenth Century, 1714–1815.* Pp. v, 365. Totowa, N.J.: Rowman and Littlefield, 1975. $12.50.

OXNAM, ROBERT B. *Ruling from Horseback: Manchu Politics in the Oboi Regency, 1661–1669.* Pp. vii, 250. Chicago, Ill.: University of Chicago, 1975. $12.50.

PATTERSON, GERALD R. et al. *Behavior Change 1974.* Pp. viii, 500. Chicago, Ill.: Aldine, 1975. No price.

PAULU, BURTON. *Radio and Television Broadcasting in Eastern Europe.* Pp. vii, 592. Minneapolis: University of Minnesota, 1974. No price.

PAXTON, JOHN. *World Legislatures.* Pp. 169. New York: St. Martin's Press, 1975. $16.95.

PEASE, JANE H. and WILLIAM H. PEASE. *The Fugitive Slave Law and Anthony Burns: A Problem in Law Enforcement.*

Edited by Harold M. Hyman. Pp. v, 103. Philadelphia, Pa.: J.B. Lippincott, 1975. $2.75. Paperbound.

PENNIMAN, HOWARD R., ed. *Britain at the Polls: The Parliamentary Elections of 1974*. Pp. 256. Washington, D.C.: American Enterprise Institute for Public Policy Research, 1975. $3.00. Paperbound.

PETROV, VLADIMIR. *U.S.-Soviet Detente: Past and Future*. Foreign Affairs Studies. Pp. 60. Washington, D.C.: American Enterprise Institute for Public Policy Research, 1975. $3.00. Paperbound.

PETTIGREW, THOMAS F., ed. *Racial Discrimination in the United States*. Pp. v, 429. New York: Harper & Row, 1975. No price.

PHILLIPS, ALMARIN, ed. *Promoting Competition in Regulated Markets*. Studies in the Regulation of Economic Activity. Pp. vii, 397. Washington, D.C.: Brookings Institution, 1975. $12.50. Paperbound, $4.95.

PINKUS, THEO, ed. *Conversations with Lukacs*. Pp. 155. Cambridge, Mass.: MIT Press, 1975. No price.

Plantation Societies, Race Relations, and the South: The Regimentation of Populations. Selected Papers of Edgar T. Thompson. Pp. viii, 407. Durham, N.C.: Duke University Press, 1975. $12.75. Paperbound, $6.75.

POLK, WILLIAM R. *The United States and the Arab World*. 3rd ed. Pp. vii, 478. Lawrence, Mass.: Harvard University Press, 1975. $15.00.

POMPER, GERALD. *Voters' Choice: Varieties of American Electoral Behavior*. Pp. vii, 259. New York: Dodd, Mead, 1975. $5.95. Paperbound.

Presidency 1974. Pp. 121. Washington, D.C.: Congressional Quarterly, 1975. $4.95. Paperbound.

PYE, LUCIAN W., ed. *Political Science and Area Studies: Rivals or Partners?* Pp. viii, 245. Bloomington: Indiana University Press, 1975. $10.95.

QUALE, G. ROBINA. *Eastern Civilizations*. Pp. ix, 508. Englewood Cliffs, N.J.: Prentice-Hall, 1975. $14.95. Paperbound, $8.95.

Racism and Apartheid in Southern Africa: South Africa and Namibia. Pp. 156. New York: Unesco Press, 1975. $4.95. Paperbound.

RADEL, J. LUCIEN. *Roots of Totalitarianism: The Ideological Sources of Fascism, National Socialism, and Communism*. Pp. iii, 218. New York: Crane, Russak, 1975. $14.00. Paperbound, $7.75.

REHMUS, CHARLES M., ed. *Public Employment Labor Relations: An Overview of Eleven Nations*. Pp. v, 170. Ann Arbor, Mich.: Institute of Labor and Industrial Relations, 1975. $9.50. Paperbound, $4.50.

REZNECK, SAMUEL. *Unrecognized Patriots: The Jews in the American Revolution*. Pp. x, 204. Westport, Conn.: Greenwood Press, 1975. $13.95.

RIPLEY, RANDALL B. *Congress: Process and Policy*. Pp. 316. New York: W. W. Norton, 1975. $9.95.

RITZER, GEORGE. *Sociology: A Multiple Paradigm Science*. Pp. v, 234. Boston, Mass.: Allyn & Bacon, 1975. $7.95.

ROKKAN, STEIN, ed. *The Scandinavian Political Studies*. Vol. IX. Pp. 276. Beverly Hills, Calif.: Sage, 1974. $15.00.

RONEN, DOV. *Dahomey: Between Tradition and Modernity*. Pp. ix, 272. Ithaca, N.Y.: Cornell University Press, 1975. $16.50.

ROSIGNOLI, GUIDO. *Army Badges and Insignia since 1945*. Pp. 218. New York: Macmillan, 1975. $6.95.

ROSSABI, MORRIS. *China and Inner Asia: From 1368 to the Present Day*. Pp. 320. New York: Universe Books, 1975. $20.00.

RUSHING, WILLIAM A., ed. *Deviant Behavior and Social Process*. 2nd ed. Pp. 515. Chicago, Ill.: Rand McNally, 1975. $7.95. Paperbound.

RUSSELL-WOOD, A. J. R., ed. *From Colony to Nation: Essays on the Independence of Brazil*. Pp. vii, 267. Baltimore, Md.: Johns Hopkins University, 1975. $12.50.

SAHOTA, GIAN SINGH. *Brazilian Economic Policy: An Optimal Control Theory Analysis*. Pp. vi, 317. New York: Praeger, 1975. $21.50.

SAXTON, ALEXANDER. *The Indispensable Enemy: Labor and the Anti-Chinese Movement in California*. Pp. 294. Berkeley: University of California, 1975. $3.95. Paperbound.

SCACCO, ANTHONY M., JR. *Rape in Prison*. American Lecture Series. Pp. vii, 127. Springfield, Ill.: Charles C. Thomas, 1975. $10.50.

SCALAPINO, ROBERT A. *Democracy and the Party Movement in Prewar Japan*. Pp. 489. Berkeley: University of California, 1975. $19.50.

SCHOTT, JOSEPH L. *No Left Turns: The FBI in Peace & War*. Pp. 214. New York: Praeger, 1975. $7.95.

SCHWARTZ, ARTHUR and ISRAEL GOLDIAMOND. *Social Casework: A Behavioral Approach*. Pp. vi, 315. New York: Columbia University Press, 1975. $12.50.

SENNHOLZ, HANS F., ed. *Gold is Money*. Pp. xiv, 299. Westport, Conn.: Greenwood Press, 1975. $11.95.

SERVICE, ELMAN R. *Origins of the State and Civilization: The Process of Cultural Evolution*. Pp. xi, 361. New York: W. W. Norton, 1975. $12.50. Paperbound, $4.95.

SHANOR, DONALD R. *Soviet Europe*. Pp. 252. New York: Harper & Row, 1975. $10.95.

SHILS, EDWARD. *Center and Periphery: Essays in Macrosociology*. Pp. vi, 516. Chicago, Ill.: University of Chicago Press, 1975. $19.50.

SIEVERS, ALLEN M. *The Mystical World of Indonesia: Culture & Economic Development in Conflict*. Pp. vi, 425. Baltimore, Md.: Johns Hopkins University, 1975. $14.00.

SIGLER, JAY A. *American Rights Policies*. Pp. ix, 316. Homewood, Ill.: Dorsey Press, 1975. $6.50. Paperbound.

SILVERT, KALMAN H. et al. *The Americas in a Changing World*. Pp. 248. New York: Quadrangle, 1975. $3.95. Paperbound.

SIPORIN, MAX. *Introduction to Social Work Practice*. Pp. vii, 468. New York: Macmillan, 1975. $12.95.

SMITH, BRUCE L. R., ed. *The New Political Economy: The Public Use of the Private Sector*. Pp. ix, 344. New York: Halsted Press, 1975. $20.00.

SMITH, ELBERT B. *The Presidency of James Buchanan*. Pp. vii, 225. Lawrence: University Press of Kansas, 1975. $12.00.

SMITH, H. W. *Strategies of Social Research. The Methodological Imagination*. Pp. vii, 423. Englewood Cliffs, N.J.: Prentice-Hall, 1975. No price.

SMITH, M. G. *Corporations and Society: The Social Anthropology of Collective Action*. Pp. 383. Chicago, Ill.: Aldine-Atherton, 1975. $17.50.

SMITH, T. ALEXANDER. *The Comparative Policy Process*. Studies in Comparative Politics. Pp. v, 184. Santa Barbara, Calif.: CLIO Press, 1975. $12.75. Paperbound, $4.75.

Smithsonian Year 1974: Annual Report of the Smithsonian Institution for the Year Ended June 30, 1974. Pp. v, 500. Washington, D.C.: U.S. Government Printing Office, 1974. $6.65. Paperbound.

SMOLKA, RICHARD G. *Registering Voters by Mail: The Maryland and New Jersey Experience*. Pp. 85. Washington, D.C.: American Enterprise Institute for Public Policy Research, 1975. $3.00. Paperbound.

SNEED, JOSEPH D. and STEVEN A. WALDHORN, eds. *Restructuring the Federal System: Approaches to Accountability in Postcategorical Programs*. Pp. iii, 261. New York: Crane, Russak, 1975. $16.00.

SONYEL, SALAHI RAMSDAN. *Turkish Diplomacy, 1918–1923*. Pp. 268. Beverly Hills, Calif.: Sage, 1975. $13.50.

Sponsored Research of the Carnegie Commission on Higher Education. Pp. ix, 397. New York: McGraw-Hill, 1975. $15.00.

STANLEY, HAROLD W. *Senate vs. Governor, Alabama 1971: Referents for Opposition in a One-Party Legislature*. Pp. xii, 112. University: University of Alabama, 1975. $6.00.

STAVENHAGEN, RODOLFO. *Social Classes in Agrarian Societies*. Pp. 266. New York: Doubleday, 1975. $3.60. Paperbound.

STAVRIANOS, L. S. *The World Since 1500: A Global History*. 3rd ed. Pp. vii, 541. Englewood Cliffs, N.J.: Prentice-Hall, 1975. $9.95. Paperbound.

STERN, FREDERICK MARTIN. *Life and Liberty: A Return to First Principles*. Pp. v, 212. New York: Thomas Y. Crowell, 1975. $7.95.

STEWART, MARGARET. *Trade Unions in Europe*. Pp. vi, 220. New York: UNIPUB, 1975. $22.50.

STOCKWIN, J. A. A. *Japan: Divided Politics in a Growth Economy*. Pp. 296. New York: W. W. Norton, 1975. $10.00. Paperbound, $3.95.

STREET, H. *Government Liability: A Comparative Study*. Pp. 223. Hamden, Conn.: Archon, 1975. $7.50.

STUART, GRAHAM H. and JAMES L. TIGNER. *Latin America and the United States*. 6th ed. Pp. vii, 856. Englewood Cliffs, N.J.: Prentice-Hall, 1974. $13.95.

SUHL, YURI. *They Fought Back: The Story of the Jewish Resistance in Nazi Europe*. Pp. 351. New York: Schocken Books, 1975. $4.95. Paperbound.

SUNSTEIN, EMILY. *A Different Face: The Life of Mary Wollstonecraft*. Pp. xiv, 383. New York: Harper & Row, 1975. $15.00.

SWIDROWSKI, JOZEF. *Exchange and Trade Controls*. Pp. v, 342. New York: UNIPUB, 1975. $32.50.

TACHAU, FRANK, ed. *Political Elites and Political Development in the Middle East*. Pp. 310. New York: Halsted Press, 1975. $17.50.

TANTER, RAYMOND. *Modelling and Managing International Conflicts: The Berlin Crises*. Pp. 272. Beverly Hills, Calif.: Sage, 1974. $11.00. Paperbound, $7.00.

TAYLOR, CHARLES LEWIS and MICHAEL C. HUDSON. *World Handbook of Political and Social Indicators*. 2nd ed. Pp. vii, 443. New Haven, Conn.: Yale University Press, 1975. $20.00. Paperbound, $6.95.

THOMAS, DOROTHY SWAINE. *The Salvage*. Pp. 649. Berkeley: University of California, 1975. $22.50.

TILLY, CHARLES, ed. *The Formation of National States in Western Europe*. Pp. vii, 711. Princeton, N.J.: Princeton University Press, 1975. $22.50. Paperbound, $4.95.

TIMMER, C. PETER et al. *The Choice of Technology in Developing Countries: Some Cautionary Tales*. Pp. v, 114. Cambridge, Mass.: Harvard University, 1975. $3.45. Paperbound.

TREVITHICK, JAMES ANTHONY and CHARLES MULVEY. *The Economics of Inflation*. Pp. 184. New York: Halsted Press, 1975. $9.95.

Turkey: Prospects and Problems of an Expanding Economy. Pp. iii, 467. Washington, D.C.: World Bank, 1975. No price.

UHALLEY, STEPHEN, JR. *Mao Tse-tung: A Critical Biography*. Pp. 233. New York: New Viewpoints, 1975. $5.95. Paperbound.

VAN LEEUWEN, AREND. *Critique of Earth*. Pp. 295. New York: Charles Scribner's Sons, 1974. $10.00.

VERBIT, GILBERT P. *International Monetary Reform in the Developing Countries: The Rule of Law Problem*. Pp. ix, 335. New York: Columbia University Press, 1975. $20.00.

VOGEL, EZRA F., ed. *Modern Japanese Organization and Decision-Making*. Pp. 370. Berkeley: University of California, 1975. $15.00.

VON BEYME, KLAUS, ed. *German Political Studies*. Vol. I. Pp. 286. Beverly Hills, Calif.: Sage, 1975. $17.50.

WANDYCZ, PIOTR S. *The Lands of Partitioned Poland, 1795–1918*. Pp. ix, 431. Seattle: University of Washington, 1975. $14.95. Paperbound, $7.95.

WATSON, BERNARD C. *In Spite of the System: The Individual and Educational Reform*. Pp. ix, 121. Cambridge, Mass.: Ballinger, 1974. No price.

WATSON, JAMES L. *Emigration and the Chinese Lineage: The Mans in Hong Kong and London*. Pp. 255. Berkeley: University of California, 1975. $10.00.

WATSON, RICHARD A. *Promise and Performance of American Democracy*. 2nd ed. Pp. viii, 616. New York: John Wiley & Sons, 1975. No price.

WAUCHOPE, ROBERT, ed. *Handbook of Middle American Indians: Guide to Ethnohistorical Sources*. Vols. XIV and XV. Pp. ix, 1034. Austin: University of Texas, 1975. $40.00 per set.

WAX, MURRAY L. and ROBERT W. BUCHANAN, eds. *Solving "The Indian Problem": The White Man's Burdensome Business*. Pp. 237. New York: New Viewpoints, 1975. $4.95. Paperbound.

WELCH, SUSAN and JOHN COMER, eds. *Public Opinion: Its Formation, Measurement, and Impact*. Pp. iii, 541. Palo Alto, Calif.: Mayfield Publishers, 1975. No price.

WELLS, JEROME C. *Agricultural Policy and Economic Growth in Nigeria, 1962–1968*. Pp. vii, 490. New York: Oxford University Press, 1975. $18.00.

WELLS, SAMUEL F., JR., ROBERT H. FERRELL and DAVID E. TRASK. *The Ordeal of World Power: American Diplomacy since 1900*. Pp. 366. Boston, Mass.: Little, Brown, 1975. $5.95. Paperbound.

WHITEHOUSE, DAVID and RUTH WHITEHOUSE. *Archaeological Atlas of the World*. Pp. 272. San Francisco, Calif.: W. H. Freeman, 1975. $17.00. Paperbound, $8.95.

WHORTON, JAMES. *Before Silent Spring: Pesticides & Public Health in Pre-DDT America*. Pp. vii, 288. Princeton, N.J.: Princeton University Press, 1975. $12.50.

WICKER, TOM. *A Time to Die*. Pp. viii, 342. New York: Quadrangle, 1975. $10.00.

WILBER, DONALD N. *Iran: Past and Present*. 7th ed. Pp. v, 355. Princeton, N.J.: Princeton University Press, 1975. $17.50.

WILCOX, CLAIR and WILLIAM G. SHEPHERD. *Public Policies toward Business*. Pp. ix, 766. Homewood, Ill.: Richard D. Irwin, 1975. $14.50.

WILLEMS, EMILIO. *Latin American Culture: An Anthropological Synthesis*. Pp. v, 423. New York: Harper & Row, 1975. $12.95.

WILSON, DICK. *The Neutralization of Southeast Asia*. Pp. v, 206. New York: Praeger, 1975. $16.50.

WILSON, EDWARD O. *Sociobiology: The New Synthesis*. Pp. v, 697. Lawrence, Mass.: Harvard University Press, 1975. $20.00.

WILSON, JERRY. *Police Report: A View of Law Enforcement*. Pp. vii, 282. Boston, Mass.: Little, Brown, 1975. $9.95.

WINICK, CHARLES, ed. *Sociological Aspects of Drug Dependence*. Pp. 327. New York: CRC Press, 1975. $39.95.

WINTER, J. M., ed. *War and Economic Development: Essays in Memory of David Joslin.* Pp. vi, 295. New York: Cambridge University Press, 1975. $22.50.

WITHERSPOON, GARY. *Navajo Kinship and Marriage.* Pp. viii, 137. Chicago, Ill.: University of Chicago Press, 1975. $9.50.

WOLF, MARGERY and ROXANE WITKE, eds. *Women in Chinese Society.* Pp. x, 315. Stanford, Calif.: Stanford University Press, 1975. $12.50.

WOLFE, WILLARD. *From Radicalism to Socialism: Men and Ideas in the Formation of Fabian Socialist Doctrines, 1881–1889.* Pp. 333. New Haven, Conn.: Yale University Press, 1975. $17.50.

WOLL, PETER and ROBERT H. BINSTOSK. *America's Political System: Urban, State and Local.* 2nd ed. Pp. v, 127. New York: Random House, 1975. No price.

WOOD, MICHAEL. *America in the Movies: Or, "Santa Maria, It Had Slipped My Mind!"* Pp. ix, 206. New York: Basic Books, 1975. $10.00.

WOODRUFF, WILLIAM. *America's Impact on the World: A Study of the Role of the United States in the World Economy, 1750–1970.* Pp. xi, 296. New York: Halsted Press, 1975. $12.95.

The World Bank: The Assault on World Poverty: Problems of Rural Development, Education, and Health. Pp. iv, 425. Baltimore, Md.: Johns Hopkins Press, 1975. $17.50.

WRIGHT, MOORHEAD, ed. *Theory and Practice of the Balance of Power, 1486–1914.* Pp. v, 152. Totowa, N.J.: Rowman and Littlefield, 1975. $9.50.

YETMAN, NORMAN R. and C. HOY STEELE, eds. *Majority and Minority: The Dynamics of Racial and Ethnic Relations.* 2nd ed. Pp. xi, 640. Boston, Mass.: Allyn & Bacon, 1975. $8.50. Paperbound.

YEZIERSKA, ANZIA. *Bread Givers.* Pp. v, 297. New York: George Braziller, 1975. $3.95. Paperbound.

ZARNOWITZ, VICTOR. *Orders, Production and Investment: A Cyclical and Structural Analysis.* Pp. x, 759. New York: National Bureau of Economic Research, 1973. $20.00.

ZASLOFF, JOSEPH J. *The Pathet Lao: Leadership and Organization.* Pp. v, 174. Lexington, Mass.: Lexington Books, 1973. $10.00.

ZAUBERMAN, ALFRED. *The Mathematical Revolution in Soviet Economics.* Pp. vii, 62. New York: Oxford University Press, 1975. $9.00.

ZOHN, HARRY, ed. *Max Weber: A Biography.* Pp. v, 719. New York: John Wiley & Sons, 1975. $19.95.

PUBLICATIONS FROM UNITED NATIONS

YEARBOOK OF THE UNITED NATIONS 1972

"Throughout its existence, the Yearbook of the United Nations has served as a unique and comprehensive record of the activities of the world organization, of profound value to all who are concerned in those activities," says Secretary-General Kurt Waldheim in his foreword to this volume.

The Yearbook, as the principal reference work of the Organization, is the only annual series containing, within a single volume, a fully-indexed, comprehensive yet succinct account—organized by subject—of the discussions, decisions and activities of the United Nations and the intergovernmental organizations related to it.

Order No. E.74.I.1   Clothbound $35.00

THE DETERMINANTS AND CONSEQUENCES OF POPULATION TRENDS

New Summary of Findings on Interaction of Demographic, Economic and Social Factors—Volume 1

Order No. E.71.XIII.5 $24.00

THE GROWTH OF WORLD INDUSTRY 1973

Vol. II Commodity Production Data 1964-1973

Order No. E.75.XVII.4 $30.00

YEARBOOK OF HUMAN RIGHTS 1971

Order No. E.74.XIV.1 $18.00

STATISTICAL YEARBOOK 1974

Important compilation of statistics from countries throughout the world covering a wide range of economic and social subjects, including: population, agriculture, manufacturing, construction, transport, trade, balance of payments, national income, education and culture. Improved statistical coverage has enabled the Yearbook to widen the territorial scope of many of its tables and to provide more comprehensive and accurate world and continental aggregates.

Order No. E.75.XVII.1 Clothbound $38.00

YEARBOOK OF NATIONAL ACCOUNTS STATISTICS 1973

Detailed estimates of national income and related economic measures for some 121 countries. Among the many subjects covered are: gross domestic product and expenditure, distribution of the gross domestic product, composition of private consumption expenditure, government and revenue expenditure and external transactions.

3 volume set (not sold separately)

Order No. E.75.XVII.2 Clothbound $48.00

DEMOGRAPHIC YEARBOOK 1973

The twenty-fifth issue of the Demographic Yearbook contains 1973 statistics of area, population, natality, mortality, nuptiality and divorce for every country of the world, latest available data on expectation of life and a 7-year trend of international arrivals and departures. Data on the economic characteristics of the population are shown, including labour force participation rates by age and sex as well as various cross-classifications of population by industry, occupation, status, age and sex.

Order No. E/F.74.XIII.1 Clothbound $38.00

YEARBOOK OF CONSTRUCTION STATISTICS 1963-1972

Order No. E.74.XVII.9 Clothbound $18.00

YEARBOOK OF INTERNATIONAL TRADE STATISTICS 1972-1973

Order No. E.74.XVII.6 $32.00

COMPENDIUM OF HOUSING STATISTICS 1971

Order No. E/F.73.XVII.4 $14.50

United Nations Publications, Room LX-2300, New York, N.Y. 10017
or
Palais des Nations, 1211 Geneva 10, Switzerland

INDEX

China's Imperial Past

An Introduction to Chinese History and Culture

Charles O. Hucker. Unique in the sweep of its design and scope and intended expressly for the general reader interested in human history and culture, this panoramic survey traces the vast course of Chinese civilization from prehistory to 1850, when China began the agonizing transition from old to new. The author's approach is primarily interpretive, emphasizing patterns of change and development rather than factual details, but he never loses sight of the particularities that made traditional Chinese civilization one of the richest in human history. Each of the three major epochs of Chinese history is examined in topical chapters on general history, political institutions, socioeconomic organization, religion and thought, and literature and the arts. Especially notable are the many translations, most of them new, of exquisite works from the great poets of the T'ang as well as selections from the philosophical writings, histories, fiction, and poetry of every age. Illustrated. $17.50

STANFORD

1925-1975—Fifty years of scholarly publishing

The American Academy of Political and Social Science

3937 Chestnut Street   **Philadelphia, Pennsylvania 19104**

Origin and Purpose. The Academy was organized December 14, 1889, to promote the progress of political and social science, especially through publications and meetings. The Academy does not take sides in controverted questions, but seeks to gather and present reliable information to assist the public in forming an intelligent and accurate judgment.

Meetings. The Academy holds an annual meeting in the spring extending over two days.

Publications. THE ANNALS is the bimonthly publication of The Academy. Each issue contains articles on some prominent social or political problem, written at the invitation of the editors. Also, monographs are published from time to time, numbers of which are distributed to pertinent professional organizations. These volumes constitute important reference works on the topics with which they deal, and they are extensively cited by authorities throughout the United States and abroad. The papers presented at the meetings of The Academy are included in THE ANNALS.

Membership. Each member of The Academy receives THE ANNALS and may attend the meetings of The Academy. Annual dues for individuals are $15.00 (for clothbound copies $20.00 per year). A life membership is $500. All payments are to be made in United States dollars.

Libraries and other institutions may receive THE ANNALS paperbound at a cost of $15.00 per year, or clothbound at $20.00 per year. Add $1.00 to above rates for membership outside U.S.A.

Single copies of THE ANNALS may be obtained by nonmembers of The Academy for $4.00 ($5.00 clothbound) and by members for $3.50 ($4.50 clothbound). A discount of 5 percent is allowed on orders for 10 to 24 copies of any one issue, and of 10 percent on orders for 25 or more copies. These discounts apply only when orders are placed directly with The Academy and not through agencies. The price to all bookstores and to all dealers is $4.00 per copy less 20 percent, with no quantity discount. Monographs may be purchased for $4.00, with proportionate discounts. Orders for 5 books or less must be prepaid (add $.75 for postage and handling). Orders for 6 books or more must be invoiced.

All correspondence concerning The Academy or THE ANNALS should be addressed to the Academy offices, 3937 Chestnut Street. Philadelphia, Pa. 19104.